Literature, Speech Disorders, and Disability

Examining representations of speech disorders in works of literature, this first collection of its kind founds a new multidisciplinary subfield related but not limited to the emerging fields of disability studies and medical humanities. The scope is wide-ranging both in terms of national literatures and historical periods considered, engaging with theoretical discussions in poststructuralism, disability studies, cultural studies, new historicism, gender studies, sociolinguistics, trauma studies, and medical humanities. The book's main focus is on the development of an awareness of speech pathology in the literary imaginary from the late-eighteenth century to the present, studying the novel, drama, epic poetry, lyric poetry, autobiography and autopathography, and clinical case studies and guidebooks on speech therapy. The volume addresses a growing interest, both in popular culture and the humanities, regarding the portrayal of conditions such as stuttering, aphasia and mutism, along with the status of the self in relation to those conditions. Since speech pathologies are neither illnesses nor outwardly physical disabilities, critical studies of their representation have tended to occupy a liminal position in relation to other discourses such as literary and cultural theory, and even disability studies. One of the primary aims of this collection is to address this marginalization, and to position a cultural criticism of speech pathology within literary studies.

Chris Eagle is Research Lecturer in the Writing and Society Research Centre at the University of Western Sydney, Australia.

Routledge Interdisciplinary Perspectives on Literature

Literature, Speech Disorders, and Disability
Talking Normal

Edited by Chris Eagle

Routledge
Taylor & Francis Group
LONDON AND NEW YORK

Library of Congress Cataloging-in-Publication Data
Literature, speech disorders, and disability : talking normal / edited by
    Christopher Eagle.
        pages cm. — (Routledge Interdisciplinary Perspectives on Literature ; 20)
    Includes bibliographical references and index.
    1. Speech disorders in literature.   2. European literature—History and
criticism.   3. American literature—History and criticism.   I. Eagle,
Christopher, editor of compilation.
    PN56.S685L58 2014
    809'.933561—dc23
    2013017405

ISBN13: 978-0-415-82304-3 (hbk)
ISBN13: 978-0-367-86778-2 (pbk)

Typeset in Sabon
by IBT Global.

Contents

Introduction
Talking Normal

Chris Eagle

In a 2005 episode of the television show *Curb Your Enthusiasm*, there is a scene in which the protagonist Larry David believes he has caught someone abusing disability tags for a parking space. Noticing the man step out of his car and walk away with no signs of physical disability, Larry David says nothing at first, but he stares at the man accusingly enough to elicit a response.

> "W-w-w-w-what?" asks the man, revealing a severe stutter.
> "What's with the walking?" replies Larry David, pointing at the man's license plate.
> "F-f-f-f-f-uck you! I have a s-s-s-s-stutter."
> "Yeah, but you can walk!"
> "L-l-l-l-look at my li-license plate. I have p-p-p-p-permission. F-f-fucking p-prick!"

With that, the man storms off, leaving David to reflect on the ethical implications of what has just transpired. As with so many scenes from *Curb Your Enthusiasm*, Larry David's semi-fictional persona has a point, but one he makes so insensitively that we're left wondering who is in the right, him or his equally unsympathetic interlocutor. Is it wrong to presume someone is not disabled, simply because there are no visible signs? Is it ever right to ask someone to verify their disability? Finally, is a vocal impairment like stuttering a legitimate disability, or is the stuttering man simply abusing the system?

These questions are connected to two other scenes within the episode, both of which stage the many pitfalls surrounding the ethics and etiquette of disability. Before the parking lot scene, David's character is chided by a man in a wheelchair for using the wheelchair-access toilet in the men's room. This awkward bathroom encounter is still on David's mind when he notices the disability tags on the parked car, and it clearly acts as the impetus for David to challenge the stuttering man. Later on, these two moments serve as thesis and antithesis to each other in a farcical climax where David finds himself at the end of a long line in another men's room.

Seeing that nobody else dares to use the wheelchair accessible toilet, David tests an unspoken hypothesis. He tries to jump the queue. When the other men yell at him to get back in line, he then feigns a rather unconvincing speech impediment:

> "I have a s-s-s-s-s-s-s-stutter you p-p-p-p-pricks."
>
> "Stutter my ass," one of the men yells, "that's for people who can't walk."
>
> "Fine fine ok ok!" David says in retreat.
>
> "Oh your stutter's gone now!" we hear one of the men yell, as David exits the bathroom.

Much of the comedic value of this scene comes from the fact that David is only indirectly victorious, by conceding defeat for a position he never truly held in the first place. The other men's reaction seems to confirm his earlier assumption that vocal infirmities, whatever their basis or personal impact, do not merit any of the benefits our society provides to those with properly physical disabilities. Stuttering, of course, has always been an easy target in popular culture, and although David's experiment demonstrates a social consensus that speech disorders have little in common with those physical disabilities that affect mobility, one cannot help but wonder how the encounter in the parking lot would have played out if the stutterer were replaced with a deaf-mute. In any case, the final question the episode leaves us with is the very same question that guides this collection of essays. If speech and language disorders are not to be understood, categorized, and treated as disabilities, then, how else are we to approach their representation in literature and other cultural forms?

In many ways, this is the ideal time to publish a collection that addresses this question. At present, there is a growing interest, both in popular culture and across the Humanities, regarding the portrayal of conditions such as stuttering, aphasia, lisping, mutism, and Tourette's syndrome. The success in recent years of films like *The King's Speech*, *Rocket Science*, and *The Diving Bell and the Butterfly* has also raised awareness about the status of the self in relation to language loss or language breakdown. But since speech pathologies are neither illnesses nor outwardly visible disabilities, critical studies of their representation have always tended to occupy a liminal position in relation to fields like literary theory, philosophy of language, medical humanities, disability studies, sociolinguistics, etc. One of the primary aims of this collection is to redress that marginalization, to position a cultural/literary criticism of speech pathology as a subfield in its own right, by placing influential essays on the subject together with new work in order to bring this topic into greater prominence. In this respect, this collection owes much to recent scholarly works like Marc Shell's *Stutter,* Benson Bobrick's *Knotted Tongues,* and L.S. Jacyna's *Lost Words,* along with the litany of popular 'aphasiographies' released over the past decade such as

Sheila Hale's *The Man Who Lost His Language* or Dr. Jill Bolt Taylor's *My Stroke of Insight*. As a collection of specifically literary essays, this volume also owes a debt to certain theoretical works by major thinkers, essays such as Gilles Deleuze's "He Stuttered" and Michel de Certeau's "Vocal Utopias: Glossolalias." Until now, works of literary criticism that took up the issue of language breakdown have existed like the separate points of a constellation, waiting to be connected. Herein lies another aim of this collection: to contribute to, as well as codify, a critical tradition that has been lying in plain sight for quite some time.

Whether or not speech and language disorders can (or should) be understood in terms of disability, it is clear to me that any new field that arises to study their representations would have to be at the very least analogous to the now well-established field of disability studies. This applies not only to the early aims of that cultural/political movement, specifically, the attempt to find a common identity amongst disparate members and the struggle to remove stigmas associated with that identity, but to the genealogy of the disability movement as well. Here I have in mind the helpful distinction made by Lennard Davis in the *The Disability Studies Reader* between "first wave" and "second wave" identity politics. "The first wave of any struggle," writes Davis, "involves the establishment of the identity against the societal definitions that were formed largely by oppression."[1] As examples of this first wave, Davis cites the "Gay Pride," "Black is Beautiful," and "Deaf Power" movements. To this list, we might add the work of the aphasic poet Chris Ireland, whose confessional poems have been described by his clinician as examples of "aphasia poetry power."[2] What follows in the "second wave" of any identity politics, according to Davis, is a diversifying and a nuancing of the rehabilitated identity. Accustomed to a now stable identity, the members of the second wave are more committed to "finding diversity with the group, and struggling to redefine the identity in somewhat more nuanced and complex ways."[3] When Davis laid out the implications of this genealogy for people with disabilities (PWDs), in the 2006 edition of *The Disability Studies Reader*, disability was in his words, "the most recent identity group on the block."[4] It is my hope that people who struggle with speech and language disorders will soon occupy that position, because what I would like to call the field of Dysfluency Studies is certainly only in its first wave at the present moment. The grunt work of sensitizing the public to disorders of speech has hardly begun. The audience I sat in for the opening of *The King's Speech* still howled with laughter as Colin Firth struggled with the ancient Demosthenean cure of speaking with marbles in one's mouth, and the satirization of famous lispers like Barney Frank or Mike Tyson still goes on in untroubled ways. Yet at the same time, we do see increasing signs of something like a grassroots 'Dysfluency Power' movement. Take recent stories like that of Philip Garber Junior. He is a college student from New York who defied his History professor's insistence that he stop speaking in class because of his disruptive stutter. Or the story of Jordan Shumate, a ninth-grader from Virginia who was asked by his teacher to recite a Langston Hughes poem to his class, only to be interrupted and told to read the poem "blacker."[5] The fact that both of these stories come from the realm of education is more than a little disheartening, but one could also reasonably ask what they even have to do with one another? Again, the field of Disability Studies directs us towards an answer. What these stories have in common is what Lennard Davis calls the enforcing of normalcy; only the normalcy being enforced here is one of the *speaking* body. Norms of speech, after all, can be no less powerful and punitive than those that regulate the body. Dating back to ancient Rome, there is a longstanding practice of denying legal rights and powers of testimony to those who lack the faculty of speech.[6] Today, our technocratic society demands that we speak not only fluently but rapidly as well.

It would seem, therefore, that a field of Dysfluency Studies, one that is compatible with Disability Studies, is not just possible but highly advisable. The potential reach of such a field, in my opinion, is quite far, for two reasons. First, the societal expectation to talk normal bears directly on race, class, gender, and sexual orientation, in addition to those more clinical categories of disordered or abnormal speech already mentioned. Commonalities of the "first wave" variety can and should be found amongst all forms of stigmatized speech, whether they be non-standard ethnic dialects, or gay men's lisps, or neurophysiological impairments like dypshasias or tourettic speech. Second, every incarnation of identity politics has depended at one point in its history on a largely unexamined notion of fluency. The politicized catchphrase "Let your voice be heard!" is heard, is it not, all the time? Although advocates of every type of identity politics have adopted this vocal metaphor for political agency, the more fundamental issue of fluency, or access to normal speech, is hardly ever raised in discussions of political marginalization. Much theoretical work in identity politics, in short, depends upon a normalization of fluency that the essays in this collection seek to challenge and interrogate. From the vantage point of an emerging field like Dysfluency Studies, it immediately becomes clearer how fluent speech itself can become politicized, as a measure of one's relative empowerment. In the same essay where Lennard Davis discusses first and second wave identity politics, he also asserts a privileged status for the Disabled subject as the quintessentially postmodern, or what he terms "dismodern," subjectivity. At the risk of adding yet another new kid to the block of identity politics, one can easily see how the figure of the stutterer, the aphasic, or the mute might also stand for the disempowered minority, the one whose voice literally cannot be heard in the public sphere.

The parameters for something like a tradition or canon of dysfluent literature should, I believe, remain as open-ended as possible, encompassing works that portray or perform clinically disordered speech as well as aesthetically defamiliarized works that force us to reassess the boundaries of normal language. Here again, this is a tradition that has been lying in plain sight for quite some time. The need in literary criticism for more study of this interaction between literary practice and speech pathology becomes apparent when one considers the list of prominent modern authors whose works portray clinical speech disorders: writers like Emile Zola, Herman Melville, Marcel Proust, James Joyce, Virginia Woolf, Zora Neale Hurston, Thomas Mann, Jerzy Kosinski, Yukio Mishima, Ken Kesey, *et al.*[7] When I speak of the performance of disordered speech in literature, it is primarily the experimental modernists I have in mind, although, I am hardly the first critic to point out the many parallels between speech pathology and the experimental styles of writers like Gertrude Stein and James Joyce, Dadaist poets like Kurt Schwitters, or members of the Trans-sense poetry movement like Majakovski or Khlebnikov. In his influential study of modernist literature, "Metaphor and Metonymy in Modern Fiction," David Lodge noted that in her poetry Gertrude Stein was, "deliberately and programmatically cultivating a kind of writing corresponding to the Similarity Disorder, or Selection Deficiency, type of aphasia."[8] In George Steiner's *After Babel,* he makes a similar observation regarding the works of James Joyce: "There is a sense in which a great poet or punster is a human being able to induce and select from a Wernicke aphasia."[9] As precursors to the experimental modernists, one might also include members of the tradition of nonsense verse such as Lewis Carroll (who spoke with a severe stutter himself), Edward Lear, or going back to the Renaissance, the prophetic nonsense poetry of Christopher Smart. Moreover, modern thinkers as seminal as William James, Sigmund Freud, Henri Bergson, Victor Shklovksy, and Roman Jakobson were all similarly preoccupied with the psychological, literary, and linguistic implications of language breakdown.

Evidently, any canon of dysfluent literature should also encompass works written by dysfluent authors, whether we are talking about works that explicitly deal with speech disorders or not. Here, I find, literary studies consistently exhibits a blind spot in appreciating the impact of these conditions on dysfluent writers. This blind spot, if we can call it that, resembles that covering over of queerness in literature that was exposed by Eve Kosofsky Sedgwick in *Epistemology of the Closet.* In one of the more ironic passages of her Introduction, Sedgwick enjoins us to ask a series of rhetorical questions along with her: has there ever been a gay Shakespeare? A gay Proust? Among many others. With a nod towards Sedgwick, I would like to pose some similar questions: has there ever been a stuttering Virgil? A stuttering Cervantes? A stuttering Moliere? A stuttering Charles Lamb? A stuttering Lewis Carroll? Somerset Maugham? Henry James? Philip Larkin? John Updike? David Foster Wallace? David Mitchell?

For any new area of study to develop, of course, it needs more than just a subject matter and a set of categories. It also needs a coherent set of critical practices, tools to apply to relevant texts. Here too I believe any critical study of representations of disordered speech would do well to learn from the practices of Disability Studies. Just as many critics working in the field of Disability Studies seek to deconstruct rigid dichotomies of able/disabled, so too the field of Dysfluency Studies would seek to destabilize rigid or facile notions of fluency. It would understand mastery over language as always already tenuous, fragile, and partial. Just as the second wave of Disability Studies counters essentializing attitudes about persons with disabilities, so too this field would investigate the socially constructed status of the 'normal' or 'able' speaker and counter the variety of assumptions made about people who stutter, lisp, etc. These are some of the ideas that guided me through the process of selecting essays for this collection, and the scope of the collection, for the reasons stated above, is wide-ranging both in terms of historical periods covered (the seventeenth to twentieth centuries) and genres (epic and lyric poetry, prose fiction, drama, autobiography, autopathograpy, etc). The theoretical approaches of the contributors are equally diverse, with poststructuralism, medical humanities, gender studies, sociolinguistics, disability studies, cultural studies, and genetic criticism all represented at different points. While the theoretical approaches have been selected to make the collection as pluralist as possible, there are several key commonalities to the chapters in this collection that need to be underscored, because it is through these commonalities that the field of Dysfluency Studies begins to emerge.

What these chapters share first and foremost is a focus on speech as a corporeal activity. We see this emphasis on the body in Joshua St Pierre's critique of the constructedness of the able-speaking body, and again in Laura Davies' study of the "frailties of speech" in the twin corpuses of Samuel Johnson, his written and physical 'bodies.' Finally, Ronald Schliefer's chapter, "The Poetics of Tourette's Syndrome," offers a fascinating examination of the somatic dimension of speech in the ticcing body. Since Tourette's Syndrome is a condition in which vocal and motor tics oftentimes coalesce, it reminds us that the line between language and the body (or between language and body language) is not so easy to draw. On a related note, I would add that this collection shares a certain tacit questioning of the validity and limitations of the influential Chomskyian distinction between competence and performance. Every chapter of this collection is attentive to those seemingly minor phenomena of actual vocalized utterance—hesitations, accents, tonalities, and somatic acts of non-verbal communication—which are often deemed irrelevant to the study of language proper.

Another distinction this collection forces us to to question is that between 'literary' and 'pathological' uses of language. For this, I would single out Herbert Marks' chapter "On Prophetic Stammering," which locates affinities between spiritually heightened states of language (e.g. glossolalia and prophetic speech) and poetic states of experimentation in a remarkable number of texts ranging from Christopher Smart's *Jubilate Agno* to Gertrude Stein's *Tender Buttons*. My own contribution to the collection similarly investigates the fine line between performance and portrayal of disordered speech in James Joyce's *Finnegans Wake*. Applying Gilles Deleuze's notion of "creative stuttering" to the uniquely disordered language of 'Wakese,' I show how *Finnegans Wake* is a work that simultaneously portrays clinically identifiable conditions like stuttering and lisping while also exploiting those conditions for various aesthetic effects. Ronald Schliefer's contribution is relevant here as well for its exploration of the creative potentialities within Tourette's Syndrome for poetic wordplay, and for the questions Schliefer raises about those involuntary aspects of the creative process laid bare by Tourette's Syndrome.

None of this is meant to suggest, however, that this collection aims to idealize or romanticize the lived experience of language breakdown. On the contrary, several contributors stress the element of crisis inherent to language loss. Laura Davies explores the personal impact of Samuel Johnson's experience of aphasia in view of his previous ideas about the nature and origin of language. Similarly, Laura Salisbury and Chris Code examine Samuel Beckett's verbal experimentation in the light of his own recovery from aphasia. Interestingly, they do this to argue that Beckett's linguistic experimentation before his aphasia in fact stems from a paradigm shift in thinking about language that was itself inaugurated by aphasiology. Gene Plunka's chapter examines the personal impact of aphasia on another playwright, Joseph Chaikin, as it was dramatized by his friend Jean-Claude Van Itallie in his play *The Traveller*. These two chapters are further linked by the fact that Chaikin was engaged in a production of *Waiting for Godot* at the time of his stroke, and it was to Chaikin that Beckett dedicated his poem "What is the Word?," a poem Beckett wrote as part of his recovery from aphasia. Lastly, there is a dual sense of crisis behind Valeria Souza's chapter on the Portugese national epic *The Lusiads*. Souza locates not only a stylistic sense of crisis in the poem's many linguistic aberrations, but also a crisis of masculinity attached specifically to stuttering in the poem. In her view, these many crises of language serve to undercut and ironize the traditional nation-building goals of epic poetry.

A final commonality to be found in this volume is a critical awareness of the stigmas and stereotypes that attach to not talking normal in modern society. On this topic, the first and last chapters offer the most stringent responses to these stigmatizations. Joshua St. Pierre's critique of the common understanding of speech disorders is grounded in a highly original phenemenological account of the moment of linguistic breakdown. For St. Pierre, broken speech is wholly dialogical, existing in a context of listener and speaker. In this sense, the 'disability' of stuttering, for St. Pierre, is one that is always shared by speaker and listener alike. Based on this dialogical account of the moment of the stutter, St. Pierre reminds us that conditions like stuttering are judged according to arbitrary (and one-sided) cultural norms of efficiency, pace, and self-mastery. This notion of self-mastery connects St. Pierre's chapter to the final contribution by Jeffrey Johnson. Johnson's study extends the collection beyond literary texts into the realms of film, television, and comic books. His chapter shares the same commitment to exposing and critiquing the kinds of assumptions that are made about people who stutter. As Johnson shows, personality traits like weakness or nervousness are regularly embedded in popular portrayals of the stutterer. Both St. Pierre and Johnson demonstrate the quick leap from these kinds of associations to a view of the stutter as a kind of moral failing to live up to the social expectation that we all must talk normal.

NOTES

1. Lennard J. Davis, "The End of Identity Politics and The Beginning of Dismodernism," in *The Disability Studies Reader: Second Edition* ed. Lennard J. Davis (New York: Routledge, 2006), 231.
2. Susie Parr, Sally Byng, Sue Gilpin and Chris Ireland, *Talking About Aphasia: Living with Loss of Language after Stroke* (Buckingham and Philadelphia: Open University Press, 1997).
3. Davis, "The End of Identity Politics and The Beginning of Dismodernism," 232.
4. Davis, "The End of Identity Politics and The Beginning of Dismodernism," 233.
5. Richard Pérez-Peña, "Professor's Response to a Stutterer," in *The New York Times* (October 10, 2011); Emma Brown, "Fairfax Investigates Allegations of Racially Insensitive Behaviour by High School Teacher," in *The Washington Post* (March 16, 2012).
6. See O'Neill, Ynez Violé. *Speech and Speech Disorders in Western Thought Before 1600*. London: Greenwood Press, 1980.
7. See Chris Eagle, *Dysfluencies: On Speech Disorders in Modern Literature*. London: Bloomsbury, 2013.
8. David Lodge, "Metaphor and Metonymy in Modern Fiction," in *Modernism 1890–1930*, ed. Malcolm Bradbury and James McFarlane (New York: Penguin Books, 1976), 83.
9. George Steiner, *After Babel: Aspects of Language and Translation* (New York: Oxford University Press, 1998), 297.

1 The Construction of the Disabled Speaker

Locating Stuttering in Disability Studies[1]

Joshua St. Pierre

To be natural is such a difficult pose to keep up.

—Oscar Wilde

INTRODUCTION

Spoken discourse is often given as the most basic and universal form of exchanging information and as such has occupied a central role in questions of human rationality, agency and identity. However, even within disability studies, very little thought has been given to the actual form of speech production as an embodied act. In this chapter, I intend to focus on stuttering, which has received attention in the emerging literature of disability studies for the most part as a pertinent example or useful anecdote. This is surprising not only because roughly 1% of the population stutters, but also because the social nature of stuttering makes it an unavoidably public disability.[2]

Discourse around stuttering and other communicative disorders is not nonexistent; several academic journals are devoted to speech pathology and therapy, support groups offer their services to stutterers, and a handful of autobiographies can be found that draw out the experience of stuttering.[3] Yet what is both interesting and telling about the existing literature is that stuttering is consistently framed as an individual, biological defect to be coped with, managed or cured. Little attention has been given to what can be learned from resisting the urge to "fix" stuttering and instead reflecting upon what it can reveal about the ways we are accustomed to understanding speech, communication and disability.[4] By gathering stuttering from the fringes of disability theory while questioning the dominant methodology surrounding stuttering discourse, this chapter seeks to understand the ways in which the disability of stuttering is not simply biological or natural, but is made meaningful by society in three interrelated ways.

Highlighting the distinctively dialogical nature of communicative disabilities, I first argue that "broken speech" is constructed by *both* a speaker and a hearer. Next, since stuttering is an embodied act, attention must be given to the construction of the speaker's body. Lastly, this chapter calls attention to the liminal nature of the stutterer, who is neither clearly abled nor disabled. This liminality can help explain the unclear and conflicting expectations forced upon stutterers, who, unlike many other disabled people, are often expected to perform on the same terms as the able-bodied. Disfluency can thus be interpreted as a distinctly *moral* failure: the failure of a stutterer's will and self-discipline, which undercuts and threatens capitalistic virtues.

Before moving on, I wish to flag quickly what might be the rather surprising de-emphasis of speech therapy within this work. Although speech therapy plays a significant pedagogical role in the stutterer learning to identify herself as such, it is simply not possible within the constraints of this work to do justice to the role of speech therapy in the construction of stuttering. I recognize that expectations of efficiency, clarity and pace are often reinforced by speech pathologists. While person-centered therapy importantly focuses on developing levels of fluency set by the client, the assumption is still that if she wants to be taken seriously, the stutterer must learn to master fluency techniques (relative to her goals) so as to present herself adequately. This concern is altruistic, and speech therapy does much good. However, given their position of authority, speech pathologists do not merely reflect how things are in the "real world," but participate in *creating* the world of normalized speech expectations and constructing the stutterer within that world. With this being said, I must largely bracket this conversation for the time being.

THE MEDICALIZATION OF STUTTERING

Insofar as stuttering has not been formally theorized, it comes as little surprise that stuttering has been understood almost exclusively through the medical model. Stuttering is accepted as a problem within the medical model, identified both clinically and medically as some*thing* to be managed and fixed. As I will show, the medicalization and management of stuttering compels stutterers to understand their stutter in a very specific way.

The prevalence of the medical model in our society's reaction to stuttering is evidenced by many recent attempts to cure or manage stuttering. For instance, in 2009 the longed for "wonder drug," Pagoclone, intended to reduce disfluencies, went into clinical testing. The initial results, which came as no surprise to many, showed that "the study did not meet its pre-specified criteria for success."[5] However, Endo Pharmaceuticals holds that there were some "trends of interest" that are currently under review. Medically, there is ongoing genetic and neurological research into the nature and causes of stuttering. To cite one example, Dennis Drayna, co-author of the 2010 study "Mutations in the Lysosomal Enzyme–Targeting Pathway and Persistent Stuttering" which revealed three genetic mutations in the brains of stutterers, comments that "the sooner that stuttering is recognized as a biological disorder, people can get down to using that understanding

. . . to better treat the disorder."[6] Drayna's optimism in the power of science to cure disability is certainly not surprising as it is emblematic of the medical model. Technologically, altered auditory feedback devices (AAF) are becoming increasingly popular; the SpeechEasy, which is worn in the ear and echoes the speaker's words at a slight delay and altered pitch, is advertised as a "discreet anti-stuttering device."[7] Though SpeechEasy has so far resulted in mixed success, technological augmentations can only be expected to increase its usage.

The medical model would have us see stuttering as a problem which must be managed through these sorts of means. The "success" or "failure" of these attempts at management is presently of little consequence, since what interests me is both the prevalence and influence of the drive to manage stuttering. What is both significant and troubling about the management of stuttering is not that it occurs but rather that management prompts stutterers to objectify their own body—specifically the speech production system—and treat it as shameful, while also extracting stuttering from its social, cultural and economic contexts, allowing the pervasive narratives of stuttering to go unquestioned and unchecked.

The quantification of disability, commonplace in the medical model, helps shape stuttering "into a concrete *individual* issue, abstracted from *interpersonal* interaction and interpretation," making it definite and easier to deal with for the medical establishment.[8] For instance, speech pathologists regularly use fluency counters to calculate the rate and percentage of disfluencies spoken per minute. Through this practice, pathologists isolate stuttering from an interpersonal communicative action to a very precise biological malfunction, thereby making stuttering into a concrete *thing* which can and should be dealt with.[9] The process of becoming arduously aware of every deviant syllable as something misspoken and out of place requires and reinforces a paradigm of objectification. That this paradigm is harmful is evidenced by Petrunik and Shearing's consideration that "stutterers experience stuttering as the work of an alien inner force (*often referred to in the third person as 'it'*) which takes control of their speech mechanism. Stuttering is something which stutterers feel happens to them, not something they do" (emphasis added).[10] Stuttering as an unwanted and an invasive "it" is evidence of the objectification and distancing stutterers are impelled to feel towards their speech through the medical model. This model is therefore woefully inadequate to resist the ways medicalization and social structures reinforce the oppression of disabled speakers through objectification and abled/disabled binaries.

COMMUNICATIVE NORMALCY AND THE CONSTRUCTION OF THE HEARER

Stuttering as a communicative action is a distinctly social phenomenon that cannot properly be reduced to the physical difficulty of producing sounds, but must be situated within its social fabric. Paralleling the way in which speech has no meaning outside of an interpretive context involving a hearer, so stuttering cannot be understood apart from expectations of "normal" hearing. What if we saw stuttering as constructed by a hearer prejudiced against "broken" speech as well as its speaker, and thus as a product of ableism? Would this allow us to dismantle the myth that stuttering is an individual defect and responsibility?

To this end, I turn to Rosemarie Garland-Thomson who locates stuttering amongst a range of disabilities that disrupt the normal expectations of human communication:

> The uncontrolled body does not perform typically the quotidian functions required by the elaborate structured codes of acceptable social behavior. Blindness, deafness, or stuttering, for instance, disturb the complex web of subtle interchanges upon which communication rituals depend.[11]

Elaborating on Garland-Thomson's reference to stuttering, prolongations—"aaaapple"—or repetitions—"p-p-p-p-potato"—disrupt subtle vocal inflections that convey meaning and similarly, speech blocks including facial grimaces, tension or freezing deny an interlocutor a significant part of communication.

In one sense then, stuttering makes the transmission of information more difficult than "normal" speech. An unaccustomed hearer often works harder to analyze non-verbal cues, to understand the meaning of words that are twisted and stretched beyond their defining phonetic structure, and to decipher syntax from sentences that are halted mid-way only to be backed up to get a running start. This interpretive process is made even more difficult by the frequent discomfort of watching / listening to a stutterer form a sentence with difficulty. However, regardless of the severity of the rupture, the responsibility for this disruption of communicative rituals does not fall singularly upon the stutterer as she deviates from "normal" speech, but also upon the hearer whose ability to pick up upon the "web of subtle interchanges" is heavily conditioned by "normal" hearing.

Necessary to detailing the hearer's role in the construction of stuttering is therefore a wider understanding of communicative normalcy as such. Opening up the notion of "normal" communication, Tanya Titchkosky's contention that "an unexamined position of normalcy is the unmarked viewpoint only indirectly available to human experience as an unobtrusive background expectation" importantly applies just as easily to expectations of hearing as to expectations of speaking.[12] For example, when a heavily accented speaker addresses a crowd straining to understand what is being said, it is common to blame the abnormal speaker because the hearers as the dominant group occupy the seemingly invisible position of normalcy. A homogenous audience does not think to question that a heavy accent presents a communicative difficulty (or is even an accent at all!) because *they* cannot adequately *hear*, since, as stated by Iris Young, "the dominant groups need not notice their own group being at all; they occupy an unmarked, neutral, apparently universal position."[13] Yet inversely, when any of those hearers travels to a place where "accented" speech is dominant, the assumed normalcy of their hearing is challenged, indicating that the normalcy of communication is settled primarily in terms of group dominance and not in simple terms of speakers vs. hearers. Dominant hearing groups hide the construction of their normalcy, passing themselves off as occupying a naturally given position.[14] When hearing *does* require extra effort, the dominant group is veiled behind its universal and unmarked position. Therefore, not only are communicative norms constructed by speakers *and* hearers, but also deviation in this communicative relation is shouldered disproportionally by the minority group.

This asymmetrical relationship is exhibited clearly in the instance of "abled" hearers and "disabled" speakers. Since "abled" hearers hold the dominant position within our society—numerically and influentially—they are unmarked and consequently it is taken for granted that to hear normally is to understand clearly recognizable and defined speech patterns. Behind a veil of universality, these expectations solidify into communicative "rules" that stutterers seem to violate. Insofar as dominant "abled" groups hide their constructed normalcy, speech becomes "broken" and the speaker *alone* is constructed as unnatural, abnormal and therefore disabled.[15]

This claim is amplified by the common assumption that hearing is passive and speaking is active, i.e. a speaker projects words and a hearer simply and neutrally absorbs them. The passivity of the senses, particularly the passivity of hearing, has a long history in Western philosophy.[16] From this perspective, it is easy to understand why stuttering is seen as an individual problem of a *speaker*, for a hearer occupies the position of an objective receptacle, whose passivity (which frees her from interpretation) reliably mirrors the objective nature of the "broken" speech. As a result, hearers have a right not to do any work in hearing and any difficulty in understanding accordingly falls upon the active speaker, not the passive hearer.

Yet this line of argumentation is quickly overturned by the widely held model of perception in the philosophy of science—"theory ladenness"—emphasizing the *active* nature of perception.[17] In this way, Anna Storozhuk contends that, "Perception is . . . active information gathering and, in many aspects, is determined by a mindset or expectations . . . The movements of the perceiver testify that perception is not a simple reflection of the reality, but is accompanied by the activity of the perceiving subject."[18] If hearing is not a passive process, but the active *collection of information* based upon expectations and former experience, then hearing cannot retain the position of a neutral recorder but is implicated in the highly politicized practice of defining and enforcing normalcy of speech based upon normalized expectations of hearing.[19]

Accordingly, the stigma encompassing stuttering must take into account the interlocutor's "faulty" hearing. Listening to someone sputter, stammer, and haltingly form words, hearers may lose patience, be unable to follow, or finish sentences for her, therein erroneously (and frustratingly!) making assumptions about what she is trying to say. In these ways, hearers are actively collecting and interpreting information in an insufficient and discriminatory way and contributing to the construction of a stutterer's speech as "broken."

Once again, the assumed normalcy of hearing hides these possible contributions to the communicative breakdown and shifts the responsibility entirely upon the speaker. It is important to emphasize that I am not arguing stuttering is merely a result of hearers constructing this variation of speech production (stuttering) as abnormal, but contrarily, that in a dialogical process the hearer and speaker are bound together in the act of communicating and thus "broken" speech is constructed from *both* the speaker and the hearer. This view reinscribes my thesis that stuttering as a disability is not necessarily or primarily natural or biological but is a discrimination against "abnormal" communicative variations.[20]

Yet while the dialogical nature of stuttering is a necessary condition of the present Western construction of stuttering, it is not a *sufficient* condition. Stuttering cannot adequately be understood as mere "interference" or "de-synchronization" between a receiver and sender, a phenomenon that can easily be imagined in various data relay systems. Stuttering is rather an embodied act involving the physical production of words—e.g. enunciation, articulation and vocalization—within a historical and socio-cultural situation. For this reason, I turn now to the construction of the speaker's body in the cultural imagining of stuttering.

THE CONSTRUCTION OF THE EMBODIED SPEAKER

The speaker cannot be cognized as an ahistorical and non-particular entity, a simple medium of communication, but must be conceived as a *body* situated in a historical context. Titchkosky, in affirming the social significance of the body, is of assistance in contending that "bodies are only found within locales of interaction, within interpretive milieus and ideological structures such as health and beauty, and the specific language or genre through which all this is expressed."[21] Outside of these contexts, bodies would mean nothing and in a substantial sense would *be* nothing.[22] Yet, the ways in which the body is inscribed with meaning are not neutral, but are often used to hierarchize and regulate. As such, this frame of reference often termed 'body politics,' is useful in tracing the social conditions and ideologies which give rise to the construction of stuttering within the domain of liberal individualism and North American capitalism.

The stutterer finds and defines herself in a context dominated by expectations of efficiency. Welded to notions of success and productivity within capitalism, expediency of both labor and communication sets the terms for participation in our socio-economic system while also enforcing the production of the sorts of subjects it requires. That is, in light of body politics, the body is *itself* interpreted as that which is meant and required to be efficient and productive. On the one hand, as I will argue below, the stutterer feels immense pressure from *without*, from environmental expectations to speak quickly and not waste anyone's time. Otherwise she may not get a chance to speak, or she may be punished for exceeding her allotted time. Yet these constructions of "normal" pace are derived from what it means to have and use a body. In failing to conform to expectations of expediency, the stutterer *herself* is constructed as a faulty instrument that is inefficient and less useful. From this angle, the stutterer feels the pressure of pace from *within*, the pressure to be the sort of efficient subject valued and required for participation.

To parse out the stutterer's failure to meet outward expectations of pace and efficiency, I draw on the valuable connection that has been made between disability and industrialization. With the onset of the Industrial Age, time took on a strong economic meaning and was carefully carved up into neat slots enabling the possibility of recording and calculating productivity with precision. Susan Wendell draws upon this idea and makes explicit the connection between time and disability: "Pace is a major aspect of expectations of performance [and] non-disabled people often take pace so much for granted that they feel and express impatience with the slower pace at which some people with disabilities need to operate."[23] As explained by Wendell, the significance of an industrialized world is not only that it brought another version of time, but also that pace and matching expectations of productivity are taken for granted and assumed as the norm. Bodies not capable of meeting expectations of pace and productivity are therefore disqualified from full participation not only in the economic sector but also in social situations.

Stuttering intersects with this theoretical re-working of time insofar as stuttering interferes with established and codified rhythms of communication. The more communication-dependent a workplace, the more perspicuity and speed in communication would be valued. Carried forward to a post-industrial capitalist world in which the mantra "time is money" is cardinal and the exchange of information gains center stage, stuttering becomes a serious economic liability. The inability to match the required "professional" pace of conversation in work situations disqualifies stutterers from full participation and therefore marks them as disabled. Wendell's contention that non-disabled people take pace for granted and subsequently are impatient with those unable to meet these expectations is particularly fitting in the instance of stuttering because stutterers lack not the ability to communicate, but the ability to communicate in the "right" way and within the "appropriate" amount of time. For example, stutterers often cannot jump into a conversation quickly enough to make their point before it moves along to another topic. Furthermore, stutterers often feel extreme pressure to be succinct, not to waste anyone's time, and therefore fearfully remain silent. Stutterers are also interrupted, ignored, or—and this is likely the most difficult—not taken seriously when their sentence takes an extra ten or twenty seconds to complete.

While the twenty extra seconds it may take a stutterer to complete a sentence can be consequential in some situations such as performing a surgery, commanding a military exercise, or alerting your child of a traffic danger, twenty seconds is clearly not pressing in the vast majority of life's situations.[24] Thus, while stuttering is in part socially constructed through social expectations of performance as related to pace, this "lost time" only gains its full significance as a meaningful lack of ability *qua* bodily deviance.

Efficiency and pace in and of themselves are inadequate in explaining why stutterers are marginalized and pitied in a way in which those who speak slowly, in a second language, or are long-winded, are not. We are often (intentionally or otherwise) inefficient with our time, so the fact that a stutterer is marginalized results from something beyond a desire to maintain a swift pace and be an efficient subject. For this reason, underlying the anxiety-riddled demands of efficiency, the stutter is more primarily constructed by the ideal of being able to master one's body. The issue is not so much that we expect speakers to be efficient, it is that we expect a speaker to *be able* to be efficient if and when they so desire.

Interpreting the significance of the extra twenty seconds it may require a stutterer to complete a sentence through the lens of body politics, it can be demonstrated that more than just a length of time, twenty seconds signifies a deviance from the liberal individualist and capitalist ideal of bodily mastery. If, as Garland-Thomson asserts, an autonomous and mastered individual within the ideology of capitalism is imagined as having "inviolate boundaries that enable unfettered self-determination," the seemingly uncontrollable repetition of words and syllables along with the involuntary facial tics that often accompany stuttering signal a susceptibility to external and hostile forces overrunning compliancy and self-government.[25] From this perspective, stutterers possess a tenuous grasp over their bodies which can at any moment be disrupted by the stutter itself.

Consider these disclosures of speech pathologist Ida Whitten: "My stuttering was a constant problem to be dealt with every time I spoke. I might at any moment feel a stuttering incident coming," and again, "The stutterer will relapse unless he continues to work *every day*, perhaps every waking hour, to keep his speech good."[26] The stutterer must continually wrestle (often in vain) with her body to subdue it and bring it back under control. In this way, the vulnerability of the stutterer's body troubles the cultural fantasy of the body as a "stable, neutral instrument of the individual will" for, though significant, it is not the stutterer's relative inability to control her body that is most troubling.[27] Rather, it is the fact that her body is not docile, that it obtrudes *at all*, which marks it as deviant. As such, twenty extra seconds tick away, not marking time so much as serving as an increasing reminder of the body's failure to be a concealed and neutral medium of communication.

In *Stuttering: A Life Bound up in Words*, Marty Jezer writes of his despair in job hunting and of one forthright interviewer who told him:

> I'm going to be frank. You've got all the qualifications to be a good copywriter. But in advertising it is image that counts. Executives aren't as impressed by talent and creativity as they are by a person's ability to fit in. They want to be comfortable with everyone they employ, and so they want the people they employ to be like them . . . Take care of your speech and come back. You'll never get a job in advertising until you learn to talk.[28]

Jezer's narrative is striking because the discrimination he faced was not due to his *ability* (or lack thereof) in itself. Rather, Jezer's interlocutor could hardly have been more lucid in his admission that to participate fully in the capitalist world, people must be normalized and thereby reinforce the identity of the North American Ideal: successful, productive and mastered. Until stutterers "learn to talk"—which is code here for not threatening the North American Ideal—they will find themselves outside full participation; for identifying with the stutterer "would remind the non-disabled," states Wendell, "that their ideals imply a degree of control that must eventually elude them too."[29]

In failing to live up to the ideals set by liberal individualism and capitalism, stutterers act as a reminder of the fragile mastery we have of our bodies and of the social downturn that quickly follows the failure to uphold and project this ideal of mastery. This "failed identity" is not limited to the economic sphere, but is superimposed over the stutterer's whole identity as a citizen, tainting and stigmatizing how she is understood by herself and others.[30]

CONCLUSION: STUTTERING AND LIMINAL OPPRESSION

By way of conclusion, I intend to reflect upon stuttering's liminal position as a disability in order to elucidate further the distinctiveness of the stutterer's "failed identity" and create space for stuttering within disability studies. Along with several other disabilities, including chronic fatigue syndrome and ADHD, a stutterer is not clearly perceived as abled or disabled. Many stutterers resist the term 'disabled' because of the associated stigma and the desire to be sensitive to those with "real" disabilities, and the lack of literature in disability studies is surely an indication that stuttering is not prominently identified as a disability. Conversely, it has been demonstrated here that stutterers are disabled insofar as they suffer from marginalization within society. Being caught in that indefinite territory between disability and ability, the conception and treatment of stuttering is thus uniquely framed.

The ambiguous boundaries of stuttering within this model can help explain the unclear and conflicting expectations forced upon stutterers. Unlike the experience of being blind or deaf, stutterers are clearly expected to perform on the same terms as the able-bodied. No one would likely tell a quadriplegic to "walk already" or a deaf person to "listen up," since it is understood that these actions are beyond their control. However, since a stutterer's disability is not understood as absolute, since the stutterer is ostensibly not *really* disabled, stuttering can evoke irritation out of listeners who wish that she could just "spit it out!" Implicit in this violence is the undergirding assumption that stuttering, unlike other disabilities, is ultimately within one's control. That stutterers are expected to communicate on the terms of the abled but cannot live up to these expectations is the basis of much of the shame and embarrassment accompanying the disability.

Stuttering, especially when diagnosed, is understood as something that *could* be fixed with enough hard work and self-discipline. I do not deny that this claim is seemingly inconsistent with my previous contention that stutterers are marginalized precisely because they lack self-mastery over their bodies. For as a liminal form of oppression, stuttering dwells in the periphery of the cultural imaginary and is the result of ambiguous social anxieties, not well-defined taxonomies. Stuttering is the aggregate of conflicting social expectations of the urgent desire and repressed impossibility to achieve mastery over oneself. Yet insofar as stuttering *can* seemingly be "fixed" with enough self-discipline, this failure can be interpreted as a distinctly moral failure.[31]

In order to illuminate the moral failure of stuttering, it may be useful to compare cultural reactions to stuttering with cultural reactions to fatness. In *Revolting Bodies: The Struggle to Redefine Fat Identity*, Kathleen Lebesco argues that anti-fat sentiment arises not only because fat people are (apparently) not as productive as the rest, but also because their body is a deliberate affront to the virtues of capitalism. Lebesco contends that "the endorsement of a Protestant ethic ideology leads one to view [fat] peoples as willful violators of traditional American values such as moral character, hard work, and self-discipline."[32] Fat people must be lazy and indulgent since they *could* control their bodies if they really wanted to.

Stuttering, as a moral failure, follows a very similar pattern. Since stuttering is constructed as an individual and invasive problem which can be managed if not cured (virtually everyone has that distant acquaintance who used to stutter), continued disfluency cuts against the philosophy of limitless individual achievement through hard work. As such, stuttering, like fatness, is not merely an affront to capitalist virtues by representing inefficiency and a lower productivity but is—tacitly perhaps—punished on moral grounds as well. If my argument holds, a stutterer cannot easily appeal to a moral high ground as a way of resisting discriminatory taunts, practices, and structures, since that ground has been shoveled onto the other side. The stutterer cannot claim to be a victim of "immoral" discrimination when they themselves are just being lazy. Defenseless in this way, the stutterer can hardly avoid identifying her stuttering body as something to be fixed, managed and controlled; something of which to be ashamed.

The liminality of stuttering places it in an unusual position with respect to disability theory. Stuttering is a "less visible" disability than many others, particularly in regards to its social effects when compared to, for example, blindness or cerebral palsy. When stuttering *is* brought to the fore, it is often not interpreted as a "severe" disability, that is, society does not discriminate against stuttering as a whole (nor recognize it through funding and support) to the same degree that it does many other forms of physical and mental disabilities. While much of this likely has to do with the stutterer's wily ability to go incognito, often passing within society, it still causes one to wonder how much discrimination is required to be classified as disabled. In this sense, I am hesitant to place stuttering categorically alongside more visible disabilities. Yet, in the same breath, stuttering comes under distinct social pressures and punishments absent from the experience of clearly defined and visible disabilities.

In building a coherent and stable understanding of disability, the pressure is to harmonize stuttering within conceptual patterns of disability studies, pigeonholing it within predetermined frameworks. I think, however, that space must be carved out in the emerging field of disability studies for liminal forms of oppression which straddle boundaries and disrupt the binaries of abled/disabled, normal/abnormal. Therefore not only does stuttering break ground for consideration of the distinctly communicative nature of disabilities such as cleft palate, autism, cerebral palsy and Tourette's syndrome, but stuttering also requires of disability studies a posture of uncertainty in order to appreciate the specific experience of liminal forms of oppression.

NOTES

1. My thanks to the *Canadian Journal of Disability Studies* for generously giving permission to reprint this article, as well as to the Living Archives on Eugenics in Western Canada project funded by the Community-University Research Alliance Program at the Social Sciences and Humanities Research Council of Canada for originally funding this project.
2. American Psychiatric Association, "Stuttering," *Diagnostic and Statistical Manual of Mental Disorders*, 4th ed., text rev. (Washington, DC: American Psychiatric Association, 1999), 307.0.
3. For example, *Journal of Fluency Disorders, The Quarterly Journal of Speech, Journal of Speech and Hearing Disorders;* National Stuttering Association, Canadian Stuttering Association; Marty Jezer, *Stuttering: A Life Bound up in Words* (New York: Basic Books, 1997); Ida E. Whitten, "The Face of All

the World is Changed," *An Autobiographical Study with the Focus on Stuttering* (Cincinnati, OH: Scott Zoller, 1989).

4. One exception might be Marc Shell's *Stutter* (Cambridge, MA: Harvard University Press, 2005), which explores the phenomenon of stuttering from the perspective of comparative literature, noting and commenting on stuttering's appearance in history and contemporary media.

5. Endo Pharmaceuticals, "Endo Pharmaceuticals, 'Research and Development'," http://www.endo.com/ClinicalStudies.aspx (accessed July 10, 2011).

6. Stephanie Smith, "Unlocking a Medical Mystery," CNN, http://www.cnn.com/2010/HEALTH/02/10/stuttering.genes.cell/ (accessed July 11, 2011); Changsoo Kang et al., "Mutations in the Lysosomal Enzyme–Targeting Pathway and Persistent Stuttering," *New England Journal of Medicine* 362 (2010): 677–685.

7. Speech Easy, http://www.speecheasy.com/ (accessed July 11, 2011).

8. Tanya Titchkosky, *Disability, Self and Society* (Toronto, ON: University of Toronto Press, 2003), 55.

9. To be fair, speech therapists do deal with the emotional side of the experience of stuttering as well as explaining how psychological stress and low self-esteem can lead to greater disfluency; however, my contention is that "disfluencies" are still the problem to be avoided or coped with.

10. Micheal Petrunik and Clifford Shearing, "Fragile Facades: Stuttering and the Strategic Manipulation of Awareness," *Social Problems* 31, no. 2 (1983): 127.

11. Rosemarie Garland-Thomson, *Extraordinary Bodies: Figuring Physical Disability in American Culture and Literature* (New York: Columbia University Press, 1997), 37.

12. Tanya Titchkosky, *Disability,* 148.

13. Iris Marion Young, *Justice and the Politics of Difference* (Princeton, NJ: Princeton University Press, 1990), 123.

14. Of course, the example of heavy accents is not a perfect fit with this claim since ethnic/cultural groupings are a relatively recognized category (though this claim is rightfully challenged by many scholars) within society. Accents thus remind hearers that they themselves *are* a hearing group since the accent is a reminder of that person's distinct culture, language, history and otherness. Disability however, is not yet recognized as a distinctive social group, but remains a lack and, to reference Beauvoir, an "inessential Other." Accordingly, stuttering does not remind hearers that their difficulty in understanding is not given.

15. It is worth noting that under this definition of communicative (ab)normalcy, ESL speakers may also be considered disabled. Such discrimination would indicate an overlap between the ableism working against stutterers and a culturally motivated linguistic ableism working against accented speakers.

16. On the passivity of the senses, Descartes notes, "the non-interpreting pure observations were considered as the unproblematic source of information about the world. Passivity of perception guaranteed independence of the world being perceived from a perceiving subject . . . Perception understood as passive provided a possibility of reliable and adequate cognition of the world." (Cited in Anna Storozhuk, "Perception: Mirror Image or Action?," *Journal for General Philosophy of Science* 38, no. 2 [2007]: 372). On the passivity of hearing in particular, in *The Hermeneutics of the Subject,* Foucault observes Plutarch taking up this very concern. Relaying Plutarch's treatise, *On Listening,* Foucault writes: "In audition, more than with any other sense, the soul is passive with regard to the external world and exposed to all the events that come from the outside world and may take it by surprise."

(Michel Foucault, *The Hermeneutics of the Subject: Lectures at the College De France 1981–1982*. New York: Picador, 2005).

17. See William F. Brewer and Bruce L. Lambert, "The Theory-Ladenness of Observation and the Theory-Ladenness of the Rest of the Scientific Process," *Philosophy of Science* 68, no. 3 (2001): 176–186.

18. Storozhuk, "Perception," 377.

19. Note also Lennard Davis's insistence that, "we do not so much listen to a speaker as try to fit that speech into preconstructed categories, so that 'we simply hallucinate word boundaries when we reach the edge of a stretch of sound that matches some entry into our mental dictionary.'" (Cited in Steven Pinker, *The Language Instinct: How the Mind Creates Language* [New York: Morrow, 1994], 159). In other words, the limpid clarity of speech is itself an illusion that conceals the extent to which the receiver of speech is continually improvising to make the act of talking make sense." (Lennard J. Davis, *Enforcing Normalcy* [New York: Verso, 1995], 19).

20. While I believe it helpful to shift attention away from the physiology of stuttering, which has monopolized the discourse, in favour of a discussion of disabling assumptions and socio-cultural structures, I am not suggesting that the stuttering body be denied. In fact, it is possible (as I am learning) that one who stutters may *want* to take pride in her stuttering body as a locus of disabled identity so as to fight against rehabilitation.

21. Titchkosky, *Disability*, 58.

22. "We are fully dependent on each other for the possibility of being understood and without this understanding we are not intelligible, we do not make sense, are not solid, visible, integrated, we are lacking." María Lugones, "Playfulness, 'World'-Travelling, and Loving Perception," in *Feminist Philosophy Reader*, ed. Alison Bailey and Chris Cuomo (New York: McGraw-Hill, 2008), 73.

23. Susan Wendell, *The Rejected Body: Feminist Philosophical Reflections on Disability* (New York: Routledge, 1996), 38.

24. Social model hardliners would argue that society is *set up* in such a way so that twenty extra seconds is consequential in such situations and therefore the structure of society which requires a certain pace is also constructing this disability. While there is obvious merit to such a view, the social model is inadequate in explaining the complex normalized construction of inefficient (communicative) bodies themselves.

25. Garland-Thomson, *Extraordinary Bodies*, 45; compare with the stutter as an unwanted outside force.

26. Whitten, "The Face of All the World is Changed," 174–175; 166–167.

27. Garland-Thomson, *Extraordinary Bodies*, 42.

28. Jezer, *Stuttering*, 151.

29. Wendell, *The Rejected Body*, 63.

30. The construction of stuttering within late-capitalism has been gestured toward, yet not thematized in this present work. It is however worth noting that interventions such as Pagoclone and SpeechEasy, as well as Jezer's experience of employability, all point toward the marketization of therapy, pathology and able-bodiedness native to late-capitalism. Important questions of the autonomy and agency of the stuttering liberal subject are raised within this sphere wherein *what* one does—that one is competent—is in many ways overshadowed by *how* these competencies are performed. The intense commodification and marketization of image within late-capitalism further oppresses one who stutters beyond what is experienced in industrialized capitalism.

31. I would be overstating my case to say that stuttering is uniquely interpreted as a moral failure, for other liminal disabilities, particularly those like chronic

fatigue syndrome which are scarcely understood, are similarly condemned. In spite of this, speech impediments present themselves as a distinctive case due to the culture of therapy pervasively surrounding the disability. Within the discourse, it is established that stuttering most often *can* be successfully managed through self-disciplinary measures.

32. Kathleen Lebesco, *Revolting Bodies: The Struggle to Redefine Fat Identity* (Boston, MA: Massachusetts University Press, 2004), 55.

WORKS CITED

American Psychiatric Association. "Stuttering." *Diagnostic and statistical manual of mental disorders* (4th ed., text rev.). Washington, DC: American Psychiatric Association.

Bordo, Susan. *Unbearable Weight: Feminism, Western Culture, and the Body.* Los Angeles, CA: University of California Press, 1993.

Brewer, William F. and Bruce L. Lambert. "The Theory-Ladenness of Observation and the Theory-Ladenness of the Rest of the Scientific Process." *Philosophy of Science* 68, no. 3 (2001): 176–186.

Corker, Marion and Tom Shakespeare, eds. *Disability/Postmodernity: Embodying Disability Theory.* New York: Continuum, 2002.

Davis, Lennard J. *Enforcing Normalcy.* New York: Verso, 1995.

Foucault, Michel. *The Hermeneutics of the Subject: Lectures at the College De France 1981-1982.* New York: Picador, 2005.

Garland Thomson, Rosemarie. *Extraordinary Bodies: Figuring Physical Disability in American Culture and Literature.* New York: Columbia University Press, 1997.

Jezer, Marty. *Stuttering: A Life Bound up in Words.* New York: Basic Books, 1997.

Kang, Changsoo, Sheikh Riazuddin, Jennifer Mundorff, Donna Krasnewich, Penelope Friedman, James C. Mullikin, and Dennis Drayna. "Mutations in the Lysosomal Enzyme–Targeting Pathway and Persistent Stuttering." New *England Journal of Medicine* 362 (2010): 677–685.

Lebesco, Kathleen. *Revolting Bodies: The Struggle to Redefine Fat Identity.* Boston, MA: Massachusetts University Press, 2004.

Linton, Simi. *Claiming Disability.* New York: New York University Press, 1998.

Lugones, María. "Playfulness, 'World'-Travelling, and Loving Perception." In *Feminist Philosophy Reader.* Edited by Alison Bailey and Chris Cuomo. New York: McGraw-Hill, 2008.

Petrunik, Micheal and Clifford Shearing. "Fragile Facades: Stuttering and the Strategic Manipulation of Awareness." *Social Problems* 31, no. 2 (1983): 125–138.

Pinker, Steven. *The Language Instinct: How the Mind Creates Language.* New York: Morrow, 1994.

Shakespeare, Tom. *Disability Rights and Wrongs.* New York: Routledge, 2006.

Shell, Marc. *Stutter.* Cambridge, MA: Harvard University Press, 2005.

Smith, Stephanie. "Unlocking a Medical Mystery." CNN. http://www.cnn.com/2010/HEALTH/02/10/stuttering.genes.cell/. Accessed July 11, 2011.

Stevenson, Robert Louis. *Lay Morals.* Cambridge: Cambridge Scholars Publishing, 2009.

Storozhuk, Anna. "Perception: Mirror Image or Action?." *Journal for General Philosophy of Science* 38, no. 2 (2007): 369–382.

Titchkosky, Tanya. *Disability, Self and Society.* Toronto, ON: University of Toronto Press, 2003.

Wendell, Susan. *The Rejected Body: Feminist Philosophical Reflections on Disability*. New York: Routledge, 1996.

Whitten, Ida E. *"The Face of All the World is Changed": An Autobiographical Study with the Focus on Stuttering*. Cincinnati, OH: Scott Zoller, 1989.

Young, Iris Marion. *Justice and the Politics of Difference*. Princeton, NJ: Princeton University Press, 1990.

2 On Prophetic Stammering[1]

Herbert Marks

Biblical prophecy is hard to read, harder even than biblical narrative, and the ostensible reasons are fairly obvious. The prophets, in Luther's words, "have a queer way of talking, like people who, instead of proceeding in an orderly manner, ramble off from one thing to the next, so that you cannot make head or tail of them or see what they are getting at."[2] Though critical analysis has improved on this formlessness, providing various maps of oral and redactional intention, the impression of sheer accumulation, of forbidding, nonsequential abundance, manages to persist. One might even argue that it helps account for the prophets' capacity to move us so powerfully, an effect that differs, at least in degree, from the continuous modulations of skillful reading, being more sudden and intermittent.

Christopher Smart, who knew as much about Hebrew poetry as Bishop Lowth or his scholarly successors, offers a profound comment on the method of these and his own cumulative "add-orations" in the third fragment of his revisionary psalter, the *Jubilate Agno*:

> For innumerable ciphers will amount to something.
> . . . .
> For the mind of man cannot bear a tedious accumulation of
>   nothings without effect. (C35–36)

Like his poetics of atonement, Smart's hermeneutic invites us to presume, in desire or aspiration, on the power of composition and the synthetic unity of form. It stresses the prerogatives of language, but it also acknowledges the transcendental agency in every act of assimilation. This presumption, which grounds the rationalists' stand against skepticism—against the radical discontinuity of all perception and the suspicion that causal relations are at best hypothetical—is the same which, strenuously exercised, allows us to read the prophets. Even the most minimal act of interpretation, as Augustine insisted, requires that we transform, or atone, succession into union. In reading the Bible, as in reading Smart's poem, we are forced to forgo the prop of authorial intention (adjacent verses in the Bible may well be the work of different authors; in the *Jubilate Agno,* where the episodic schizophrenia of the author is confirmable, of radically disjunctive states of mind). But Smart's lines also remind us how tenuous the prop of intentionality can be, and that our opportunity in forgoing it is to move the battle with skepticism indoors: behind the essentially erotic problem of intercommunication to the stark arena where the one and the many would defy one another.

Rephrased in the language of contemporary idealism, Smart's rule conforms almost precisely to a more influential eighteenth-century theory, Kant's analytic of the sublime, particularly that subdivision sometimes known as the sublime of magnitude or the "mathematical sublime." In his third *Critique,* section 29, Kant describes the sublime object as one "the representation of which determines the mind to think the unattainability of nature as a presentation of [reason's] ideas."[3] The relation by means of which "unattainability" (*Unerreichbarkeit*) becomes a mode of "presentation" (*Darstellung*) depends on the substitution of a cognitive for a perceptual failure, but the same structure may be applied to objects outside nature, in the first place to literature but in the end perhaps even to memory traces or to affective impulses that display the compulsive structure of repetition. Accordingly, Thomas Weiskel, in his discussion of Kant's theory, argued for a broadening of the definition: "We call an object sublime," he writes, "if the attempt to represent it determines the mind to regard its inability to grasp wholly the object as a symbol of the mind's relation to a transcendent order."[4] "We call" simply records a linguistic fact; for in Kant's theory sublimity is properly referred to the *subject* and to the extension of its power, the "supersensible destiny" that follows upon its collapse before the innumerable ciphers, and not to the ciphers themselves. The indefinite plural or unassimilable excess that defeats the ordinary understanding becomes the occasion of a reactive identification that depends on the negative relation of unattainability. In Weiskel's semiological translation: "The absence of a signified itself assumes the status of a signifier, disposing us to feel that behind this newly significant absence lurks a newly discovered presence."[5] Daunted initially by a repetition that defies assimilation, the mind posits the same potential infinity within itself, thereby both capitulating to repetition and defending against its ostensive form.

One of the virtues of Kant's theory is the ease with which it allows itself to be translated into a hermeneutic, to yield a "reader's sublime" as well as a "mathematical sublime," and it thus seems to me a useful model for approaching my proper topic—prophetic calling. A second model, from poetic rhetoric, will figure later on, but I believe that even here our operative categories are abstractions from our own experience as readers. The grammatical ambiguity in the conjunction of prophet and call is already thematic. Is the prophet subject or object, we ask. But the voice that cries calls only "Cry" (Isa 40:6). The cry itself is a repetition, and our understanding of the identity, or, as we shall see, the identifications, that conditioned it must proceed via the dynamics of transference if we are to escape from the empty labeling of traditional scholarship, with its purely formal typologies.

In limit cases, what the prophet himself transfers or conveys is finally nothing more than the fact of conveyance itself, a reflexive figure that culminates in the gospel of Mark, whose content is its own proclamation, and in John's treatment of the messiah as the Word. The Kantian sublime might be said to operate by two submodes, negation and tautology, and the self-referential oracle is perhaps the strongest example of the latter, whose paradigm is YHWH's self-originating and self-circumscribed gloss on his own name, *'ehyeh 'asher 'ehyeh,* "I will be what I will be" (Exod 3:14). One example is the isolated but climactic oracle immediately preceding the first of the three doxologies strategically placed by the editors of Amos to solemnize the divine judgments:

> Therefore, thus I will do to you, O Israel;
>> because I will do this to you,
>> prepare to meet your God, O Israel! (Amos 4:12)[6]

Here, the logical order, accusation-threat, elsewhere followed by Amos (3:11, 5:11, 5:16, 6:7, 7:17) has been reversed, a metalepsis emphasized by the unusual conjunction *('eqev ki)* with its intensive force, "precisely because." Concurrently, the two ostensives, "thus" and "this," have no referent other than each other. The result is another *idem per idem* formula in which temporality is collapsed in a promise (or threat) of manifestation. Teased out, the logic of the oracle is double: "because of God's action, therefore manifestation of God's action," with the floating sense of futurity in the imperfect aspect left to hover ambiguously between the two clauses. One is reminded of the deuteronomistic superscription in which what Amos sees is the word of Amos: "The words of Amos . . . which he saw concerning Israel" (1:1).

Another example is God's response to the renewed complaint of Habakkuk, whose satisfaction must derive not from the vision but from the annunciation of the vision:

> And the Lord answered me:
>> Write the vision;
>> make it plain upon tablets,
>> so that he may run who reads it.
> For still the vision awaits its time;
>> it hastens to the end—it will not lie.
> If it seem slow, wait for it;
>> it will surely come, it will not delay.
> Behold, he whose soul is not upright in him shall fail,
>> but the righteous shall live by his faith (Hab 2:2–4)

—or, following Gerald Janzen, "by his confidence in it [the vision]" *(be'emunato,* objective pronoun).[7] In its literary context this vision may be the theophany described in the closing hymn—YHWH the divine warrior riding forth from Mount Paran attended by pestilence and plague (Hab 3); but the power of the prophetic word is independent of the content of the vision which in Chapter 2 is indefinitely deferred in favor of attentiveness to the announcement itself—a purely kerygmatic program. Here no less than in the negative sublime the "absence of a signified itself assumes the status of a signifier." The epistemological breakdown is resolved by substitution, and we ourselves experience the freedom or power that corresponds to the *active* apprehension of terms independent of causality. To recall Kant's phrase, "unattainability" becomes a form of "presentation."

A similar dialectic explains the effectiveness of the more prevalent sub-mode of negation. Here the paradigmatic instance for interpreters since Hegel is from Psalm 104: "who coverest thyself with light as with a garment: who stretchest out the heavens like a tent"; but the "great veil," as Maimonides calls the juxtaposition of revelation and concealment, figures in all of the prophets where it is incident to, or even definitive of, prophetic speech: "obscuris vera involvens" (*Aeneid* 6.100)—the difficult ornament universally associated with prophecy.[8]

I invoke this Renaissance commonplace critically, for I want to contest the notion that the rhetorical forms that prophecy takes are secondary embellishments, or even parabolic correlatives of their object, as if this could be independently known. Obscuration corresponds rather to the moment of blockage that marks the mind's defeat before the unattainability of the object. It symbolizes not the transcendent order but the prophet's relation to the transcendent order, a relation that includes his mute intuition of his own infinitude. The rhetoric of obscuration which follows upon the prophetic call demonstrates—like the rhetoric of threat—the prophet's identification with the blocking agent that *he himself* has constructed in a reaction against the indefinite magnitude (Smart's "innumerable ciphers") which threatens to overwhelm him. In the Kantian model, this magnitude is external, a sum of natural percepts or, in our hermeneutic translation, of legible signs. From a Freudian perspective, we might rather say that an external effect provokes the deferred mobilization of unbound "energy"—a metapsychological notion homologous to Weiskel's "excessive signifiers"—which assails the mind from within. Defenseless against such an assault, the ego calls upon repression to block the excess to which no phenomenal signified corresponds.

In the dramatizations of prophetic calling, this central moment of blockage before the reactive identification takes place is represented by the prophetic stammer—the "slow tongue" of Moses and its variations, the "unclean lips of Isaiah," the demur of Jeremiah, the mutism of Ezekiel. The topos has had a full career in secular literature, invariably marking the subject's resistance to an overwhelming influx. Thus Dante, when abandoned to himself by Virgil toward the end of the *Purgatorio*, will stand mute, his voice broken "like an overstretched bow," following the unique invocation of his proper name by Beatrice (his version of the prophetic call); while Vico, followed by Joyce, will make stammering the original utterance, an imitation of—but also a reaction to—the senseless iteration of the thunder.[9] The complex dynamics behind all these uses are captured most subtly in the stammering of the bride in the *Cántico espiritual* of St. John of the Cross:

> Y todos cuantos vagan
> de ti me van mil gracias refiriendo
>   y todos mas me llagan,
>   y dejame muriendo
> un no se que que quedan balbuciendo.

[And all who pass tell me as they go of your thousand graces, and each wounds me more, and I am left dying by I don't know what that they keep stammering.]

The thousand rumored graces of vague provenance which wound the poet provoke, by their unassimilable magnitude, a sense of inundation. Meaningless iteration is then projected out onto the others, who are represented as stammering ("balbuciendo"). In between, however, the ego's own blockage is figured by a phonic and grammatical stammer in the verse itself ("un no se que que quedan").

The most extraordinary representation of the prophetic stammer in the Hebrew Bible is Ezekiel's prophecy to the mountains of Israel in Chapter 36, which with its disordered plethora of commissions to the prophet, summonses to attention, causal conjunctions, and introductory formulae resembles nothing so much as the *qua qua* of Lucky's speech in *Waiting for Godot*. The effect may well be the result of editorial overlaying, but even Walther Zimmerli, the most comprehensive of Ezekiel's modern critics, confesses himself thwarted by the dense tangle of inceptions, each turning on the last, which precede the climactic announcement of YHWH's turning toward Israel in verse 11:[10]

> And you, son of man, prophesy to the mountains of Israel, hear the word of the Lord. Thus says the Lord God: Because the enemy said of you, 'Aha!' and, 'The ancient heights have become our possession,' therefore prophesy, and say, Thus says the Lord God: Because, yea, because they made you desolate . . . ; therefore, O mountains of Israel, hear the word of the Lord God: Thus says the Lord God to the mountains and hills, the ravines and the valleys, the desolate wastes and the deserted cities, which have become a prey and derision to the rest of the nations round about; therefore thus says the Lord God: I speak in my hot jealousy against the rest of the nations, and against all Edom, who gave my land to themselves as a possession. . . . Therefore prophesy concerning the land of Israel, and say to the mountains and hills, to

the ravines and valleys, Thus says the Lord God: Behold, I speak in my jealous wrath, because you have *suffered* the reproach of the nations; therefore thus says the Lord God: I swear [literally, '*lift* my hand'] that the nations that are round about you shall themselves *suffer* reproach. But you, O mountains of Israel, shall shoot forth your branches, and *bear* your fruit to my people Israel; for they will soon come home . . . (Ezek 36:1–8)

Here the conjunctions "because" and "therefore" give a promise of discursive movement, but in fact the phrases are logically independent. If one tries to analyze the speech grammatically, one finds only abstract patterns: the triple recurrence of the command to "prophesy," as of the pseudo-illative "because," suggesting one purely formal model; while the sixfold repetition of the phrase "Thus says the Lord God," which with the injunction to "hear the word of the Lord God" makes seven occurrences of the divine name, recalls the numerological schemes encoded in the priestly account of creation. As if in comment upon this extended epanaphora or "carrying back," the actual oracle, marked by the long-delayed eruption of the first person ("I speak"), turns about the recurrent stem *nasa'* 'to carry' ("suffer," "lift," "bear"), whose nominal form, *massa'* 'burden,' is in fact the technical term for oracle.

Ezekiel himself, in contrast to Isaiah, Jeremiah, and many of the Twelve, never uses the nominal form *massa'*, but the verb occurs throughout the book as a figure for prophetic calling: "Then the Spirit *lifted* me up . . ." (3:12, 14; 8:3; 11:1, 24; 43:5). The meaning of this avoidance may be covertly at issue in our passage, which seems to allude to the celebrated speech by Jeremiah expressly prohibiting the use of *massa'* in prophetic discourse:

When one of this people, or a prophet, or a priest asks you, 'What is the burden of the Lord?' you shall say to them, 'You are the burden, and I will cast you off, says the Lord.' And as for the prophet, priest, or one of the people who says, 'The burden of the Lord,' I will punish that man and his household. . . . Surely I will *lift* you up and cast you away. (Jer 23:33–39)

(Similar puns appear in Numbers 11—a text concerned with the office of the prophet—where Moses resents the weight of the public "burden" that has been placed on him and compares himself to a nurse who has to *"carry a sucking child"*—a figure enlarged by the analogy between the prophetic word and manna in the same chapter.)

Since Jeremiah's speech, at least in the canonical arrangement, follows directly on his imprecation against prophets "who steal my words from one another" (23:30), Ezekiel's appropriation is particularly sly. Yet the allusive strategy is darkly apposite given his larger revisionary project. Where "reproach" and "disgrace" in Jeremiah are to be the portion of the Isra-elites, who flaunt the verbal forms of prophecy while ignoring its ethos, Ezekiel, writing a few years later in the wake of the Babylonian conquest, has YHWH promise to turn the same threat against the surrounding nations (Ezek 36:6, 7, 15; the words echo those of Jer 23:40 and stand moreover with the verb *nasa'*). For both prophets, however, the double sense of *massa'* represents their own ambivalence toward the prophetic commission.

The ambivalence that binds the stammerer is finely diagnosed by St. John's modem admirer, Gertrude Stein, who transposes it, in Kantian fash-ion, into the realm of aesthetics ("Pigeons on the grass, alas"). In Stein's cri-tique, stammering is a response to the crisis of inception, best represented in her early poem "Orange In" (read "origin") from *Tender Buttons,* whose final paragraphs oppose a premolecular "pain soup" to the obstructed wish for a creation ex nihilo ("only excreate, only excreate a no since"). The result is a second stalemate: a spontaneous generation of non-sense, which refuses to abandon causality, and hence to proceed:

> A no, a no since, a no since when, a no since when since, a no since when since a no since when since, a no since, a no since when since, a no since, a no, a no since, a no since, a no since, a no since.

For Stein as for many poets, the impasse of origination (inseparable from originality in the modern sense) is manifest primarily in the insistence of semantic phantoms, which gather about every rhythmically or phonetically modulated text like dead souls about a sacrifice. But the crisis of inception has a deeper structure, suggested most clearly in the striking figure used by the Priestly writer to signify the barrier of resistance or verbal blockage in his version of the call of Moses (Exod 6). In this revision of the burn-ing bush story, Moses is sent directly to Pharaoh: "But Moses said to the Lord, 'Behold, the people of Israel have not listened to me; how then shall Pharaoh listen to me, who am a man of uncircumcized lips?'" (6:12). To be like Moses *'aral sephatayim,* "of uncircumcized lips," is to be vulnerable to the threat of annihilation, represented—in the symbolic structure that Freud wanted to call a phylogenetic inheritance—by the anxiety of castra-tion. Weiskel, in his treatment of the psychology of the sublime, traces the sequential movement in which this anxiety takes its place:

> In a first moment, the excessive object [in the Sinai prototype figured both by the burning bush and by the repetition of Moses' name (Exod 3:2–4)] excites a wish to be inundated, which yields an anxiety of incor-poration [marked by the divine warning to approach no nearer]; [next] this anxiety is met by a reaction formation against the wish which precipitates a recapitulation of the oedipus complex [a double move-ment elided by the Exodus text, although the transformation of the rod of authority into a serpent and the leprous contamination of the hand

thrust into the bosom (4:1–7) both suggest the redirection of an aggressive aim]; [finally this recapitulation] in turn yields a feeling of guilt. . . and is resolved through identification.[11]

The failure of speech which marks the final crossing in the prophetic call would, according to this scheme, be induced by a turning back upon the self of a destructive drive, a drive that testifies to the crucial moment of revulsion in which the prophetic ego reasserts itself, at considerable cost, against the original incommensurability of signifier and signified, form and content, outside and inside.

In the main, it is the initial and final terms of this sequence that are most apparent. Let us begin with the former. The "excessive object" (excessive with regard to its recuperable meaning or relation to the self) is especially manifest in the visions of Isaiah and Ezekiel. In the throne vision or "call" in Isaiah 6, the mind is thwarted immediately by the supernumerary wings of the seraphim and the repetitiveness of the hymn they sing to one another, a redundancy reinforced by the one echoing word *qadosh*, "holy," even before the magnitude of the calling voice makes itself felt and "the [mental] house fills with smoke" (6:4). In Ezekiel 1, the inundation is even more violent. The merkabah, or divine chariot, is a paradoxical icon of mobility, a literal and figurative vehicle whose only goal is to evade by constant transference all recuperative translation. The superabundance of its external forms defies assimilation: four cherubs with four faces and four imbricated wings, all shadows of a disembodied spirit, and thus figures not of totality but of infinity. The sound they make is indefinable: "like the sound of many waters, like the thunder of the Almighty, a sound of tumult like the sound of a host" (1:24). Neither the singing nor the words that were still prominent in the story of Micaiah ben Imla (1 Kings 22) and in the call of Isaiah—the two precursory texts—are audible any more. In the expansion that follows in the middle of the chapter, each creature is further provided with a "wheel upon the earth," the immanent extension or complement of the transcendent vehicle, yet no more comprehensible, "their construction being as it were a wheel within a wheel" (1:16), and the rims that might have marked their integral boundary being inset with eyes (1:18). If one were to take the chariot as an object for contemplative exercise, a higher instrument of accommodation rather than a vehicle of war, these eyes might seem to carry the incarnational movement a step farther, evoking the notion of mutuality. Such a figure would resemble the statues, which Rilke exhorts us to regard with total intensity until each surface begins to return our gaze.[12] As Ezekiel's prostration shows, however, the eyes of the wheels work more like the gaze of the Medusa, turning back the effort of vision and transfixing the beholder.

In Jeremiah 1, the initial excess is represented by a temporal metalepsis rather than a visual paradox. The prenatal commissioning—"Before I formed you in the womb I knew you, and before you were born I consecrated you"(1:5)—implies an infinite regress of call and response in which the prophet's attention can never bind or catch up with the original invocation. Despite the difference in form, its effect is thus similar to the unassimilable visions on the Isaianic model. At the same time, its function within the context of the deuteronomistic redaction is rather to identify Jeremiah as the "prophet like Moses" announced in Deuteronomy 18:18, a verse deliberately echoed in the unusual expression *natati debaray bepikha,* "I have put my words in your mouth," in verse 9 (where normal usage would have rather required the verb *sim).* That such overdeterminations pose no obstacle to the prophet is confirmed by the final pun on *shaqed,* which points to the duplicity of the prophetic word itself. The almond *(shaqed),* an untimely bloomer, represents the word as seen by Jeremiah, likewise called to flower before his time. But YHWH takes back even this prerogative, incorporating the word into his own *shoqed,* a providential "watching," which again objectifies the prophet and makes him into the spectacle (1:11–12). Moreover, the association with Moses will play a part in the antithetical or reactive movement of the identification, to which we may now turn, only pausing to note that in the two prophetic calls in the narrative books— the call of Moses in Exodus 3 and the call of Samuel in 1 Samuel 3—the sublime of magnitude is conveyed most simply and effectively by the bare repetition of the prophet's name—"Moses, Moses"; "Samuel, Samuel."

The identification that frees the prophet to speak is apparent in the very form of the oracle and in the phrase "word of YHWH," which occurs some 240 times in the Hebrew Bible, of which over nine-tenths relate to prophetic oracles. However, the underlying mechanism, which involves a double movement of introjection and projection, absorbing the desired presence and spitting out the destructive threat, is figured most dramatically in the scenes of oral incorporation in which the prophet actually eats the word or the scroll, YHWH places his—or perhaps Moses'—words in Jeremiah's mouth at his commissioning (1:9), but the trope is developed more fully in the course of his "second lament":

> Thy words were found, and I ate them,
>> and they became to me a joy
>> and the delight of my heart;
> for I am called by thy name,
>> Lord, God of hosts. (Jer 15:16)

The name itself, with its military epithet, suggests the prophet's commission "to pluck up and break down, to destroy and overthrow" (1:10), upon which even the word of mercy must build. In Ezekiel, a "writing prophet" in the full sense, the divine words become a written scroll, which the prophet eats following his prostrating vision, "and it was in my mouth as honey for sweetness" (Ezek 3:3). Again, the ingested words are sweet, but the prophetic speech which they unleash is bitter, a dynamic contrast made explicit by the author of Revelation, where this text is revised: "It was sweet as honey in my mouth, but when I had eaten it my stomach was made bitter" (10:10). The two effects are rather complementary than sequential, although formally one might say that the projection of punishment precedes the introjection of presence. This was the pattern in Ezekiel 36, reconfirmed at the redactional level—the promise to the mountains of Israel having been split off from its original counterpart, the oracle of judgment against the same mountains at the beginning of the collection (Ezek 6), and attached to the judgment against Edom at the end. The same pattern is reflected by the conventional tripartite arrangement of several of the minor prophets and of the Greek text of Jeremiah. The book of Zephaniah is particularly revealing by virtue of its strategically placed tropes of incorporation. Thus, in Chapter 1, the imminent "day of the Lord" is conceived, following Amos, as a "day of wrath" on which Judah will be judged and the whole earth "devoured [te'akhel] by the fire of his jealousy" (Zeph 1:18). At the end of the central section of oracles against the nations—culminating with Assyria and Nineveh "the oppressing city"—the same phrase recurs: "For all the earth shall be devoured with the fire of my jealousy" (3:8); but now the judgment has been displaced onto the foreign nations who were the object of the preceding oracles. The ensuing gospel of redemption then culminates with a literal image of internalization in which YHWH the "devourer" assumes a place "in the midst" of Israel:

> The Lord has taken away the judgments against you,
>> he has cast out your enemies.
> The King of Israel, the Lord, is in your midst;
>> you shall fear evil no more. . . .
> The Lord, your God, is in your midst,
>> a warrior who gives victory;
> he will rejoice over you with gladness,
>> he will renew you in his love;
> he will exult over you with loud singing. (3:15, 17)

Referred to the individual prophet, such incorporation is the active counterpart of the original anxiety produced by the desire for inundation, and the bitterness of the law derives its flavor from the intensity of the prophet's own defense against the intrusion of the sublime.

In the one place where Freud discusses stammering directly (the case history of Frau Emmy von N.), he traces it to a moment of childhood panic during which his patient had fought back a strong urge to scream. The convulsive inhibition of speech had then become a mnemic symbol, involuntarily repeated years later whenever there was an analogous conflict between an intention and an antithetic idea or "counter-will."[13] The prophetic stammer might be thought to mark a similar conflict between the wish to cry out and the fear of crying, except that in prophecy, which represents the abrogation of temporality, the three phases of the Freudian model—trauma, repression, and return in the symptom—would have to be collapsed.

The attraction of the hysterical model within the context of the Kantian sublime is that it develops from an initial overwhelming of the ego. The stammer is a secondary transposition of the psychical conflict provoked by the original influx; in economic terms, the energy released by repression (by the dissociation of idea and affect) is converted into a somatic symptom. The primary symptom of the first stage of hysteria, which always presupposes a passive experience of unpleasure, is fear "accompanied by a *gap* in the psyche."[14] It is because of the gap that the source or object of the fear is never accessible, as it would be in the case of an external danger, against which the primitive defense would be flight. (It is because Jonah is a devout student of biblical tradition, and thus clear about the source of his call, that he commits the mistake of fleeing.)

If the stammer resembles a hysterical response to YHWH's "call," the call itself might rather come within the defensive structure of paranoia, in which "the repressed affect seems invariably to return in hallucinations of voices."[15] Since hallucinations are themselves irrepressible, they provoke a secondary defense on the part of the ego, which, instead of dismissing them as alien, adapts itself through an often elaborate system of intellectual formations, which Freud called "assimilatory" or "interpretive" delusions.[16] This whole process is subsequent to an original act of projection, understood, at least in the early writings, as a form of *méconnaissance*, in which one escapes from self-reproach by recognizing one's own forbidden tendencies only as they appear in others.

Where hysteria begins with the overwhelming of the ego, paranoia leads indirectly to the same effect. Perhaps then the prophetic texts should be considered "interpretive delusions," which in turn employ the hysterical model as a representational strategy. This would suggest that the tropes and displacements of representation, its endless deferrals and extraneous versions, are precisely the inaccessible "experience" one seeks in vain as the original cause of defense. Such circular reasoning would narrow the divide between prophets and redactors, both of whom are excluded from knowledge of the first cause. More specifically, it would confirm our intuition that if the oracles "bear witness," it is only insofar as they themselves are inspired interpretations—attempts to understand what such a thing as prophecy could be. Similar intimations of our exclusion from knowledge eventually led Freud to formulate a more radical model of defense—a "splitting of the ego," in which disavowal and acknowledgment "persist side by side."[17] In disavowal (*Verleugnung),* the gap within the psyche is replaced by a gap between the psyche and the world. Thus "what was abolished internally returns from without"—from the inaccessible dimension both Lacan and the prophets would label "the real."[18] Disavowal and the consequent splitting of the ego are brought about by experiences of presence *and* absence, in which self-preservation demands that the absence be denied. This returns us to the prophetic trope of circumcision; for Freud's prototypical instance involves sexual difference, and what the subject denies or disavows is castration.

If, like Freud and the biblical authors, we are prepared to take the bedrock of sexual difference figuratively, we may draw a further lesson on the stammering of the prophet from the uncanny story of the bridegroom of blood, which follows the call of Moses in Exodus:

> At an encampment on the way, the Lord met him and sought to kill him. Then Zipporah took a flint and cut off the foreskin of her son and touched his feet with it and said, "Surely you are a bridegroom of blood to me!" So he let him go. At that time she said "bridegroom of blood" in reference to the circumcision. (Exod 4:24–26)

The passage seems to allude to a more extensive tradition, long since lost, but in its present context it concerns Moses on his way to Egypt to execute the prophetic commission he has only just received. Since there is no antecedent for the "him" whom YHWH meets, we cannot say who precisely is threatened (a calculated uncertainty, as in the similar story of Jacob and the angel, Gen 32). However, the fact that the son is specified in the following verse suggests that the attack was originally against Moses. If we assume further that Zipporah's words are addressed to her husband and that it is thus his genitals she touches with the son's foreskin ("feet" is a conventional euphemism), we may interpret the scene as extending a symbolic, or second, circumcision to Moses himself. Precritical interpreters, beginning with the ancient versions, read the circumcision as a symbolic sacrifice, in which the blood of the son shed by Zipporah atones for the guilt of Moses—incurred, as the rabbis made explicit, by his failure to perform the rite himself. The final verse, which appears to be an editorial gloss, tends to support this reading, the repetition drawing attention away from the demon-god, to whom the title "bridegroom of blood" would originally have belonged, and redirecting it to his would-be representative.

In the Priestly version of Moses' call in Exodus 6, however, the need for circumcision is transferred back onto the scene of commissioning itself, where, as already mentioned, it interprets the prophet's stammer: "slow of speech and tongue" in the earlier account (4:10) becoming "of uncircumcized lips" (6:12). This conflation opens up the possibility of a less ritualistic reading of the bridegroom passage, in which Zipporah's act is not a sacrificial atonement but, on the contrary, a symbolic castration. From the moment he removes his sandals at the burning bush, Moses is alive and potent only by virtue of the potency of YHWH. On the road to Egypt he has to come to terms with the reality of his new office—to renounce his own prerogative in favor of an otherness he is still tempted to disavow. The acknowledgment of castration is the recognition of that otherness, or of the other's presence as absent other: hence the urgency of the circumcision, which can only be carried out by the wife—the one marked by absence here acting as surrogate for the absent one. For the prophet to repudiate circumcision would be to disavow the absence that assails him and so to remain captive to the demonic power of the real which only symbolization can undo. Stammering is the sign of this "captation" by the real, resolved in the passage through oral circumcision—a passage to the symbolic dynamics of projection and identification.

In Exodus 4 the circumcision is performed on the son, that is, on the sign of the prophet's past encounter with the uncanniness of the surrogate in coition. This substitution of son for father, enlarged by the oscillation of the pronouns, qualifies the status of Moses as first or archetypal prophet, replacing origin with originary repetition. The initiation at Sinai is shadowed by the attack on the road to Egypt; YHWH's relation to Moses is shadowed by Moses' relation to Aaron; and so on. Such repetitions cut both ways. On the one hand, they provide against cultic fixation, thereby freeing us from the immobility of worship; but they also weaken the linearity of history, which can no longer be felt as progressive. In the Priestly call narrative, the description of Moses as "of uncircumcised lips" at 6:12 is recapitulated, with the syntax reversed, at 6:30. Between the two verses, we are given the genealogy of the Levites, in which Aaron and Moses both appear. Biblical history is here the blank space within the stammering of the text. In Kantian terms, it passes from the mode of permanence into the mode of succession in pursuit of the mode of simultaneity. We cannot hear the voice of Moses except in the voice of Aaron; we cannot touch the bridegroom of blood but only those marked by his absence.

The identification of the prophet with YHWH is thus dependent on a second identification with the son, which defends against the pressures of historical supersession. Ultimately, this Oedipal son is a figure for the people of Israel. A similar doubling of prophet and people is evident in the accounts of prophetic calling, though it is often obscured by the more obvious signs of antagonism. The call of Jeremiah, for instance, ends with a figure of fortification that can be read from two sides:

> And I, behold, I make you this day a fortified city, an iron pillar, and bronze walls, against the whole land, against the kings of Judah, its princes, its priests, and the people of the land. They will fight against you; but they shall not prevail against you, for I am with you, says the Lord, to deliver you. (Jer 1:18–19)

The "bronze wall," which seems at first to be an image of separation between YHWH—or Jeremiah—and the Israelites, is also, in the context of the Babylonian sieges, an image of protection: YHWH will make Jeremiah himself the wall of protection which the city lacks. In part, then, Jeremiah identifies himself with the people, that is, with the externalized object of condemnation required by the logic of prophetic transference. Such an identification is clearly second-order, but it is the crucial movement that distinguishes prophetic calling from other manifestations of the sublime, whether mystical or aesthetic. One sees it most clearly at the beginning of Deutero-Isaiah, where the portrayal of the heavenly council is resolved into a call scene with the conversion of the indeterminate voice that generates or controls the various rhetorical voices into the voice of the "herald Zion" (Isa 40:1–9). The corporate title picks up and effectively transfigures the initial response of the solitary "I" unable to reconcile the call to prophesy with the dire knowledge of his own mortality or limitation: "A voice says, 'Cry!' And I said, 'What shall I cry? All flesh is grass.'" The repeated phrase "the grass withers" dramatizes not the influx of sublimity, but the fixation of the blocked prophet before an inaccessible word until, in a paronomastic inversion of "the word made flesh," the flesh that is grass (*habbasar hatsir*) becomes the herald Zion (*mebasseret tsiyon*).

I want to return in concluding to the perspective of the reader; for the prophet's heteropathic or centripetal identification with the people of Israel is as it were a mirror of the reader's own. The absolute importance of this element is that it distinguishes prophecy as a literary genre from lyric, in which the reader identifies with the poetic "I"—most intensely perhaps when the poem pretends to address him or her as "you." Lyric poetry, in Mill's famous phrase, is always "overheard"; but the word is only prophetic if it is heard directly. This is not a distinction that corresponds to biblical/ classical or sacred/secular but is independent of the institutionalization of historical traditions and generic forms.

In classical rhetoric, apostrophe, the figure of direct address, is commonly placed beside prosopopoeia, the trope which "gives a face" to inanimate objects and nonperceptual categories such as time. According to Quintilian, prosopopoeia may serve equally "to bring down the gods from heaven and to raise the dead."[19] Raising the dead is elsewhere the specific function of "eidolopoeia," which may also refer to the petrifying impact the trope can have on the audience. Thus, Paul de Man only develops a rhetorical commonplace when he writes of "the latent threat that inhabits prosopopoeia, namely that by making the dead speak, the symmetrical structure of the trope implies, by the same token, that the living are struck dumb, frozen in their own death."[20]

The same effect applies to the experience of hearing a prophetic oracle, as the example of Dante at the end of the *Purgatorio* "turned to stone in the mind and stonelike" illustrates (33.73–76). Beatrice's command to the poet paralyzed by the prophecy of the DVX is to "carry" the obscure words away within him—"if not written, at least depicted"—a command that seems designed to allay the poet's (or perhaps the reader's) misgivings about the imminent transition from direct address to literary inscription. The meaning of this transition is the obsessive concern of Romantic poetry, most overt in Wordsworth, and we may turn to it briefly here as a way of testing the relation of prophet to poet, hitherto simply assumed. The classic prooftext is the "Intimations Ode," which revises the peculiar paradigm of prophetic calling at the end of Virgil's fourth eclogue—source for the blessed babe passage in Book Two of the *Prelude* as well. The final lines of Virgil's "messianic" poem mark at once the actual inception of the new age, invoked with perlocutionary force, and, in their chiastic structure, the impossibility of ever finding a point of entry into its perfected economy:

> incipe, parve puer, risu cognoscere matrem:
> matri longa decem tulerunt fastidia menses,
> incipe, parve puer: cui non risere parentes,
> nec deus hunc mensa, dea nec dignata cubili est.

> [Begin, baby boy, to know thy mother with a smile—to thy
> mother ten months have brought the weariness of travail.
> Begin, baby boy! Him on whom his parents have not smiled,
> no god honours with his table, no goddess with her bed.][21]

Like the mutual infusions of the blessed babe passage, the circulation of interdependent smiles has no obvious point of origin, unless it is the poet's own timely utterance, the "incipe, parve puer." The important difference is that in Wordsworth's work utterance can only follow the *disruption* of this interdependence; the subject may indeed think with (by virtue of) its object, but can only *speak* without it. Thus, the babe that "leaps up on his mother's arm" at the end of the joyous awakening in stanza four of the "Ode" may incite the poet to realize his calling—to pass from "I have heard the call" to "I hear, I hear, with joy I hear!"—but the leap, like the oracle which evoked it, is premature. As a result, the vision collapses before the end of the stanza, and composition, as we know, was suspended for two years.

I am inclined to read this intermittence in the "Ode" as a more extended version of the prophetic stammer, analogous to the mutism of Ezekiel, only at a somewhat higher level of abstraction—since it is now the entire scene of election, with its self-reflexive calls and conversions, rather than the more daemonic eruption of a personified demand, that constitutes the intolerable burden. Yet there can be no doubt that the poet's intimations extend to the very pattern of intermittence itself, which seems to have been an essential part of the poem's initial agenda. One cannot ignore the almost programmatic shrillness of the opening allegro or discount the echo of Spenser's poignant address to Colin Clout on Mount Acidale, about to be bereft of his vision ("Pype iolly shepheard, pype thou now apace," *Fairie Queene* 6.10.16), in the reflexive apostrophe at the end of stanza three: "Thou Child of Joy / Shout round me, let me hear thy shouts, thou happy / Shepherd Boy!" Wordsworth's defaults, on closer reading, are often ironically self-conscious, which is another reason why critics can speak of his tone as anti-apocalyptic. In his work, the shadow of the object has become so long that its darkness acquires a generic outline of its own, recognizable in the elegiac frame that at once limits and composes every representation of the call.

When the poet's block finally lifted and he resumed composition of the "Ode" at stanza five, it was with a mythical account of the theory of anamnesis, in which the soul comes to birth "trailing clouds of glory." Now however, Wordsworth has a subtler attitude toward the "Mighty Prophet" who is the youthful subject of this myth. Not yet schooled in the "fallings" and "vanishings" which will free him to remember and recreate his own life, he remains a captive to presence: "Thou, over whom thy Immortality / Broods like the Day, a Master o'er a Slave, / A Presence which is not to be put by." Why this brooding, and why these figures of bondage? The allusion through Milton to the mysterious wind of God "brooding" over the primal waters (*Paradise Lost* 1.21) is only background for the figure, although the ambiguous identity of a spirit that impregnates after, or even *by* incubating is analogous in several respects to a breeze, at once correspondent and creative, that "vexes its own creation" (1805 *Prelude*, 1.47) or to a voice, both concordant and transgressive, that through the hollow of woven fingers inaugurates by mimicking (5.390–414). For the "Boy of Winander," the subject of this last passage, the dawn of consciousness, equivalent to a commissioning, is attendant upon the intermittence of sound and the concurrent access of vision: it is the shadow of the object that falls upon the ego. The suspension of voice, which marked the translation of the natural self in the original (first-person) Winander fragment, is represented again in the muteness of the poet himself, whose half-hour vigil by the grave (5.422–423) recalls the half-hour of silence that ushers in the synaesthetic vision of trumpets and incense at the opening of the seventh seal (Rev 8:1). Until immortality gives way to loss, the poet remains overmastered and silent. So too in the "Ode," where, with the sobering of the eye, the soul of the future poet who did "gather passion" becomes the soul that recollects or reads, transcending that primordial "Eye among the blind, / That, deaf and silent, read[s] the eternal deep."

What becomes clear in these texts is that Wordsworth abandons the direct simulation of the prophetic call (in its Virgilian as well as its Hebraic mode) and represents us instead in our reading of the call. But he does so from the conviction that these two postures are ultimately the same. The history of the prophetic movement with its ever-mounting burden of intertextuality illustrates in the end a similar intuition. Against the tumult of its echoes, critical debates between the proponents of logos and the proponents of graphe are scarcely audible. The distinctive feature of the prophetic oracle is not, as Harold Bloom has suggested, its relative freedom from influence anxieties, but simply its greater compression—the directness with which it addresses its audience.[22] In the oracle, as opposed to the Romantic lyric, the temporal, narrative, and allegorical dimensions are all omitted (or better, to use

the language of the epitaph poem itself, "by-passed," transgressed—
though they still continue to operate at the level of expectation), and the
threat revolves less literalistically around the concept of "sin," a more
difficult figuration for death.

To hear a prophetic oracle is to be totally arrested in the state of sin,
which, it must be emphasized, is not an effect of some previous act or
mental attitude, *but of the fact of being addressed.* The sinner is the one
who stands arrested under the prophetic address—outside of temporal or
natural continuity. The only possible consequences within the frame of
the address itself are fixation, or what the prophets figure forth as turning
and its emotional correlative, repentance. One might say therefore that
within the prophetic frame, trope or conversion is the sufficient and only
condition of life. The dead that are made to speak in Romantic lyrics are
generally inanimate objects or forms of nature: prosopopoeia is a rhetorical function of animism. But just as theism can be seen as animism of a
more abstract order (without thereby implying any hierarchy or evolution
from one to the other), so the prophetic oracle or divine word is a hyper-
bolic prosopopoeia. Theology represents the impulse to apostrophe as the
initiative of the other. It is thus the other that both arrests and restores us
by two movements of transformation. The critical reader, pondering all
this, is in something of the position of Leontes at the end of *The Winter's
Tale*; he recognizes the reality of the first transformation only by witness-
ing the second.

The other has several modes in which it addresses us, however: besides
the modes of judgment and promise (arrestation or literalization, and
animation or trope), there is the important mode of command. Interpretation of this final mode must eventually become objective, as in the
Abraham stories, for example, where it inheres in blind acts of obedience.
It seems to have been the peculiar trick of the prophets (at least up to
Jeremiah) to have projected the petrifying element of condemnation onto
the audience, while personally responding to an interpreted command.
Thus, for Amos, the fear of one who hears the lion's roar (Amos 3:8)—of
one arrested before the sudden manifestation in the "real" of the rent in
the ego's relation to the world—is superseded by a fiction of authority.
Amos must prophesy; it is Israel who must fear. The prophet needs the
audience so that he can project the sense of judgment or threat involved in
the apperception of the other, while retaining a sense of inalienable mission. If the mode were narrative or allegorical, it might be possible for the
one called to respond to the command—as Abraham does in Genesis 12
and 22—without implicating an audience. It could become a command
to go. But oracle, more radically even than lyric, suspends succession or
movement. Its antitemporal conventions prohibit the prophet from real-
izing the command within a narrative frame or translating it into the
first term of a sequence (thereby opening the moment up to supersession).
He is unable to evade the guilt by repressing it as Abraham does—by

transforming it into the shrouded, inaccessible occasion for the drives; all he can do is to project it onto the audience—Israel.

The crisis of Jeremiah is bound to his recognition that command and accusation cannot be so readily separated. In him, for the first time, the reflexive basis of the prophet's aggression becomes fully apparent. Whether this is the cause or the effect of the fact that he no longer has any audience is hard to say. The pronominal agitation characteristic of all apostrophic modes here becomes a subjective confusion, in which the stammering cry, *me'ay, me'ay,* "My bowels, my bowels!" (4:19) is simultaneously a transmission of divine pathos and an expression of personal outrage. Like Freud's psychotic Dr. Schreber unmanned by the *Gottesstrahlen,* he feels he has been "raped" *(patah,* 20:7–9), and he responds with the full set of negations from erotomania to jealous delusion. Ezekiel likewise suffers schizophrenic episodes and a period of muteness. In their wake, postexilic prophecy can be said to give up the oracle of judgment, to revert, in the words of the late exilic watchman, to the "burden of silence" *(massa' dumah):*

> To me, calling from Seir:
> > Watchman, what of the night?
> > Watchman, what of the night?
> The watchman says:
> > Morning comes, and also the night.
> > If you will inquire, inquire;
> > return, come. (Isa 21:11–12)

The call that comes here to the waiting prophet imposes a question rather than a command. Indeterminately emanating from a site of origin that seems to have become a land of alienation or exile, it manifests itself only as anxiety—or rather, since its subjective status is in doubt (not *qol qore',* "a voice calls," as in Isaiah 40, but only the prophet's *'elay qore',* "to me calling . . ."), it is under this mode that it is apprehended. Reiteration is its sign as well as its burden. In a sense, its burden has become a refrain.

Is this refrain fixation or the tautology representative of one mode of the sublime? An answer would be possible only if we could separate the active personae of the scene. To schematize briefly, there are three possible "voices" here: those of YHWH, his people, and the prophet. The scene offers only two personae however: the one (offstage) who questions the watchman and the watchman who answers. If the "me" addressed by the questioner is the prophet, the transition to the third person which introduces his response may again suggest the self-alienation that allows the threatened subject to escape fixation. Alienation enables the culminating identification which marks the watchman's response. His words are now YHWH's command to Israel in exile—but also an expression, albeit a weary one, of the prophet's ambiguous triumph. Henceforth, the prophetic stammer will be refigured less violently as temporal syncope, the poetic gap between an experience of presence and its recollection. We in turn are left with the agrammaticality of reading, a literary "stammering" ("un balbutiement, que semble la phrase")—in which, as Mallarmé insisted, "unfailingly the blank returns."[23]

NOTES

1. An earlier form of this essay appeared originally in *The Yale Journal of Criticism* 1, no. 1 (1987), 1–20.
2. *D. Martin Luthers Werke*, Kritische Gesamtausgabe, 70 vols. (Weimar: Hermann Böhlaus, 1883), 19.350.
3. Immanuel Kant, *Kritik der Urteilskraft* [1788, 1790], section 29, *Gesammelte Schriften* (Berlin: Preussiche Akademie der Wissenschaften, 1900–1942), 5.268.
4. Thomas Weiskel, *The Romantic Sublime: Studies in the Structure and Psychology of Transcendence* (Baltimore: The Johns Hopkins University Press, 1986), 23.
5. Weiskel, *The Romantic Sublime*, 28.
6. Biblical quotations follow the Revised Standard Version with occasional modifications.
7. See J. Gerald Janzen, "Habakkuk 2:2–4 in the Light of Recent Philological Advances," *Harvard Theological Review* 73 (1980): 53–78.
8. Moses Maimonides, *The Guide of the Perplexed*, 3.9, trans. S. Pines, 2 vols. (Chicago and London: University of Chicago Press, 1963), 2.437.
9. For Dante's "call," see *Purgatorio* 30:55; for his failure of voice, 31:16–21. Giambattista Vico describes the emergence of human speech in Chapter 4 of Book II, ii of *La Scienza Nuova*, 3rd edition (Naples, 1744), paragraph 448; cf. paragraphs 228, 462–463 on stuttering and the origins of poetry. The first of Joyce's hundred-letter thunderclaps, composed of foreign words for "thunder," appears–following an allusion to Vico's "recorso"–in the third paragraph of *Finnegans Wake*, where it sets off a volley of batrachian echoes ("Brékkek Kékkek Kékkek Kékkek! Kóax Kóax Kóax! Ualu Ualu Ualu!") and prepares the entrance of the hero, "Bygmester Finnegan, of the Stuttering Hand."
10. See Walther Zimmerli, *Ezekiel 2, II. Teilband*, Biblischer Kommentar Altes Testament, Band XIII/2 (Neukirchener-Vluyn: Neukirchener Verlag, 1969), ad loc.
11. Weiskel, *The Romantic Sublime*, 105.
12. See especially "Früher Apollo" and "Archaïscher Torso Apollos" ("denn da ist keine Stelle, / die dich nicht sieht" ["for there is no place that does not see you"]), the opening poems, respectively, of *Neue Gedichte* (1907) and *Der Neuen Gedichte Anderer Teil* (1908).
13. Sigmund Freud, *The Standard Edition of the Complete Psychological Works*, ed. and trans. James Strachey et al., 24 vols. (London: The Hogarth Press and the Institute of Psychoanalysis, 1953–74), 2.57–58, 91–92. Subsequent references are to this edition.
14. Freud, "Draft K. The Neuroses of Defence," *Standard Edition*, 1.228.
15. Freud, *Standard Edition*, 1.227.
16. Freud, *Standard Edition*, 1.227; cf. "Further Remarks on the Neuro-Psychoses of Defence," *Standard Edition*, 3.185
17. Freud, "An Outline of Psycho-Analysis," *Standard Edition*, 23.203.
18. Freud, "Psycho-Analytic Notes on an Autobiographical Account of a Case of Paranoia," *Standard Edition*, 12.71.

19. Quintilian, *Institutio Oratoria*, 9.2.31, trans. H.E. Butler, 4 vols., Loeb Classical Library (London: Heinemann, 1920–22), 3.391.
20. Paul de Man, *The Rhetoric of Romanticism* (New York: Columbia University Press, 1984), 79.
21. Translation by H. Rushton Fairclough in his edition of Virgil, Loeb Classical Library (London: Heinemann, 1916).
22. Harold Bloom, *A Map of Misreading* (Oxford: Oxford University Press, 1975), 50.
23. Stéphane Mallarmé, "Le Mystère dans les lettres" (1896), in *Oeuvres complètes*, ed. Henri Modor and G. Jean-Aubry, Bibliothèque de la Pléiade (Paris: Gallimard, 1945), 386, 387.

WORKS CITED

Bloom, Harold. *A Map of Misreading*. Oxford: Oxford University Press, 1975.
Dante Aligheri. *La Commedia secondo l'antica vulgata*. Ed. Georgio Petrocchi. 4 vols. Milan: Mondadori, 1967.
De Man, Paul. *The Rhetoric of Romanticism*. New York: Columbia University Press, 1984.
Freud, Sigmund. *The Standard Edition of the Complete Psychological Works*. Edited and translated by James Strachey et al. 24 vols. London: The Hogarth Press and the Institute of Psychoanalysis, 1953–74.
Janzen, J. Gerald. "Habakkuk 2:2–4 in the Light of Recent Philological Advances," *Harvard Theological Review* 73 (1980): 53–78.
Kant, Immanuel. *Kritik der Urteilskraft* [1788, 1790]. *Gesammelte Schriften*. Berlin: Preussiche Akademie der Wissenschaften, 1900–1942.
Luther, Martin. *D. Martin Luthers Werke*. Kritische Gesamtausgabe. 70 vols. Weimar: Hermann Böhlaus, 1883–.
Maimonides, Moses. *The Guide of the Perplexed*. Translated by S. Pines. 2 vols. ChicagoLondon: University of Chicago Press, 1963.
Mallarmé, Stéphane. "Le Mystère dans les lettres" (1896). *Oeuvres complètes*. Ed. Henri Modor and G. Jean-Aubry. Bibliothèque de la Pléiade. Paris: Gallimard, 1945.
Quintilian. *Institutio Oratoria*. Trans. H.E. Butler. 4 vols. Loeb Classical Library. London: Heinemann, 1920–22.
Smart, Christopher. *The Poetical Works of Christopher Smart: Vol. 1: Jubilate Agno*. Ed. Karina Williamson. Oxford: Oxford University Press, 1980.
Spenser, Edmund. *The Fairie Queene*. Ed. J.C. Smith. 2 vols. Oxford: Oxford University Press, 1961.
Virgil. *Eclogues. Georgics. Aeneid. The Minor Poems*. Trans. H. Rushton Fairclough. 2 vols. Loeb Classical Library. London: Heinemann, 1916.
Weiskel, Thomas. *The Romantic Sublime: Studies in the Structure and Psychology of Transcendence*. Baltimore: The Johns Hopkins University Press, 1986.
Wordsworth, William. *The Poetical Works of William Wordsworth*. Ed. Ernest de Selincourt. Oxford: Clarendon Press, 1949.
Zimmerli, Walther. *Ezekiel 2, II. Teilband*. Biblischer Kommentar Altes Testament. Band XIII/2. Neukirchener-Vluyn: Neukirchener Verlag, 1969.

3   Samuel Johnson and the Frailties of Speech

Laura Davies

The names of only a handful of authors have become eponymous with the age in which they lived. In the literature of the West, Chaucer, Shakespeare and Milton are notable examples, as too is Samuel Johnson (1709–1784). In such figures, this alignment suggests, we find the distinctive features of a particular historical period reflected. At the same time, we see evidence that its contours were shaped by their work. In the case of Johnson, this is absolutely the consensus: "[he] was a figure in whom certain cultural trends received magnification through the force of his personality and the extent of his writing" and at the same time he was "an influential creator of the ideological impressions that, in turn, would inform the way people behaved in every facet of English life."[1] The status of literary giants such as these is paradoxical, however, in that their preeminence derives from their extraordinary abilities but, as consequence of their achievements, they are also constitutive of the canon. They are, in other words, at once exceptional and normative. In Johnson's case, this tension is intensified for a number of reasons: the concept of an English literary canon was a product of his age, and even in part of his own efforts; the extent of his idiosyncrasies and bodily afflictions; and the strength and the nature of his afterlife, or what is known as the "double tradition of Dr Johnson" in which the conversational Johnson is separated from his authorial persona.[2] For Bronson, who first conceptualized this division, its source lay in Boswell's biographical agenda, but as Catherine Parks has argued more recently, its persistence has been reinforced by a further dichotomy: between "Johnson the talker, of popular tradition and Johnson the writer of scholarly tradition."[3]

This chapter aims to bring Johnson's talk and his attitude towards it back into the sphere of academic investigation and to argue that in so doing we can learn more not only about Johnson and his age, but also about the complexity of his influence upon our ideas of what it means to 'talk normal.' It will take the form of a series of case studies, allowing us to move chronologically through a series of different contexts in which Johnson spoke, listened to other voices and thought about speech, before reaching the final aphasic crisis at the end of his life.

CONVERSATION

Johnson's close friend Hester Thrale Piozzi believed conversation to be at least as important to him as writing, if not more so: "his life, at least since my acquaintance with him, consisted in little else than talking, when he was not absolutely employed in some serious piece of work."[4] Therefore, whilst the preponderance of conversational scenes within Boswell's *Life* is probably an exaggeration, it seems not to be a fundamental distortion of the rhythm of Johnson's life. Indeed, the Doctor himself was certain of its unparalleled value: "the most eligible amusement of a rational being seems to be that interchange of thoughts which is practiced in free and easy conversation."[5] It is not surprising then that he should have sought it out all his life, in clubs, taverns, and private houses, often talking his interlocutors to exhaustion and usually unwilling to "retreat from the conversational company." By avoiding solitude, he believed, he could best defend himself from the depression—'the black dog'—that constantly threatened to overwhelm him.[6]

Whatever Johnson may have claimed about "free and easy conversation," however, he could see no harm in "rough" conversation and those who knew him report that his voice was "naturally loud, and often overstretched."[7] They also agreed that the "desire of shining in conversation was in him, indeed, a predominant passion" and, thus, that there was "no arguing with Johnson; for if his pistol misses fire, he knocks you down with the butt end of it."[8] For him conversation was a battle and an opportunity to exert power over others, even to the point of rudeness.[9] On account of his quick intellect and eloquence, it was clearly also an activity at which he excelled: "Johnson's dexterity in retort, when he seemed to be driven to an extremity by his adversary, was very remarkable."[10]

For those who encountered Johnson in the flesh, however, his conversation was also extraordinary for another reason. It was punctuated by a range of curious movements and sounds, bodily tics and involuntary vocalizations. This did not go unnoticed: "His mouth is almost constantly opening and shutting as if he were chewing [. . .] His body is in continual agitation seesawing up and down."[11] It is a characteristic of which Boswell writes infrequently but with close attention. For example:

> In the intervals of articulating he made various sounds with his mouth, sometimes as if ruminating, or what is called chewing the cud, sometimes giving a half whistle, sometimes making his tongue play backwards from the roof of his mouth, as if clucking like a hen, and sometimes protruding it against his upper gums in front, as if pronouncing quickly under his breath *too, too, too.*[12]

Boswell also records the shock that Johnson's appearance generated in those who knew him only by reputation. The most famous of these anecdotes centres on the first meeting between Johnson and the artist William Hogarth at the house of Samuel Richardson. Both men clearly knew of one another but had never met. Whilst talking with his host, Boswell records, Hogarth "perceived a person standing at a window in the room, shaking his head and rolling himself about in a strange ridiculous manner. He concluded that he was an ideot, whom his relations had put him under the care of Mr. Richardson." But "to his great surprise" the figure then "took up the argument" and "displayed such a power of eloquence" that Hogarth, still not catching on, believed the "ideot had been at the moment inspired."[13]

This is an illuminating vignette on a number of counts. First it reinforces the connection that we have already seen between speech and power. Here Johnson moves from the margins of the scene to its centre, from silence to speech, and from idiocy to excellence. Second, it reveals an assumption that remains all-too common—that an afflicted body is indicative of an enfeebled mind. Third, it generates a narrative in which Johnson's astonishing intellect and capabilities as a speaker compensate for and allow him to overcome his problematic body, forcing Hogarth to switch his attention from the extraordinary body of the great Doctor to his extraordinary conversation.

Whilst this tale of triumph over adversity may well suit Boswell's biographical agenda, and has embedded itself into Johnson's posthumous reputation, it is not in fact a helpful framework through which to interpret either how Johnson understood his speech or the nature of his legacy. Its heroic strains, Lennard Davis has shown, derive from a simplistic and "moralized narrative" of selfhood embedded within the very idea of disability as "something over which the individual triumphs"; a notion that, as he points out, was in its nascent form during the eighteenth century but which is firmly established today.[14] It is problematic too, I would add, in its suggestion that Johnson's voice was an uncomplicated conduit for his intellectual powers, rather than a series of sounds produced by and from within his body. And, indeed, that as such it was under the direct control of his highly functioning mind, in contrast to his apparently wayward and afflicted body.

That this clear separation of Johnson's mind from his body and his alignment of Johnson's speech with the former, is generated at least to a degree by Boswell's desire to memorialize the great Doctor, is evidenced by the fact that on other occasions he lists Johnson's voice amongst his many peculiar bodily characteristics: "Mr. Johnson is a man of a most dreadful appearance. He is a very big man, is troubled with sore eyes, the palsy, and the king's evil. He is very slovenly in his dress and speaks with a most uncouth voice."[15] It is apparent too in Boswell's deliberate evasion here of the issue of control, and the degree to which Johnson was able to regulate his bodily tics. He attributes Johnson's clarity of expression to the "force of habit and the customary exercises of his powerful mind," but he is less forthcoming on this aspect of his speech behavior.[16] We know that Johnson's friends did speculate about the cause of Johnson's movements and vocalizations, and Boswell does record hearing Johnson refer to them as a "bad habit."[17] None of this comes through in this scene though. As Helen Deutsch has pointed out, for us, the subsequent history of scholarship on Tourette's syndrome, which many medical professionals now believe to be the most likely explanation of Johnson's symptoms, complicates the matter still further because the condition itself challenges "the limits between body and mind, and between intention and its lack."[18]

For Deutsch, Boswell's equivocation in this scene extends beyond the question of control to that of Johnson's agency and authority. In his characterization of Johnson as an "inspired ideot," she argues, a process of disembodiment is enacted and Johnson's `speech, rather than his tics' are depicted as "the product of another."[19] This is not an unreasonable interpretation. Clearly Johnson has lived on in numerous biographies and anecdotes as a voice represented on the page, and absolutely it is true that in this transferral Boswell is able to mitigate the fact that Johnson represented "a mind and body in potentially monstrous conflict."[20] It is equally the case, however, that Boswell is not entirely committed to this disembodiment. The simplest indication of his doubt lies in his attribution of this model of inspiration to Hogarth's perception of the situation: he "actually imagined that this ideot had been at the moment inspired."[21] Less overtly, but no less significantly, his turn to the language of inspiration, which is etymologically and conventionally associated with the breath, foregrounds Johnson's body not only as a receptacle into which the breath of any external force of genius must be inhaled, but also as the frame from which this inspired speech must be exhaled.[22] We see the same equivocation as to the relationship between Johnson's mind, body, voice, and authority on other occasions. It is present when Boswell discusses Johnson's voice through the analogy of "the Canterbury organ . . . that majestic medium" and it is even more so when he describes his early "admiration of his extraordinary colloquial talents" and characterizes the process by which he became familiar with the Johnsonian mode as one in which his "mind was, as it were, strongly impregnated with the Johnson aether."[23] In so doing he suggests both that Johnson merely breathed the diviner air of the Gods, but also that he did so because he was one. And, in the contrast between the rarified, insubstantial "aether" and the definitively corporeal verb "impregnated," he withholds judgment as to the extent to which Johnson's affective power operates on a bodily plane.

Boswell, it would seem, is conflicted in his desire to represent Johnson in all of his complexity, but at the same time, to depict him in a manner that would do justice to his greatness. His ambivalence with regard to the location of Johnson's voice within the mind-body problem is a key focus of this conflict, as is his bringing together of the two very different ways in which Johnson's speech was extraordinary. Both are vital components of Boswell's construction of Johnson, as a man both distinguished by his difference and yet held apart from it, or in the analysis of Lennard Davis, as a figure whose disabilities are both central to his character and yet at the same time something that he is "not really allowed to have."[24]

LEXICOGRAPHY

In his lexicographical writing Johnson approaches the subject of speech from an entirely different perspective. Where he is reticent on the subject of his own peculiarities of speech, he writes at length in his *Dictionary of the English Language* (1755) and its associated *Plan*, "Preface", and "Grammar" about the ways in which speech can both become disordered and, more importantly, how speech can itself constitute a form of disorder.[25] These arguments are advanced in a number of different ways but each essentially develops from the same starting point: Johnson's fervent belief in "the stability of truth."[26] One manifestation of this belief emerges, as DeMaria has observed, within the *Dictionary* definitions themselves, where "very often" truth "is described as a substance: solid, tangible, independent, and inflexible."[27] In the *Plan* and the "Preface", Johnson articulates this position explicitly, arguing that: "All change is of itself an evil"; "inconstancy is in every case a mark of weakness"; and that "There is in constancy and stability a general and lasting advantage."[28] It is on this basis that Johnson argues for a division between writing, which is valuable because it is permanent and resistant to decay and upon whose truths "the mind can only repose," and speech, which is transient and always in flux.[29] *Permanent*, which the *Dictionary* defines as "durable, not decaying, unchanged" is an essential quality of the Horatian ideal that Johnson claims as the goal of Western literature—"to raise monuments more durable than brass, and more conspicuous than pyramids"—whilst the first illustrative quotation of *oral* makes clear the unsuitability of speech for this noble endeavor: "Oral discourse, whose transient faults dying with sound that gives them life, and so not subject to a strict review, more easily escapes observation."[30] On this account the *Dictionary* not only takes written language, specifically that of the "writers before the restoration" whose works are regarded "as *the wells of English undefiled*" as its standard, but authorizes its definitions through illustrative literary quotations.[31]

Johnson's lexicographical position relies, however, on a particular interpretation of the nature of language itself and, more precisely, upon an assumed synonymy between language and speech: he defines *language* as "human speech" and "language" is offered as the second definition of *speech*.[32] In the *Plan* and the prefatory material to the *Dictionary* this is most neatly expressed by the synecdochic noun "tongue," by which is meant both language in general ("of English, as of all living tongues") and its spoken form specifically ("every tongue that speaks it").[33] Johnson was not unusual in this conception of language but his *Dictionary* is undoubtedly one of the publications that formalized its use. As Nicholas Hudson has shown it was only from the start of the century that grammarians and scholars started to make a "clear distinction" between the intrinsic qualities of writing and speech. Prior to this, although it was acknowledged that they differed as forms of transmission, accounts of language were constructed primarily with written reference.[34] It was through the work of lexicographers, as well as those who investigated the origins of languages, alphabetic script, and the development of civilized society from its savage roots, that this consciousness developed. As a lexicographer, therefore, Johnson believed himself to be grappling not only with the instability of speech, but also with the very nature of language itself. He acknowledges this early on in the *Plan*, in a statement that challenged the view of many of his contemporaries that language was a gift from God, but which also aligned his conception of language with that of its transient and unstable oral expression. To Johnson's mind, although the "faculty of speech" may be considered the consequence of "inspiration," language understood in terms of the manifestation of this capability in particular words or grammatical forms "did not descend to us in a state of uniformity and perfection," but rather is "the work of man, of a being from whom permanence and stability cannot be derived."[35]

Consequently, in the *Dictionary* Johnson makes a series of judgments that are ostensibly about language but which refer primarily to its spoken form. The first of these concerns the matter of order and regulation. The English language, he argues, has been "neglected, suffered to spread, under the direction of chance, into wild exuberance," meaning that his task was more difficult that it need have been: "I found our speech copious without order, and energetick without rules; wherever I turned my view, there was perplexity to be disentangled, and confusion to be regulated."[36] Reinforcing this slippage from a critique of the "wild exuberance" of language to the "confusion" of its oral form, he then is forced to acknowledge that the "boundless chaos of living speech" actually precludes any hope of regained control: "Sounds are too volatile and subtile for legal restraints; to enchain syllables, and to lash the wind, are equally the undertakings of pride; unwilling to measure its desires by its strength."[37] The French Academicians may have refused to face this, he argues, but his own work would be less naïve.

It is not coincidental then that the key characteristics of these descriptions of language as speech and of speech itself mirror those by which Johnson defines *disorder:* "irregularity," "confusion," "immethodical distribution," "tumult" and "neglect of rule." However, the embeddedness of disorder within Johnson's conception of speech also makes itself felt through his frequent recourse to metaphors of corruption and decay. For example, he argues that the language has been "resigned to the tyranny of time and fashion, and exposed to the corruptions of ignorance, and caprices of innovation."[38] For this reason, he advocates a written standard: "Much less ought a written language to comply with the corruptions of oral utterance, or copy that which every variation of time or place makes different from itself."[39] Yet at the same time, he insists that "because the first change will naturally begin by corruptions in the living speech," the "stability" of pronunciation is of signal importance for the endurance of a language.[40]

This definition of *disorder* also shapes Johnson's rejection of linguistic variety, both in terms of diction and of pronunciation. In his view, speech corrupts the ideal correctness and uniformity that can be achieved in literature. The *"wells of English undefiled"* that he quotes represent these "pure sources" and, therefore, his rule is "to consider those as the most elegant speakers who deviate least from the written words."[41] For this reason, the diction of the "laborious and mercantile part of the people" is excluded from the dictionary: "This fugitive cant, which is always in a state of increase or decay, cannot be regarded as any part of the durable materials of a language, and therefore must be suffered to perish with other things unworthy of preservation."[42] On the same grounds, he is opposed to regional dialects and accents as well as to individual idiosyncrasies of pronunciation. Thus his pronouncements that "while our language is yet living" it is "variable by the caprice of every tongue that speaks it," and that words are "so capriciously pronounced, and so differently modified, by accident or affectation, not only in every province, but in every mouth," are value judgments.[43] With the idea of caprice, which as we have seen appears on a number of occasions, Johnson's argument takes on a distinctly moral dimension. *Caprice,* as the *Dictionary* defines it—"freak, fancy, whim, sudden change of humour"— imperils the sense of order and stability he so values, and, moreover, is associated through its illustrative quotations with "ill-design," "folly" and even "vice." In the "Grammar," Johnson argues that it is only by adherence to the written word that this corruption can be avoided:

> of English, as of all living tongues, there is a double pronunciation, one cursory and colloquial, the other regular and solemn. The cursory pronunciation is always vague and uncertain, being made different in different mouths by negligence, unskillfulness, or affectation. The solemn pronunciation, though by no means immutable and permanent, is yet always less remote from orthography, and less liable to capricious innovations.[44]

As John Barrell has argued, what Johnson suggests here is that there are no valid variations in English speech. There is "one language only" and merely "different degrees of skill or care" with respect to its utterance. [45] In the *Dictionary*, therefore, Johnson aimed to encourage and assist individuals in a process of self-improvement that would transform their speech, both in its diction and pronunciation, replacing variability with uniformity, chaos with order, and corruption and disease with "purity" and health.[46]

Johnson is of course well aware that the *Dictionary* will never achieve what he hopes, and despite all his arguments about the superiority of a written standard, he admits at the close of the 'Preface' that "the pen must at length comply with the tongue."[47] Nevertheless, he refuses to relinquish his dream, certain that the fight is worth fighting:

> it remains that we retard what we cannot repel, that we palliate what we cannot cure. Life may be lengthened by care, though death cannot ultimately be defeated: tongues, like governments, have a natural tendency to degeneration; we have long preserved our constitution, let us make some struggle for our language.[48]

The expression here is distinctively Johnsonian, in its periods and analogies as much as its preoccupation with the body and its death. How singular though is his attitude?

In his conception of the relative value of writing and speech Johnson certainly accords with the mind-shift Foucault has attributed to the invention of printing, the arrival of European and oriental manuscripts, and the privileged position of textual interpretation relative to oral tradition in the church: "Henceforth it is the primal nature of language to be written [. . .] The sounds made by voices provide no more than a transitory and precarious transcription of it."[49] Equally, although his *Dictionary* was innovative in its structure and was to become enormously influential, it was not an isolated endeavor. In Europe and in England it formed part of a much wider movement of linguistic standardization and regulation through the publication of hundreds of grammars and dictionaries, and an even greater number of elocutionary guides designed to assist individuals to improve their speech.[50] With regard to pronunciation, the basic efforts offered by Johnson's *Dictionary*, which comprise the printing of "an accent upon the acute or elevated syllables" and the construction of a short list of rules in the "Grammar," were within a few decades superseded by pronouncing dictionaries, such as those compiled by Thomas Sheridan and later John Walker.[51] There were two key effects of this push towards the codification of language and speech. The first was the emergence of a clear standard pronunciation "identified with the pronunciation of the socially higher classes in London and its surroundings" by the end of the eighteenth century. This standard functioned as "a yardstick with which to measure others and very quickly became a prerequisite for social advancement. The view that mastering the standard improves one's lot in life becomes increasingly apparent."[52] The second was the confirmation of a particular idea about the nature of speech, not only as "the result of an intellectual act of will but also a bodily habit." Since this idea "revealed the possibility of a structured, repetitive regimen of intervention that could reorganize habitual behavior from deviance to normality," it was to become an important factor in the rapid growth of the elocutionary movement.[53]

Clearly, Johnson's *Dictionary* had a role to play in this. In one important respect, however, it cannot be mapped in any simple way onto later historical iterations of this class-based model of speech variation. As John Barrell has demonstrated, there was a "double valence" at the heart of the process of linguistic standardization. On the one hand, it was "egalitarian" in that it was concerned with "fitting all men to communicate with each other on the equal terms of reason." On the other, it would have seemed to many, and particularly those whose native speech was targeted (as it was in Scotland for instance) as "an attempt to reduce, to subjugate, varieties of provincial English, and the modes of expression of different social classes to the norms of that élite."[54] Clearly, there are traces of both interpretations in Johnson's lexicographical writing, which both upholds the notion of an ideal language of truth and virtue and advocates the reduction of speech variation. What Barrell is right to point out though is that for Johnson there is no one single group who can be said to represent 'correct' speech, because the standard that he requires does not derive from actual speech but from literature, and not even from contemporary literature, but a carefully selected pre-Restoration canon.[55] Acknowledging this difference is important. Without it the nuances of Johnson's argument are obscured, as is the complex manner in which he both engages with and yet at the same time rejects the very notion of a 'standard' in relation to speech.

ETHNOGRAPHY

Johnson's decision to travel to the Highlands of Scotland with Boswell in 1773, nearly twenty years after the publication of the *Dictionary*, afforded him new speech experiences. Beyond a desire for adventure, it seems that he and the Scotsman Boswell made this unlikely and treacherous journey at least in part to investigate the validity of the claims made by James Macpherson's Ossianic publications. This controversy raised questions about the kind of poetry that could be expected from an early oral culture and was fuelled by a vogue for antiquarianism and for conjectural histories of linguistic and social development. Johnson was famously skeptical of Macpherson's claims to have discovered and translated the works of the third-century bard Ossian, but nevertheless, as Boswell records, their "desire of information was keen" and they did make every effort to learn as much as they could about Highland culture and its oral tradition.[56]

As literate outsiders intent upon investigating the native Gaelic people, Johnson and Boswell were essentially ethnographers.[57] For this reason, their trip was deliberately structured around oral performances, including recitations of poetry given by Highlanders and conversations with those who claimed to have knowledge of the Ossianic material. Clearly this perspective also shaped their expectations of and responses to these performances. Johnson in particular reflects upon this, recording that almost immediately after their arrival it became apparent that what they had hoped for could not be found because the ancient Highland culture has already been substantially eroded: "We came thither too late, to see what we expected, a people of peculiar appearance and a system of antiquated life." This realization adds urgency to his belief that whatever he hears must be recorded: "Narrations like this, however uncertain, deserve the notice of the traveler, because they are the only records of a nation that has no historians, and afford the genuine representation of the life and character of the ancient Highlanders."[58]

Nothing that Johnson hears, however, leads him to change his mind regarding the Ossian question. Aside from the conspicuous absence of the manuscripts that Macpherson had ostensibly translated, Johnson simply cannot believe that the sophisticated poetry attributed to Ossian could be genuine. The first reason for this doubt is implicit in the arguments regarding speech we have already encountered: the oral tradition by which the poems must have been carried, in the absence of a written language, is to his mind precarious and unreliable and thus unable to transmit works of such length and refinement. This argument is reiterated in the *Journey* in the form of a generalized assertion: "In nations, where there is hardly the use of letters, what is once out of sight is lost for ever." It is then underscored by a judgment about the Highlanders in particular: "The traditions of an ignorant and savage people have been for ages negligently heard, and unskillfully related."[59]

The second reason centers on Johnson's rejection of the idea that an ancient pre-literate culture could have produced poetry of the quality Macpherson claimed. It could not have done so, he asserts, because such cultures are primitive and barbarous, and they are so primarily because they lack literacy. Unlike Rousseau, he finds no genius or nobility in the state of savagery.[60] Instead, he roots his negative assessment of the Highland culture in a judgment about the state of its language, arguing that whilst the progress of the Saxons from "barbarity" to a "civilized people" arose through the development of a standardized orthography, since "Earse never was a written language" it remained, even to the present day, "the rude speech of a barbarous people." The alignment made here between linguistic and cultural development reveals the influence of a deeper presupposition—the sense that "language revealed the mind."[61] A standardized orthography, Johnson argues, is crucial: "When a language begins to teem with books, it is tending to refinement; as those who undertake to teach others must have undergone some labor in improving themselves [. . .] speech becomes embodied and permanent [. . .] By degrees one age improves upon another. Exactness is first obtained, and afterwards elegance, but diction merely vocal, is always in its childhood."[62] A written language not only allows a language to develop, but it facilitates and then reflects a parallel maturation of the culture that employs it and strives to do so excellently.

It is on this account that Johnson finds the Highlanders to be not simply without letters, but also without intelligence, imagination, or industriousness. This is not peculiar to them as a group, but rather the consequence of their illiteracy: "In nations, where there is hardly the use of letters, what is once out of sight is lost for ever. They think but little and of their few thoughts, none are wasted on the past, in which they are neither interested by fear nor hope." The Highlanders whom he meets, however, do conform entirely to this model, having "few thoughts to express" and being "content, as they conceived grossly, to be grossly understood."[63] Thus Johnson binds the Highlanders' inadequacies inextricably to their mode of communication, and their mental failings to the impermanence of their speech, and yet at the same time, as in the *Dictionary* with the idea of *caprice,* his language reveals a note of moral condemnation, not of their state but of their apparent lack of effort. They are charged with hearing "negligently" and relating "unskillfully" (again adverbs we recall from the *Dictionary*), with a lack of curiosity and a "laxity" in merely being "content" with their "gross" state of thought and of communication.[64] By contrast, the "scholars" whom he meets at Braidwood's "college of the deaf and dumb" at the close of his expedition, are full of enthusiasm and desire for improvement; despite laboring under the "most desperate of calamities," they work hard to learn to read and speak and are "delighted with the hope of new ideas."[65] Thus Johnson brings together two different criticisms of the Highlanders' speech, mapping the primitive onto the vulgar and judging their earlier state of development by contemporary standards. That they can only speak is in itself an impairment; but to compound the matter, their speech is also improper, inaccurate, and careless.

Johnson is by no means alone in his adherence to this model of human progress. As Olivia Smith has argued, the idea that "Civilization was largely a linguistic concept" was a commonplace by the later decades of the eighteenth century and would go on being so well into the nineteenth.[66] The strength of his conviction and its forthright expression are, however, distinctively Johnsonian. That his ideas were influential during his lifetime and after is beyond doubt; that from a twenty-first-century perspective, many seem both untenable and unacceptable, is no less so. What we find, nevertheless, in Johnson's account of his travels in the Highlands remains valuable, as an exceptionally personal expression of a connection between speech and mortality that is more commonly explored in the abstract. As an aging man, fearful of the onward march of time and with "the contemplation of his own approaching end" always in his mind, he is forced to confront the inevitable transience of human existence in the voices that surround him: in the transient faults of the Highlanders' speech, "dying with sound that gives them life," in their history that cannot live beyond the moment of its utterance, in the "passing fast away" of the ancient Highland culture itself, and, even in the lowlands, in the "peculiarities" of the "dialect" which also he knows will soon also "wear fast away," leaving no trace, even of its imperfection.[67]

APHASIA

The loss of his own voice, when it occurred in the early hours of the morning on June 17, 1783 as the result of a minor stroke, cements this bond between the transience of speech and human mortality. Much to Johnson's surprise, though, it did not intensify his fear of death: "I had no pain, and so little dejection in this dreadful state that I wondered at my own apathy, and considered that perhaps death itself when it should come, would excite less horror than seem[s] now to attend it."[68] Despite the fact that the aphasia began almost immediately to lift, the evidence left in the letters he wrote to his doctors and friends in the days and weeks that followed suggests that far from being apathetic Johnson was in fact deeply affected by the experience. The nature of his response to it is illuminating. It was comprised of three distinct components: a belief that his voice has been taken from him by God; an assumption that the problem was an "impediment" of the "vocal organs" rather than the mind; and finally a sense that the disorder of this crisis had to be brought under control.[69]

Whilst he may have argued in the *Dictionary* against the divine origin of language, in this context the agency of God is uppermost amongst his thoughts. His immediate response to the discovery of his speech loss is to pray, and even when requesting the medical assistance of Dr. Heberden at daybreak, this is his explanation of the situation: "It has pleased God by a paralytic stroke in the night to deprive me of speech."[70] Furthermore, even as he welcomes the treatments offered to him by Heberden and also by another physician, Dr. Brocklesby, Johnson continues to pray that God should "forgive" his sins and "relieve" his suffering.[71]

His spiritual torment notwithstanding, Johnson is certain that this expression of the will of God took the form of a bodily affliction. This is quickly established, as is the separation of body from mind: "I was alarmed and prayed God, that however he might afflict my body he would spare my understanding. This prayer, that I might try the integrity of my faculties I made in Latin verse. The lines were not very good, but I knew them not to be very good, I made them easily, and concluded myself to be unimpaired in my faculties."[72] From thence he describes his condition as one of "disease," of "organs" which need to be "rous[ed]," and later, as he recovers, of weakened "nerves."[73] In this, Johnson agrees with contemporary medical opinion, which focused on the tongue, rather than as would be the case after Broca's groundbreaking work of 1861, upon lesions in the brain.[74] It is for this reason that he takes "two drams" of wine and puts himself into "violent motion," enquires about "stimulants" and the efficacy of a "vomit violent and rough." It is also why he endures the application of multiple "vesicatories," swallows "salt of Hartshorn," and follows dietary advice.[75]

It is Johnson's hope that through the mercy of God and the treatment of his doctors, his speech will be "restored," by which he means not only that his capacity for utterance will return as it was before but also that he will be able to gain control of his disorder, understood in its final *Dictionary* definition as a "breach of that regularity in the animal oeconomy which causes health; sickness; distemper."[76] The language through which he describes the stroke and its effects suggests his inability to resist an external force: it is a "heavy blow," God has "deprived him" of his speech, it has been "taken" from him, he has been "attacked."[77] Afterwards, however, as Julia Epstein has observed, what is astonishing about Johnson's response to his aphasia is the intensity of determination "to remain in control of his own mind and of his body."[78] He does so by closely directing his medical treatment, refusing some treatments and suggesting others, and also by transforming his disordered speech into a series of orderly written narratives. Initially he reports some "difficulty" with his "hand"—a symptom now definitive of an accompanying agraphia—but he does not mention this again, despite evident transpositions, omissions, and errors of spelling in the surviving manuscripts of his letters.[79]

What Johnson may have suspected, but could not have known, is that he would not live long enough to achieve a full restoration of his vocal powers. Until the final days of his life, his voice would remain "like any other weak limb" which "can endure but little labor at once."[80] Paradoxically, however, thus afflicted Johnson becomes not more exceptional, but less so. This is something he himself writes into the record: "Palsies are more common than I thought. I have been visited by four friends who have had each a stroke, and one of them, two." He then remembers how three of his acquaintances had "lost their voices, of whom two continued speechless for life." [81] He even remarks that his own case was not particularly extreme: "When the Physicians came they seemed not to consider the attack as very formidable."[82] From a historical perspective too, this is apparent. Davis, for instance, identifies the eighteenth century as the period in which the term "disability" evolves, in contradistinction to the earlier term "deformity" and cites Johnson as a key figure in whom this development inheres. For Davis, this is due in large part to Boswell's representation of Johnson in the *Life*. However, a number of characteristic features implied by "disability," as Davis defines it, are as strongly present in Johnson's own letters. In them we find the implication of "weakness or evil as well as personal culpability and the effect of divine justice." Only the unusual intensity of Johnson's faith precludes the final feature Davis suggests, namely that disability is "random" and "impersonal."[83] Equally, it is possible to argue that Johnson's interpretation of his aphasia is amongst the cultural productions that have instantiated a diction of disability based on the "ascription of passivity," which many today interpret as limiting and discriminatory, through his emphasis on the "attack" that he suffers, and the deprivation that he must endure.[84]

AFTERLIFE

In other ways too, this Johnsonian case study can shape our understanding of what it may mean to talk normal. Most distinctively, I would argue, Johnson conceptualizes human speech as inherently *frail*, by which he means "weak; easily decaying; subject to causalities." Its transient sounds make it an unstable and unreliable form of expression, and in its variable pronunciation and unauthorized neologisms, it is disorderly. In this respect, speech for Johnson is intimately connected with the *frailty* of the human mind and body: with "weakness of resolution; instability of mind" and with "infirmity." Consequently, his point of reference for ideal standards of speech is a carefully selected canon of pure and permanent literary sources, against which all spoken utterances are liable to fail.

It is an equally distinctive feature of both Johnson's experiences of speech and his writing about it, that they resist interpretation from the perspective of normality. Most straightforwardly, this derives from the fact that the word *normal* and its associated forms, *normality, normalcy,* and *normative,* do not appear in Johnson's *Dictionary* and indeed did not enter the English lexicon until the 1840s; only with the development of statistics and the invention of the bell curve did the idea as we now know it of "constituting, conforming to, not deviating or differing from, the common type of standard" emerge.[85] Even when applied retrospectively, however, it proves an unhelpful framework through which to consider Johnson's own speech. Epstein, for example, points out that even so defined, "normal" nevertheless implies a "lack of difference, of conformity, of the capacity to blend in invisibly," none of which are descriptions that can reasonably be applied to Johnson for much of his life, and only in the smallest degree when he finds himself an unexceptional patient.[86] On this, one of his more recent biographers John Wain writes perceptively, suggesting that it was not merely a matter of Johnson's speech or even his body, but rather the fact that "Johnson as individual, was highly independent and unbiddable. He did not fit smoothly into any system. Intellectually, on the other hand, he approved systems."[87]

So, Johnson's speech is notable not because it exemplified either his own ideal or the demands of speech propriety as it was understood in eighteenth-century England, but rather because it brings together multiple forms of the extraordinary: it was exceptionally eloquent, distinctive in its tone, volume, and expression (what one contemporary described as his "bow wow way"), and at times bizarre and oddly out of control.[88] Furthermore, for those who knew him, there was no comparing of Johnson to any other. His "singularities" were the subject of imitation, in jest by his friends, and in endless satires by those less won over by him, but ultimately he was his own standard.[89] More specifically, his talk and his writing were judged reciprocally, not only as they were held by many who knew him to be practically identical, but also because his achievement in one sphere seems to have shaped his reputation in the other. When Hester Thrale remarks that each of his *Rambler* essays "breathes indeed the genuine emanations of its great author's mind, expressed too in a style so natural to him, and so much like his common mode of conversing," we see this reinforcement in action.[90]

Thrale echoes Boswell here; like him she turns to the metaphor of the breath in order to capture the nature of Johnson's authority, but to do so without precisely identifying the relationship between his mind, body, and voice. She does so, I would suggest, because like Boswell, her thoughts of Johnson are bound up with his living, breathing form and because she was uncertain how else to explain him. She was his intimate confidante, however, and thus it seems likely that in this she also reflects Johnson himself. As Alvin Kernan explains, "the talking world" appealed to Johnson because it was "socially reassuring and sensorially fulfilling, almost an animal contact with other bodies of your own kind."[91] This, I would suggest, we see incorporated into Thrale's sense of him, as a man afraid of solitude and silence, and hence always seeking the company and the conversation of others.

Although this language is familiar, and appears to recall the nexus of voice, presence and being articulated most exhaustively by Derrida, Johnson's case is testament to a different but equally significant resonance. Where Derrida, like Husserl, is primarily concerned with the phenomenological structure of the voice, with respect to Johnson, it is the connection of the voice not only with the body but with the situation of its utterance and the mode of its performance, which requires our attention.[92] And where one consequence of the Derridean project is a flattening of different types of speech into the category of *voix*, Johnson alerts us to the variety not only of modes and forms of speech, but also to the fact that it is possible to have one opinion about speech in the context of conversation and entirely another with regard to oral poetry recitation. Finally, I would suggest that through the example of Johnson a case can be made for a productive analysis of the concept of "presence" that pays less heed to the idea of interiority and instead attends to what Johnson loved: the presence of individuals within a group and the power of a voice to capture the attention and shape the response of an audience. This is not to suggest that the "determination of absolute presence" as "self-presence," or in other words, as "the experience—or consciousness—of the voice: of hearing (understanding)-oneself-speak" has no bearing on his life, writing, and the nature of his legacy. It is simply to point out that Derrida's argument is shaped by the belief that the eighteenth century was the Age of Rousseau, and that this is a judgment open to challenge.[93] To judge oral performances, Johnson learns in the Highlands, requires an attendance to the whole event, or what the folklorist and linguistic anthropologist Richard Bauman describes as "the performance situation, involving performer, art form, audience, and setting."[94] What he teaches us is that this is no less true of any attempt to examine representations of speech and its disorders; after all, once the sounds and the body that breathed them have "fast died away," these will always remain "subject to strict review."

NOTES

1. Jon Klancher, *The Making of English Reading Audiences 1790–1832* (Madison: University of Wisconsin Press, 1987), 3–4; Nicholas Hudson, *Samuel Johnson and the Making of Modern England* (Cambridge: Cambridge University Press, 2004), 222, 226.
2. Bertrand Bronson, "The Double Tradition of Dr Johnson," *English Literary History*, 18 (June, 1951). See also Helen Deutsch, *Loving Dr. Johnson* (Chicago: University of Chicago Press, 2005).
3. Catherine Parks, "Johnson and the Arts of Conversation," in *The Cambridge Companion to Samuel Johnson*, ed. Greg Clingham (Cambridge: Cambridge University Press, 1997), 18.
4. *Johnsonian Miscellanies,* ed. G.B. Hill, 2 vols. (Oxford: Clarendon Press, 1897 repr. 1966), I.160.
5. Samuel Johnson, *The Rambler*, ed. W.J Bate and Albrecht B. Strauss, 3 vols., no. 89 (New Haven: Yale University Press, 1969), IV: 108.
6. Hester Thrale Piozzi, in *Johnsonian Miscellanies*, I.160; *The Letters of Samuel Johnson*, ed. Bruce Redford, 5 vols. (Oxford: Clarendon Press, 1992–1994),Vol IV (1782–1784), to Mrs Thrale, 28 June 1783, 160.
7. James Boswell, *The Life of Samuel Johnson, LL.D*, 2 vols. (London: printed by Henry Baldwin, for Charles Dilly, 1791), II.494; Arthur Murphy, "An Essay on Johnson's Life and Genius (1792)," in *Johnsonian Miscellanies*, I.451.
8. Joshua Reynolds, in *Johnsonian Miscellanies*, II.231; Oliver Goldsmith reported in Boswell, *Life*, II.100.
9. Hester Thrale Piozzi, *Anecdotes of the Late Samuel Johnson, LL.D, during the Last Twenty Years of His Life* (London: T. Cadell, 1786).
10. Boswell, *Life*, II.100.
11. Fanny Burney, *Memoirs of Dr. Burney*, 3 vols. (London, 1832), II.91.
12. Boswell, *Life*, I.265.
13. Boswell, *Life*, I.77.
14. Lennard J. Davis, "Dr Johnson, Amelia, and the Discourse of Disability in the Eighteenth Century," in *Defects: Engendering the Modern Body* ed. Helen Deutsch and Felicity Nussbaum (Ann Arbor: University of Michigan Press, 2000), 62.
15. *Boswell's London Journal*, ed. by Frederick A. Pottle (London: Heinemann, 1950), 260.
16. Boswell, *Life*, II.464.
17. For example Joshua Reynolds in *Johnsonian Miscellanies*, II.222; James Boswell, *The Life of Samuel Johnson, LL.D. comprehending an account of his studies and numerous works, in Chronological order* [. . .] 3 vols. (London: for Charles Dilly, 1793), III.446.
18. Deutsch, *Loving Dr. Johnson*, 91. See also T.J. Murray, "Dr Samuel Johnson's Movement Disorder," *British Medical Journal*, (1979), and L.C. McHenry,

Jr., "Neurological Disorders of Dr Samuel Johnson," *Journal of the Royal Society of Medicine* 78, no. 6 (June, 1985).

19. Deutsch, *Loving Dr. Johnson*, 102.
20. Deutsch, *Loving Dr. Johnson*, 118.
21. Boswell, *Life* (1791), I.77.
22. Timothy Clark, *The Theory of Inspiration: Composition as a Crisis of Subjectivity in Romantic and Post-Romantic Writing* (Manchester: Manchester University Press, 1997).
23. James Boswell, *The Journal of a Tour to the Hebrides with Samuel Johnson LL.D* (London: for Charles Dilly, 1785), 8–9; Boswell, *Life* (1791), I.421.
24. Davis, in *Defects*, 69.
25. Samuel Johnson, *The Plan of a Dictionary of the English Language* (London: for J. and P. Knapton, et al., 1747); Samuel Johnson, *A Dictionary of the English Language*, 2 vols. (London: for J. and P. Knapton et. al., 1755–56).
26. *Preface to Shakespeare*, The Yale Edition of the Works of Samuel Johnson, ed. Allen T. Hazen, John Middendorf et. al. (New Haven: Yale University Press, 1958-), VII: 62.
27. Robert DeMaria Jnr, *Johnson's Dictionary and the Language of Learning* (Oxford: Clarendon Press, 1986), 78.
28. Johnson, *Plan*, 11; Johnson, *Dictionary*, "Preface," 2.
29. *Preface to Shakespeare*, 59.
30. John Locke, in *Dictionary*; *The Rambler*, no. 106, IV.200.
31. Johnson, *Dictionary*, "Preface," 8.
32. The first definition is "the power of articulate utterance."
33. Johnson, *Dictionary*, "Preface," 6.
34. "Constructing oral tradition: the origins of the concept in Enlightenment intellectual culture," in *The Spoken Word: Oral Culture in Britain 1500–1800*, ed. Adam Fox and Daniel Woolf, (Manchester: Manchester University Press, 2003), 244.
35. Boswell, *Life* (1791), II.447; Johnson, *Plan*, 18, 20.
36. Johnson, *Dictionary*, "Preface," 1.
37. Johnson, *Dictionary*, "Preface,"5, 10.
38. Johnson, *Dictionary*, "Preface," 1.
39. Johnson, *Dictionary*, "Preface," 2.
40. Johnson, *Plan*, 12.
41. Johnson, *Dictionary*, "Grammar," 7.
42. Johnson, *Dictionary*, "Preface," 9. The wider context of this issue is explored in Janet Sorenson, "Vulgar Tongues: Canting Dictionaries and the Language of the People in Eighteenth-Century Britain", *Eighteenth Century Studies*, 37, no. 3 (Spring, 2004), 435–454.
43. Johnson, *Dictionary*, "Preface," 6, 2.
44. Johnson, *Dictionary*, "Grammar," 7.
45. John Barrell, *English Literature in History, 1730–80: An Equal, Wide Survey* (London: Hutchinson, 1983), 156.
46. *Plan*, 4, 32, 35; *Dictionary*, "Preface," 1.
47. Johnson, *Dictionary*, "Preface," 10.
48. Johnson, *Dictionary*, "Preface," 11.
49. Michel Foucault, *The Order of Things: An Archaeology of the Human Sciences* (New York: Vintage Books, 1970), 42.
50. See Olivia Smith, *The Politics of Language 1791–1819* (Oxford: Clarendon Press, 1984); Lewis H. Ulman, *Things, Thoughts, Words, and Actions: The Problem of Language in Late Eighteenth-Century British Rhetorical Theory* (Carbondale: Southern Illinois University Press, 1994); Carey McIntosh, *The Ordering of English: Style, Rhetoric, Politeness, Print Culture, and the*

Evolution of Prose from 1700–1800 (Cambridge: Cambridge University Press, 1998).

51. Johnson, *Dictionary*, "Preface," 2; Thomas Sheridan, *A General Dictionary of the English Language. One main Object of which, is to Establish a Plain and Permanent Standard of Pronunciation* (London: for J. Dodsley, C. Dilly and J. Wilkie, 1780) and John Walker, *A Critical Pronouncing Dictionary and Expositor of the English Language* (London: sold by G.G.J. and J. Robinson; and T. Cadell, 1791).

52. *Eighteenth-Century English: Ideology and Change*, ed. Raymond Hickey (Cambridge: Cambridge University Press, 2010), 15.

53. Terence MacNamee, "Normativity in Eighteenth Century Discourse on Speech," *Journal of Communication Disorders* 17 (1984), 408.

54. Barrell, *An Equal Wide Survey*, 111–112. See also, John Guillory, *Cultural Capital: The Problem of Literary Canon Formation* (Chicago: University of Chicago Press, 1993), 100.

55. Barrell, *An Equal Wide Survey*, 112, 144.

56. Samuel Johnson, *A Journey to the Western Islands of Scotland* (London: for W. Strahan and T. Cadell, 1775), and Boswell, *The Journal of a Tour to the Hebrides with Samuel Johnson LL.D*; *Journey*, 252.

57. Here I draw on the definition offered by Tim Ingold in "Anthropology is *not* Ethnography," *Proceedings of the British Academy* 154 (2008), 69–92.

58. Johnson, *Journey*, 127–128, 109.

59. Johnson, *Journey*, 145, 112.

60. Jean-Jacques Rousseau, *Discourse on the Origin of Inequality*, trans. Franklin Philip (Oxford: Oxford University Press, 1994).

61. Smith, *The Politics of Language*, 2.

62. Johnson, *Journey*, 268.

63. Johnson, *Journey*, 65, 267.

64. Johnson, *Journey*, 112.

65. Johnson, *Journey*, 382.

66. Smith, *The Politics of Language*, vii.

67. Johnson, *Journey*, 313, 380; Arthur Murphy, in *Miscellanies*, I; 439.

68. *Letters*, 151.

69. *Letters*, 159, 151.

70. *Letters*, 149.

71. *Letters*, 153.

72. *Letters*, 151.

73. *Letters*, 151, 164.

74. Arthur L. Benton and Robert J. Joynt, "Early Descriptions of Aphasia," *Archives of Neurology* (August, 1960).

75. *Letters*, 149, 153–155. For medical analysis see Macdonald Critchley, "Dr. Samuel Johnson's Aphasia," *Medical History* 6, no. 1 (January, 1962).

76. *Letters*, 162.

77. *Letters*, 150, 149.

78. Julia Epstein, *Altered Conditions* (London: Routledge, 1995), 70.

79. This is discussed in detail by Critchley.

80. *Letters*, 162.

81. *Letters*, 157, 177.

82. *Letters*, 177.

83. Davis, in *Defects*, 62.

84. Simi Linton, "Reassigning Meaning," in *The Disability Studies Reader* ed. Lennard J. Davis, 2nd edn. (London: Routledge, 2006), 169.

85. Davis, in *Defects*, 24, 62.

86. Epstein, *Altered Conditions*, 11.

87. John Wain, *Samuel Johnson* (London: Macmillan, 1974), 45–46.
88. Boswell, *Journal*, 8–9.
89. Boswell, *Life*, I.265.
90. Hill, *Johnsonian Miscellanies*, I.248.
91. Alvin Kernan, *Printing Technology, Letters, and Samuel Johnson* (Princeton: Princeton University Press, 1987), 209.
92. On Derrida and the disabled body see Lennard Davis, *Enforcing Normalcy: disability, deafness, and the body*(London: Verso, 1995), 103.
93. Jacques Derrida, *Of Grammatology* trans. Gayatri Chakravorty Spivak (Baltimore: Johns Hopkins University Press, 1997), 97–98.
94. Richard Bauman, "Verbal Art as Performance," *American Anthropologist* 77, no. 2 (June, 1975), 290.

WORKS CITED

Barrell, John. *English Literature in History, 1730–80: An Equal, Wide Survey.* London: Hutchinson, 1983.

Bauman, Richard. "Verbal Art as Performance." *American Anthropologist* 77, no. 2 (June 1975): 290–311.

Benton, Arthur L., and Robert J. Joynt. "Early Descriptions of Aphasia." *Archives of Neurology* (August 1960): 205–222. Boswell, James. *The Life of Samuel Johnson, LL.D*, 2 vols. London: printed by Henry Baldwin, for Charles Dilly, 1791.

Boswell, James. *The Life of Samuel Johnson, LL.D. Comprehending an Account of His Studies and Numerous Works, in Chronological Order* [. . .], 3 vols. London: for Charles Dilly, 1793.

Boswell's London Journal, edited by Frederick A. Pottle, London: Heinemann, 1950.

Boswell, James. *The Journal of a Tour to the Hebrides with Samuel Johnson LL.D.* London: for Charles Dilly, 1785.

Bronson, Bertrand. "The Double Tradition of Dr Johnson." *English Literary History* 18 (June 1951): 90–106.

Burney, Fanny. *Memoirs of Dr. Burney,* 3 vols. London, 1832.

Clark, Timothy. *The Theory of Inspiration: Composition as a Crisis of Subjectivity in Romantic and Post-Romantic Writing.* Manchester: Manchester University Press, 1997.

Critchley, Macdonald. "Dr. Samuel Johnson's Aphasia." *Medical History* 6, no. 1 (January 1962): 27–44.

Davis, Lennard. *Enforcing Normalcy: Disability, Deafness, and the Body.* London: Verso, 1995.

Davis, Lennard J. "Dr Johnson, Amelia, and the Discourse of Disability in the Eighteenth Century." In *Defects: Engendering the Modern Body*, edited by Helen Deutsch and Felicity Nussbaum, Ann Arbor: University of Michigan Press, 2000, 54–74.

DeMaria, Robert, Jnr. *Johnson's Dictionary and the Language of Learning.* Oxford: Clarendon Press, 1986.

Derrida, Jacques. *Of Grammatology.* Translated by Gayatri Chakravorty Spivak. Baltimore: Johns Hopkins University Press, 1997.

Deutsch, Helen. *Loving Dr. Johnson.* Chicago; London: University of Chicago Press, 2005.

Eighteenth-Century English: Ideology and Change, edited by Raymond Hickey, Cambridge: Cambridge University Press, 2010.

Epstein, Julia. *Altered Conditions*. London: Routledge, 1995.

Foucault, Michel. *The Order of Things: An Archaeology of the Human Sciences*. New York: Vintage Books, 1970.

Guillory, John. *Cultural Capital: The Problem of Literary Canon Formation*. Chicago; London: University of Chicago Press, 1993.

Hudson, Nicholas. *Samuel Johnson and the Making of Modern England*. Cambridge: Cambridge University Press, 2004.

Ingold, Tim. "Anthropology is *not* Ethnography." In *Proceedings of the British Academy* 154 (2008).

Johnson, Samuel. *The Rambler*, edited by W.J. Bate and Albrecht B. Strauss, 3 vols. Yale: Yale University Press, 1969.

Johnson, Samuel. *The Plan of a Dictionary of the English Language*. London: for J. and P. Knapton, et al., 1747.

Johnson, Samuel. *A Dictionary of the English Language*, 2 vols. (London: for J. and P. Knapton et. al., 1755–56).

Johnson, Samuel. *A Journey to the Western Islands of Scotland*. London: for W. Strahan and T. Cadell, 1775.

Johnsonian Miscellanies, edited by G.B. Hill, 2 vols. Oxford: Clarendon Press, 1897 repr. 1966.

Kernan, Alvin. *Printing Technology, Letters, and Samuel Johnson*. Princeton: Princeton University Press, 1987.

Klancher, Jon. *The Making of English Reading Audiences 1790–1832*. Madison: University of Wisconsin Press, 1987.

Linton, Simi. "Reassigning Meaning." In *The Disability Studies Reader: Second Edition*. New York: Routledge, 2006.

McIntosh, Carey. *The Ordering of English: Style, Rhetoric, Politeness, Print Culture, and the Evolution of Prose from 1700–1800*. Cambridge: Cambridge University Press, 1998.

MacNamee, Terence. "Normativity in Eighteenth Century Discourse on Speech." *Journal of Communication Disorders* 17 (1984): 407–423.

McHenry, L.C., Jr. "Neurological Disorders of Dr Samuel Johnson." *Journal of the Royal Society of Medicine* 78, no. 6 (June, 1985): 485–491.

Murphy, Arthur. "An Essay on Johnson's Life and Genius (1792)," in *Johnsonian Miscellanies*, ed. G.B. Hill, 2 vols. (Oxford: Clarendon Press, 1897 repr. 1966).

Murray, T.J. "Dr Samuel Johnson's Movement Disorder." *British Medical Journal* (1979): 1, 1610–1614.

Parks, Catherine. "Johnson and the Arts of Conversation." In *The Cambridge Companion to Samuel Johnson*, edited by Greg Clingham, Cambridge: Cambridge University Press, 1997, 18–33.

Preface to Shakespeare. The Yale Edition of the Works of Samuel Johnson, edited by Allen T. Hazen, John Middendorf et. al., New Haven: Yale University Press, 1958.

Rousseau, Jean-Jacques. *Discourse on the Origin of Inequality*. Translated by Franklin Philip. Oxford: Oxford University Press, 1994.

Sheridan, Thomas. *A General Dictionary of the English Language. One main Object of which, is to Establish a Plain and Permanent Standard of Pronunciation*. London: for J. Dodsley, C. Dilly and J. Wilkie, 1780.

Smith, Olivia. *The Politics of Language 1791–1819*. Oxford: Clarendon Press, 1984.

Sorensen, Janet. "Vulgar Tongues: Canting Dictionaries and the Language of the People in Eighteenth-Century Britain." *Eighteenth Century Studies*, 37, no. 3 (Spring, 2004): 435–454.

The Letters of Samuel Johnson, Vol IV (1782–1784), edited by Bruce Redford, Oxford: Clarendon Press, 1992–1994.

Thrale Piozzi, Hester. *Anecdotes of the late Samuel Johnson, LL.D, during the Last Twenty Years of His Life*. London: T. Cadell, 1786.

The Spoken Word: Oral Culture in Britain 1500–1800, edited by Adam Fox and Daniel Woolf, Manchester: Manchester University Press, 2003.

Ulman, Lewis H. *Things, Thoughts, Words, and Actions: The Problem of Language in Late Eighteenth-Century British Rhetorical Theory*. Carbondale: Southern Illinois University Press, 1994.

Wain, John. *Samuel Johnson*. London: Macmillan, 1974.

Walker, John. *A Critical Pronouncing Dictionary and Expositor of the English Language*. London: sold by G.G.J. and J. Robinson; and T. Cadell, 1791.

4   "Irate, with no grace of style"

Stuttering, Logorrhea, and Disordered Speech among Male Characters in Luís Vaz de Camões' *The Lusiads* (1572)[1]

Valéria M. Souza

In the transition between the seventh and eighth cantos of *The Lusiads*, something extraordinary happens: the poet, Camões, stutters.[2] An occurrence of this type would not necessarily be remarkable in a modern literary work, since many of these feature stuttering narrators and protagonists, but *The Lusiads* is a sixteenth-century epic poem—and not just any epic poem, but *the* national epic of Portugal. By definition, epics are narratives of power designed to linguistically "restage" the imperial conquests of the victors who produce them.[3] An epic written by a member of a "winning" people—in this case the Portuguese—should represent a display of textual mastery, acting simultaneously as a written record of the group's achievements and an infinitely repeated (and repeatable) performance of masculine imperial projects of expansion and colonization. What, then, are we to make of this epic poet's stutter?

The crucial stumble takes place in a part of the poem that deals with the arrival of the Portuguese in Calicut. A Moor named Monçaíde visits the ship and describes Malabar, after which Captain Vasco da Gama and his crew disembark and are received by a local official called the Catual and then by the king, or Samorim. Having met Gama, the Samorim's curiosity is piqued and he sends the Catual, along with Monçaíde, back to the Portuguese ships on a reconnaissance mission. Paulo da Gama, Vasco's elder brother, greets the Catual on board and proceeds to inform him about the ship's silk flags, which depict relevant individuals and events from Portuguese history. The scene is narrated by Camões:

> [Catual] rose, and with him Gama rose as well,
> And on their side Coelho and the Moor.
> His glance on a white, noble ancient fell,
> Depicted in a warlike portraiture,
> Whose name undying in the world shall dwell
> While human intercourse shall still endure.
> Dressed in the true Greek manner did he stand,
> *A branch for ensign held in his right hand.*

A branch in his hand he held . . . But I, Ó blind!
Who thus launch forth, a madman desperate,
Mondego's nymphs and Tagus' left behind,
On paths so various and rough and great.
Nymphs, I invoke your grace, for I must find
My course through high seas where such gales frustrate
That, if you help me not, my fear is strong,
My fragile cockboat will go down ere long.

Lo! What long years since fate first made me sing
Songs of your Tagus and your Portuguese,
The fate that still has kept me wandering,
Seeing new labors and new pains increase,
Now seaward gone, now suffering everything
'Mid perilous battle's inhumanities.
Like Cânace, resolved herself to kill,
One hand still holds the sword and one the quill
        (VII.77–79, italics mine, trans. slightly altered).[4]

This interlude continues for eight more stanzas, with Camões outlining in exhaustive detail the suffering he has endured, including poverty, the "degradation" of being forced to accept "charity" from others, and in general being underappreciated in his occupation as a bard. The stammer ("A branch for ensign held in his right hand / A branch in his hand he held . . . But I, Ó blind!") heralds a poetic breakdown or crisis, marking the divide between epic and lyric modes of narration. It is comprised of the final line of the first octave and the beginning line of the second octave, which together effect a dual "bracketing off" of the primary, heroic narrative from the poet's secondary, autobiographical tale. The graphic separation between stanzas functions as the original disfluency.

When the poet realizes that he is on the verge of faltering, he tries to buy time by repeating and slightly reformulating the verse about the branch. He then seems to experience what stutterers refer to as a "block" or inability to produce any sound whatsoever, as indicated by the presence of ellipses and a space preceding the "But"—both rendered typographically in the Portuguese text—before veering completely off course and launching into lyric mode. This final maneuver, which postpones the development of the scene involving Paulo da Gama and the Catual for nearly ten stanzas, can be read as an extreme example of circumlocution, in which stutterers rearrange words in a sentence or add in extra, often unnecessary, interjections so as to purposely delay the utterance of a term or phrase with which they expect to encounter difficulty.[5]

The poet's reaction post-stutter is to cry out: "But I, Ó blind!" Camões is unable to *speak* about the designs on the flags and hence temporarily ceases to be able to *see* them. The primacy of vision in the Renaissance in general, and in *The Lusiads* in particular, has been amply discussed in existing criticism but is nonetheless worthy of brief mention here.[6] Within the context of European imperialism, masculine beholding was a precursor to possession. Camões' epic places great emphasis on direct acquisition of knowledge, which includes seeing, touching, and "discovering" with one's own eyes, hands, and so forth. If being unable to speak is tantamount to being blinded then being unable to speak properly—or not at all—poses very serious consequences. The poet's exclamation regarding his "blindness" at once grounds his experience of stuttering in the body and likens his disfluency to an ocular disability that threatens to undermine masculine identity as expressed through performances of physical conquest.[7]

During the digression, Camões induces parallels between his situation and that of a frail nautical vessel in danger of capsizing, thereby linking the autobiographical stanzas to a long tradition of Portuguese shipwreck narratives. Josiah Blackmore identifies the shipwreck scene as one of disruption, "when things break away from order, when the integrity of the whole begins to dissolve, when the ordered trajectory of the road (*caminho*) or the itinerary (*itinerário*) is threatened (and often disintegrates altogether)" and as a site of potential resistance, a "place without a place" that exists outside of empire and, in so doing, opens up a space in which stories of human suffering, failure, and death can be counterposed to official, state-sponsored versions of events.[8] In *The Lusiads*, the verbal breakdown occurs when the poet is about to introduce Lusus, Portugal's founding father. This is especially significant given the patriarchal bent of the poem, which glorifies "vertical continuation" through procreation equally as much as horizontal expansion via "discovery".[9]

When the episode featuring Paulo da Gama and the Catual finally resumes, it is in a new canto (VIII). The interval between cantos VII and VIII can be viewed as another form of "blocking" in that it acts as a substantial hesitation, or pause, after which the poet makes an effort to pick up where he left off:

> By the first image would the Catual stay
> To view the figure he saw painted there,
> *The branch in hand for emblem did display.*
> The beard was white and combed with care.
> "Who may the old man be? And in what way
> Is the symbol fitting, he in hand doth bear?"
> Paul made him answer, whose intent discreet
> The wise Moor in translation would repeat
> (VIII.1, italics mine, trans. slightly altered).[10]

This stanza was supposed to start off with the remark about the branch, but it gets deferred, in yet another instance of hesitancy, until the third verse. Camões also elides the word that caused him to falter: "ensign" has been replaced by "emblem." In Portuguese the linguistic swap is more evident, since the word for "emblem" [*divisa*] sounds nothing like the one for "ensign" [*insígnia*]. Through the clever deployment of a synonym, the poet avoids repeating a term that threatens to trip him up.[11] Similarly, the "autobiography" sandwiched between cantos operates like a "starter," a movement of the body or "certain words, phrases, or lead-ins that a stutterer uses to try to initiate speech or to avoid stuttering".[12] The purpose of "starters" is to create a distraction for both speaker and listener, in the hopes of downplaying the noticeability of the stutter.[13] In the case of bodily motion and some forms of verbal repetition, "starters" also afford the stuttering speaker an opportunity to delay and sometimes mitigate his or her impediment. In *The Lusiads*, it appears as though the poet seeks to draw attention away from the stumble in canto VII. Deviating from the central narrative makes it easier to forget about his stammer, and judging by Camonian criticism the tactic has been successful; for over 400 years, nothing has been written about Camões' disfluency.

The updated version of the verse about the branch in Lusus' hand that debuts in canto VIII is an amalgam of the bard's first and second attempts at it back in canto VII. Camões refashions the sentence on semantic and syntactical levels, using a combination of devices including word substitution, circumlocution, repetition, and re-organization. Notwithstanding this clever repertoire of stunts, the "new" verse in canto VIII maintains its status as another repetition—through permutation—of the stammered verses from canto VII, becoming a prolongation of the disfluency. The three verses read together leave no room for doubt:

A branch for ensign held in his right hand (VII.77)
[. . .]
A branch in his hand he held . . . (VII.78)
[. . .]
The branch in hand for emblem did display (VIII.1).

After hijacking the narrative in canto VII and veering off into his protracted overshare, the bard is strangely quiet in canto VIII. He reiterates the line about the branch in stanza 1, but then switches gears and allows Paulo da Gama to do the rest of the talking for him. A long section (40 stanzas) follows, in which the conversation between Gama and the Catual regarding the flags is presented via direct quotation. While citation of other characters is not uncommon in *The Lusiads,* an epic with many different speakers, it is difficult to overlook the placement of this episode, which relies heavily on the technique of direct quotation. Based on the transition from canto VII to VIII, it is clear that the poet himself was originally going to furnish the description of Lusus. Only in the wake of his stutter and rambling autobiographical tangent does he cede control to Gama in canto VIII. The latter takes up where Camões stopped, weaving details about the branch into his account (VIII.4). The shift over to Paulo recalls Marc Shell's observations surrounding ventriloquism and stuttering.[14] Like Moses—a stutterer who speaks through his fluent brother Aaron in the Bible—the stammering poet in *The Lusiads* relies on an eloquent character to relay his thoughts. The ventriloquism serves as Camões' final corrective measure against the poetic failure of canto VII.

When the poet laments that he is "Like Cânace, resolved herself to kill, / One hand still holds the sword and one the quill," he is evoking the *topos* of arms and letters—the idea that both military and literary training are vital to the education of the young male citizenry—while drawing on a classical text to put a unique twist on the concept.[15] Cânace, the daughter of Aeolus, lord of the winds, is a Greek mythological figure. According to legend, she fell in love with her brother, Macareus. The pair committed incest and Cânace became pregnant. Their father was outraged and ordered Cânace to kill herself, sending her a sword for this purpose. In *Heroines*, Ovid depicts Cânace as writing a final letter to Macareus while carrying out her father's will by stabbing herself to death. Upon identifying with Cânace, Camões does more than just equate poetry with suicide.[16] The bard's reference to her story cements the relationship between verbal stuttering and "aberrant" physical activity by figurally translating his stammer in VII.77–78 into an image of corporeal violence. In a manner reminiscent of the vociferation "Ó blind!," Camões uses Cânace to comment on his gender identity, suggesting through analogy that his stutter is emasculating. When he momentarily loses his grip on the quill (verbal dexterity), he is no longer the prototypical virile subject confidently wielding pen and sword, but rather its self-destructive feminine inverse.

The arms and letters *topos* provides a fitting bridge between the poet's stutter and the oral ineptness of another key character, Dom Nuno Álvares Pereira. Pereira appears twice in the poem: once in canto IV, during the "Battle of Aljubarrota" (IV.14–45), and then again in canto VIII, when Paulo da Gama includes him in the roster of personalities who contributed to Portugal's glory (VIII.28). Historically, the "Battle of Aljubarrota" was waged on August 14, 1385. A Portuguese army of 7,000 led by Dom João I and Pereira, his commandant, clashed with Don Juan I's Castilian militia of 40,000. In essence, the Battle was a civil war, because although technically waged between armies from two different monarchies, it was motivated by Queen Leonor Teles' insistence that she and the recently deceased Dom Fernando I's daughter Beatriz (widow of Don Juan I), were the rightful heirs to the Portuguese throne. The Portuguese people vigorously resisted Teles' proposal, rejecting the formation of a "personal union" with Castile. Despite being outnumbered in the conflict, the Portuguese emerged victorious.

The "Battle of Aljubarrota" episode offers a stimulating opportunity for analysis precisely because it fails poetically on so many levels. In the epic, it is preceded by a dramatic speech on the part of Nuno Álvares as he attempts—galvanized by his brothers' lack of motivation—to incite his fellow countrymen to war:

But such erroneous thought could never dwell
In the stout Nuno Álvares, who still,
Though in his brothers he saw treason well,
Sternly rebuked every inconstant will.
In words more forceful than elegant,
He spake to all men whom such doubts might fill,
Hand on sword, irate, with no grace of style,
But the whole world threatening, land and sea, the while:

"What?! Has the glorious race of Portugal
Bred men who will not like good patriots fight?
What?! In this province, princess of them all
In world-wide war, is there one man in sight,
Who to defend her disobeys the call,
Refusing faith, love, soldier skill, and might
Proper to Portugal, for no reason known?
Does he hope to see his country overthrown?
What?! Have you ceased to be their right descent,
Who, with the great Afonso's flag before,
Proved themselves fiery and armipotent
And this martial nation overbore,
When they beat back so vast an armament,
Whose soldiers with their banners fled the war,
And seven Counts illustrious were ta'en,
Prisoners, beside what other booty they might gain?
[. . .]
I only, with my men and this beside
(Which saying, forth he drew the sword half way)
Will against hateful foes defense provide
For the country none has conquered to this day.
With the King, and with the Kingdom sadly tried,
And the mere loyalty which you gainsay,
I'll beat not only those our present foes
But whosoever shall my King oppose"
            (IV.14–16; 19, trans. slightly altered).[17]

Prior to his speech (punctuated by indignant repetitions of "What?!" that recall Camões' stutter) Nuno Álvares has already placed his hand on his sword, the blade of which he partially withdraws for emphasis during the final lines. The message of these verses, wherein the character is described as "forceful" and "irate, with no grace of style," could not be stronger: on the poem's own terms, Nuno Álvares lacks even the most basic degree of eloquence, relying instead on flashy exhibitions of weaponry as his primary method of persuasion. The combination of clumsy vocalizations peppered with threats of violence is repeated by members of Álvares' army, who, following their leader's example, "brandish" and "swing about" their weapons, while "screaming, their mouths hanging open" (IV.21). Overall, the utilization of arms during the Battle of Aljubarrota highlights a linguistic lack for which its participants attempt to compensate using artillery. Nuno Álvares is not a cogent speaker. Deficient in the art of rhetoric, the character employs his weapon as a verbal prosthesis. At the same time, his disordered speech mirrors his body language, and he is as rough with words as he is with arms.

But it is not merely Nuno Álvares' language that is inarticulate in this section of the poem. The battle sequence comprises one of the most maladroit and redundant passages in all of *The Lusiads*, featuring an astonishing number of phonetic and semantic repetitions packed into its 32 stanzas. In Portuguese, unlike in English, linguistic replication is frowned upon. The phenomenon, known as "cacophony," goes beyond stylistic forms such as alliteration or anadiplosis (though these also figure prominently in the aforementioned verses). In Romance languages, "cacophony" occurs when similar constructions are repeated in close proximity to one another, and even today it is considered highly undesirable in written Portuguese. To give an idea, the sentence "Your reac**tion** shows no imagina**tion**" is perfectly acceptable in English but would be regarded as "cacophonous" in Portuguese due to the repetition of the suffix "-tion." The "Battle of Aljubarrota" sequence is exceedingly cacophonous and lexically impoverished, recycling identical words as well as variations on the same root words over and over again. Leonard Bacon's translation eliminates these repetitions—even though they would have been easy enough to mimic in English—presumably because the translator felt the need to clean up Camões' aesthetically displeasing phraseology.

The awkward way in which the Battle of Aljubarrota is recounted complicates what would otherwise be a straightforward victory tale. Through slips, stutters, and cacophonous stanzas, Camões inscribes an anti-epic palimpsest beneath the poem's overtly epic program. The encrypted lesson of the "Battle of Aljubarrota" seems to be that the Renaissance ideal of arms and letters is unsustainable, and that, in moments of weakness, the sword will inevitably triumph over the pen. If the quintessential man is supposed to be equally proficient in handling both instruments, only the less than perfect male will choose one over the other. Based on their respective performances in the "autobiographical stanzas" (VII.77–79) and the "Battle of Aljubarrota," both Camões-the-poet and his bellicose hero Nuno Álvares are exposed as deeply flawed masculine subjects.

In contrast to Camões and his ferocious, sword-wielding war hero, the sea captain Vasco da Gama strikes one at first glance as a model of verbal dexterity. With a massive, uninterrupted discourse spanning nearly three cantos (III.3–V.91), in addition to numerous shorter utterances interspersed throughout the poem, Gama communicates more than anyone else in *The Lusiads* with the exception of the poet, and whenever he speaks those around him "hang on every word, drinking" from the captain's mouth (V.90). Yet Vasco da Gama's speech is not unproblematic either. Hélio J.S. Alves underscores the extent to which Gama's responses to questions mismatch what has been asked of him, making the captain a poor interlocutor for his unfortunate conversational partners.[18] Gama's most famous instance of dialogical incongruence is his longest. Having arrived in Malindi, the Portuguese captain is warmly received by the local king, who requests that Gama tell him about Portugal's climate, as well as the genealogy of the Portuguese people and details of their military exploits (II.109). Gama, ignoring the king's invitation, replies: "Thou hast commanded, Ó great king, that I / My nation's splendid lineage should narrate. / Thou dost not ask me for some foreign story, / But plainly bidst me praise my people's glory" (III.3, trans. slightly altered).[19] By echoing the king's request in his rejoinder, the captain demonstrates that he has heard and understood it. In spite of this, Gama will not (even for the sake of diplomacy) oblige, instead seizing the opportunity to "praise [his] people's glory".[20]

What follows is a gargantuan chunk of text in which the captain does nothing but uninterruptedly brag. Gama's assessment of his speech does not match the poet's, for while the seaman guarantees the king that he'll "be brief" (III.4), Camões—once he can get a word in edgewise—refers to the captain's narrative as a "long tale" (V.90). Critics have rightly sided with the poet, for the captain's spiel is very long indeed. The sheer size of the monologue, coupled with the fact that Gama delivers it with the understanding that he is not actually answering the question asked of him *and* exhibits cognitive dissonance in labeling the diatribe "brief" suggests that he suffers from logorrhea, a communication disorder manifested by excessive, often incoherent talkativeness. Interestingly, grandiloquence falls under the umbrella of communication disorders characterized by verbosity, and the captain's speech—a constant stream of praise about his people—is nothing if not pure bombast. The issue at stake is not simply that Gama refuses to properly address the king's query. Before the captain even begins speaking, the king states that he is familiar with Portugal's greatness. Specifically, he says that, while he does not know the minutiae of Portuguese military victories, he has heard of their "worth" (II.109). He then proceeds to underscore this comment by asking rhetorically: "For who is he, by fame, who doth not know / That actions of the Portuguese are great?" (II.111).[21] Vasco da Gama thus knows that his interlocutor *already knows* of the Portuguese people's "glory," but still chooses to ignore what has been asked of him in favor of regurgitating a long-winded and pragmatically useless lecture.[22]

The captain's verbal glut is consistent with his physical excess in the form of displays of artillery and manpower. Earlier in the voyage, for example, he made a point of laying out a colossal number of arms in front of a group of largely defenseless Mozambicans for no other reason than to threaten them (I.67–68). Vasco da Gama's linguistic domination is an extension of his imperial impulse towards any non-Portuguese people he meets. Just as he preemptively shows off munitions and weaponry in order to subdue, so too does he prophylactically quash the voices of his interlocutors, monopolizing the conversation. Camões affirms as much when he compares da Gama to "Caesar [who] in triumph subjugated France, / But in Arms in him the Arts did not repress. / One hand, the pen, the other the lance, / Cicero yet matching in persuasiveness" (V.96). If Camões-the-poet and Nuno Álvares each fail to strike a balance between arms and letters, then Vasco da Gama represents the monstrous surplus of both these values. By overplaying his hand with brutal spectacles of linguistic and physical force, the captain reveals himself a political failure. He, too, falls short of the Renaissance model; far from judiciously handling pen and sword, he abuses both to bully everyone he encounters.

One of the captain's most memorable exchanges is with a giant called Adamastor, a personification of the Cape of Good Hope (aka Cape of Storms) who has been identified with Africa and Africans, and as a guardian of disputed territory who "dwells along the line, on the margin or frontier or in limbo".[23] Adamastor is a figure so great in stature—literally and figuratively—that it would be impossible to do him justice in just a few pages.[24] This study will therefore offer only a preliminary inquiry into the issue of disordered speech as pertains to the character. In canto V, at the center of both the poem and the voyage, the captain and his crew are preparing to round the Cape when suddenly menacing a figure rises up out of thin air.[25] The scene is narrated by Vasco da Gama and is part of his monologue before the king of Malindi:

> I had not finished when a form appeared,
> High in the air, filled with prevailing might.
> The face was heavy, with a squalid beard.
> Misshaped he was but of enormous height.
> Hollow the eyes, and bad and to be feared
> The gesture, and the color earthen-white,
> And, thick with clay, the lank hair twisted hangs.
> And the mouth was black and full of yellow fangs.
>
> So huge of limb he was, I swear to thee,
> That the thing's equal only could be found
> In the Rhodian's colossal prodigy,
> One of the Seven Wonders world-renowned.
> And the voice seemed to thunder from the sea,
> As he spoke thickly with a ghastly sound.
> Our hair stood up on end, our flesh went cold,
> Only to hear the monster, and behold. (V.39–40)[26]

Once the giant has taken shape, he immediately begins to speak, menacing the Portuguese with a series of dire prophecies regarding the losses and deaths they will incur as a result of their insatiable desire for global takeover. The monster is prevented from completing his discourse by none other than Gama, who audaciously interrupts him and demands to know "Who art thou?" (V.49). For the captain, this is another moment in which he seizes control of the narrative, forcibly silencing his interlocutor.

Adamastor is muted for a stanza and, by the time he resumes speaking, the captain's interrogation has completely altered the giant's demeanor. He responds to Gama's question with obvious discomfort: "Heavily, harshly his reply he made, / As one on whom the answer gravely weighed" (V.49). Adamastor explains that he was a Titan who fell in love with a nymph named Thetis. Thinking himself "ugly" (V.53), he resolved to take Thetis by force until her mother, Doris, intervened and offered to set the monster up with her daughter. Like any enamored suitor, Adamastor brimmed with hope and desire as he awaited the rendezvous. One night, after seeing Thetis' nude, white form in the distance and judging this to be the hour of the much anticipated date, he ran towards her and flung himself into her embrace, kissing her face and hair. Then, tragedy—for Doris had cruelly tricked him:

> "What bitterness do I not know, who this recount!
> I deemed my love was in my arms, no less,
> But found I had embraced a rugged mount,
> Full of rough woods and thickset wilderness,
> And with the high crag standing front to front,
> When I thought that angelical face to press,
> I did not become a man, no, but mute, and still,
> Became a rock joined to another rock.
> [. . .]
> This flesh of mine was changed into hard clay.
> My bones, of crags and rocks, took on the cast.
> These limbs you see, this form and body, lay
> Stretched out in the great waters. And at last
> Into this promontory faraway
> The gods transmuted all my stature vast.
> And, that I might endure redoubled sorrow,
> The seas of Thetis circle round me still"
>   (V.56; 59, trans. slightly altered).[27]

After telling his life story, Adamastor, "weeping wild" (V.60), disappears, leaving Vasco da Gama and his men to continue their journey and the captain to continue his verbosity for the remainder of canto V.

The Adamastor episode can be read as a commentary on the interplay of muteness and speech. The giant is dumbstruck—once by his astonishment at Doris' scam, and then again by Gama's refusal to let him communicate. The interaction between the Portuguese captain and the Titan draws attention to the dialogic nature of speech disorders, which do not exist in a vacuum but—as Joshua St. Pierre argues in his chapter of this collection—are always constructed in part by listeners.[28] It is Vasco da Gama, Adamastor's auditor, who interrupts the flow of the giant's speech and drives him off narrative course by demanding to know his identity. (By the same token, we can only judge the captain's speech to be "disordered" when examining it within the larger context of the poem's total number of speakers and listeners; in *comparison* to other characters, Gama suffers from logorrhea.) Adamastor's unfortunate fate is the product of failed communication with Doris. Just as Gama willfully ignores the king of Malindi's question, Adamastor overlooks the possibility that Doris might be deceiving him. Both circumstances produce disordered speech (verbal diarrhea on one hand, mutism on the other).[29]

Adamastor's mournful autobiography prefigures the poet's own in canto VII. Like Camões, the monster links his inability to communicate and to "see" (Thetis) with failure to live up to masculine expectations. For the giant, the connection between speech and masculine sexual identity is even more explicit: his miscommunication with Doris directly results in his inability to ever physically consummate his love for Thetis. This violent negation of the creature's sexuality represents a third, very permanent state of enforced muteness. The character is prevented from giving *bodily* expression, whether through speech or sex, to his innermost thoughts, feelings, and desires. Adamastor recognizes the implications of his entrapment when he bemoans that he "did not become a man, no, but mute, and still" (V.56). Yet again in *The Lusiads*, the capacity for fluent speech is associated with the successful enactment of masculinity through conquest. Significantly, Adamastor is also the only male character in the epic who weeps; every other crying character is female (II.39–41; III.102–106; IV.89–92).

The organization of Camões' epic further complicates analyses of speech disorders. It is in fact Camões-the-poet who talks more than anyone else in *The Lusiads*. This assertion may appear self-evident, even facile, but it has major ramifications for my overarching argument. The way in which the poem is structured has been compared to a Russian doll, with Camões as the only true "subject of enunciation," and all other characters' speech encased inside his own via direct quotation.[30] This assessment is accurate: when Vasco da Gama "speaks" for almost three consecutive cantos, he is not so much speaking as taking part in a ventriloquist's show, for before the captain manages to open his mouth, the poet has taken up two stanzas invoking the Muse Calliope to "instruct me now [. . .] what to the king great Gama might declare" (III.1). When Dom Nuno Álvares Pereira exhorts his contemporaries to battle in canto IV and Adamastor pines for Thetis in canto V, their vocalizations are part of Gama's discourse before the king of Malindi, which in turn is actually the poet's speech, which in turn is actually the language of the Muses that the poet repeatedly summons and who speak *through* him.

Because the poet uses female Muses to speak and everyone else speaks through the poet, all verbal production in *The Lusiads* is ultimately ventriloquized *and* gendered as female. This may explain why speaking is an activity fraught with anxiety for male characters: to speak is to risk inserting oneself into the realm of the "feminine." Moreover, the very existence of Camões' poem is premised on the idea of "disordering" or disrupting the speech of others, namely the poet's precursors. In the epic's proposition, Camões brashly tells the "ancient Muse" to "shut up" so that he can have a chance to say his piece:

> Enough of the wise Greek and of the Trojan
> The great voyages they made;
> Shut up about Alexander the Great and Trajan, leave untold
> Triumphant fame in wars which they essayed.
> For I sing of the illustrious Lusitanian spirit,
> That Mars and Neptune equally obeyed.
> Enough of everything the ancient Muse sings,
> For valor superior yet now rings. (I.3, trans. altered)[31]

He then immediately enlists the "nymphs of Tagus" to assist him with the task at hand (I.4).

If epic poetry and its correlate activities of empire building are essential to early modern constructions of masculinity, what follows is that constructions of masculinity per se are inherently "disordered" by the presence of "abnormal" speech in *The Lusiads*. The prevailing effect created in the poem recalls Deleuze's discussion of the third way in which a text can stutter. The first way is by "doing," or incorporating stuttering into characters' written speech. The second is by "saying without doing," usually through the use of verbs like "he stuttered," "he stammered," and so on, but without any actual transcription of the stutter. The third way occurs when "saying is doing" and "[i]t is no longer the character who stutters in speech [but] the writer who becomes *a stutterer in language*".[32] Camões' text can be said to stutter in the third sense proposed by Deleuze. Against the epic agenda of his poem, the poet pits numerous unmistakably anti-epic voices. These voices stammer, spill over, ramble, fall silent. In the process, they challenge the epic framework and, by extension, notions of masculine identity and empire.

NOTES

1. This chapter is part of a larger project on gendered speech patterns in Camões' poem which also includes analyses of female speakers and an exploration of the limits of discursive agency associated with constructions of "femininity" in the epic.

2. In *The Lusiads*, "Camões" and "poet" are interchangeable terms. A pair of paronomasic verbs—"sing" [*cantar*] and "tell" [*contar*]—are employed to signal narration and to differentiate between the verbal activities of the poet and those of all other figures. Without exception, "cantar" refers to the poet's speech, as well as to that of various supernatural beings. "Contar," on the other hand, designates language produced by Vasco da Gama and other characters; these utterances are set off by quotation marks.

3. David Quint, *Epic and Empire* (Princeton, NJ: Princeton University Press, 1993), 45–50, 99.

4. Here are the three stanzas in Portuguese:

> Alça-se em pé, co ele o Gama junto,
> Coelho, de outra parte, e o Mauritano;
> Os olhos põe no bélico e trasunto
> De um velho branco, aspeito venerado,
> Cujo nome não pode ser defunto,
> Enquanto houver no mundo trato humano:
> No trajo a Grega usança está perfeita;
> Um ramo, por insígnia, na dereita.
>
> Um ramo na mão tinha . . . Mas, ó cego,
> Eu, que cometo insano e temerário,
> Sem vós, Ninfas do Tejo e do Mondego,
> Por caminho tão árduo, longo e vário!
> Vosso favor invoco, que nevago
> Por alto mar, com vento tão contrário,
> Que, se não me ajudais, hei grande medo
> Que o meu fraco batel se alague cedo.
>
> Olhai que há tanto tempo que, cantando,
> O vosso Tejo e os vossos Lusitanos,
> A Fortuna me traz peregrinando,
> Novos trabalhos vendo e novos danos:
> Agora o mar, agora esprimentando
> Os perigos Mavórcios inumanos,
> Qual Cânace, que à morte se condena,
> Nua mão sempre a espada e noutra a pena[.]

Luís Vaz de Camões, *Os Lusíadas* (Porto: Porto Editora, 2000), VII.77–79 (Portuguese); Luís Vaz de Camões, *The Lusiads*, trans. Leonard Bacon (New York: Hispanic Society of America, 1950) (English). All subsequent citations are from these editions and are included within parentheses within the text (English) and endnotes (Portuguese).

5. Marc Shell, *Stutter* (London: Harvard University Press, 2005), 176–180, 204; Franklin H. Silverman, "The 'Monster' Study," *Journal of Fluency Disorders* 13, no. 3 (June 1988), 229.

6. See Sergei Lobanov-Rostovsky, "Taming the Basilisk," in *The Body in Parts: Fantasies of Corporeality in Early Modern Europe*, ed. David Hillman and Carla Mazzio (New York: Routledge, 1997), and Fernando Gil and Helder Macedo, *Viagens do Olhar: Retrospecção, Visão e Profecia no Renascimento Português* (Porto: Campo das Letras, 1998), 77–120.

7. Brazilian sociologist and anthropologist Gilberto Freyre famously described *The Lusiads*' "distinguished barons" (I.1) as "'discoverers not just with their eyes, but with their sexes.'" Cited in Anna Klobucka, "Lusotropical Romance: Camões, Gilberto Freyre, and the Isle of Love," *Portuguese Literary & Cultural Studies 9: Post-Imperial Camões* (Fall 2002), 124 (my translation).

8. Josiah Blackmore, *Manifest Perdition: Shipwreck Narrative and the Disruption of Empire* (Minneapolis: University of Minnesota Press, 2002), 63, 61.
9. Klobucka, Lusotropical Romance, 130; Saúl Jiménez-Sandoval, "Love and Empire in Os Lusíadas." *Portuguese Literary & Cultural Studies 7: A Repertoire of Contemporary Portuguese Poetry* (Fall 2001), 240–241. For an illuminating analysis of patriarchal dysfunction in Lusophone literature, see Phillip Rothwell's *A Canon of Empty Fathers: Paternity in Portuguese Narrative.*
10. In Portuguese:

    Na primeira figura se detinha
    O Catual, que vira estar pintada,
    Que por divisa um ramo na mão tinha,
    A barba branca, longa e penteada.
    Quem era e por que causa lhe convinha
    A divisa que tem na mão tomada?
    Paulo responde, cuja voz discreta
    O Mauritano sábio lhe interpreta (VIII.1).

11. On these and other common strategies employed by stutterers, see the work of Shell, Gerald F. Johnson, "A Clinical Study of Porky Pig Cartoons," *Journal of Fluency Disorders* 12 (1987), 237, and George G. Helliesen, *Therapy for the Severe Older Adolescent and Adult Stutterer: A Program for Change* (Newport News, VA: Apollo Press, 2006), 7–9.
12. Helliesen, *Therapy for the Adult Stutterer*, 7.
13. Helliesen, *Therapy for the Adult Stutterer*, 8.
14. Marc Shell, *Stutter*, 106–129.
15. Robert Ernst Curtius, *European Literature and the Latin Middle Ages* (Princeton, NJ: Princeton University Press, 1953), 178–179.
16. João R. Figueiredo, *A Autocomplacência da Mimese: Uma Defesa da Poesia, Os Lusíadas e a Vida de Frei Bertolameu dos Mártires* (Coimbra: Angelus Novus, 2003), 45–46.
17. From the original text:

    Mas nunca foi que este erro se sentisse
    No forte Dom Nuno aluerez; mas antes,
    Posto que em seus irmãos tão claro o visse,
    Reprovando as vontades incostantes,
    Àquelas duvidosas gentes disse,
    Com palavras mais duras que elegantes,
    A mão na espada, irado e não facundo,
    Ameaçando a terra, o mar e o mundo.
    "Como?! Da gente ilustre Portuguesa
    Há-de haver quem refuse o pátrio Marte?

    Como?! Desta província, que princesa
    Foi das gentes na guerra em toda parte,
    Há-de sair quem negue ter defesa?
    Quem negue a Fé, o amor, o esforço e arte
    De Português, e por nenhum respeito,
    O próprio Reino queira ver sujeito?

    Como?! Não sois vós inda os descendentes
    Daqueles que, debaixo da bandeira
    Do grande Henriques, feros e valentes,
    Vencestes esta gente tão guerreira,
    Quando tantas bandeiras, tantas gentes

Puseram em fugida, de maneira
Que sete ilustres Condes lhe trouxeram
Presos, afora a presa que tiveram?

[. . .]

Eu só, com meus vassalos e com esta
(E, dizendo isto, arranca meia espada),
Defenderei da força dura e infesta
A terra nunca de outrem sojugada.
Em virtude do Rei, da pátria mesta,
Da lealdade já por vós negada,
Vencerei não só estes adversários,
Mas quantos a meu Rei forem contrários" (IV.14–16; 19).

18. Hélio J.S. Alves, *Camões, Corte-Real e o Sistema da Epopeia Quinhentista*, (Diss. University of Coimbra, 2001), 480, 502–503.
19. In Portuguese: "'Mandas-me, ó Rei, que conte declarando / De minha gente o grão genealosia; / Não me mandas contar estranha história, / Mas mandas-me louvar dos meus a glória" (III.3).
20. Alves, *Camões, Corte-Real e o Sistema da Epopeia Quinhentista*, 480.
21. From the original text:

"Mas antes, valeroso Capitão,
Nos conta (lhe dezia) diligente,
Da terra tua o clima e a região
Do mundo onde morais, distintamente;
E assi de vossa antiga geração,
E o princípio do Reino tão potente,
Cos sucessos das guerras do começo,
Que, sem sabê-las, sei que são de preço.

[. . .]

E não menos co tempo se parece
O desejo de ouvir-te o que contares;
Que quem há que por fama não conhece
As obras Portuguesas singulares?
Não tanto desviado resplandece
De nós o claro Sol, pera julgares
Que os Melindanos tem tão rudo peito,
Que não estimem muito um grande feito" (II.109; 111).

22. Alves denounces da Gama's speech as "linguistic waste," *Camões, Corte-Real e o Sistema da Epopeia Quinhentista*, 502.
23. Lawrence Lipking, "The Genius of the Shore: Lycidas, Adamastor, and the Poetics of Nationalism," *PMLA* 111, no. 2 (Mar. 1996), 214.
24. See the work of Monteiro, Lipking, Pierce, Banks, Blackmore, Klobucka and Martz for an introduction to the existing body of criticism on Adamastor.
25. Frank Pierce, "Camões' Adamastor," *Hispanic Studies in Honour of Joseph Manson* (Oxford: Dolphin, 1972), 207.
26. From the source text:

Não acabava, quando hua figura
Se nos mostra no ar, robusta e válida,
De disforme e grandíssima estatura;
O rosto carregado, a barba esquálida,
Os olhos encovados, e a postura

Medonha e má, e a cor terrena e pálida;
Cheios de terra e crespos os cabelos,
A boca negra, os dentes amarelos.

Tão grande era de membros, que bem posso
Certificar-te que este era o segundo
De Rodes estranhíssimo Colosso,
Que um dos sete milagres foi do mundo.
Cum tom de voz nos fala, horrendo e grosso,
Que pareceu sair do mar profundo.
Arrepiam-se as carnes e o cabelo,
A mi e a todos, só de ouvi-lo e vê-lo! (V.39–40).

27. Here is Adamastor's dirge in Portuguese:

"Oh! Que não sei de nojo como o conte!
Que, crendo ter nos braços quem amava,
Abraçado me achei cum duro monte
De áspero mato e de espessura brava.
Estando cum penedo fronte a fronte,
Que eu polo rosto angélico apertava,
Não fiquei homem, não, mas mudo e quedo
E, junto dum penedo, outro penedo!

[. . .]

Converte-se-me a carne em terra dura;
Em penedos os ossos se fizeram;
Estes membros, que vês, e esta figura
Por estas longas águas se estenderam.
Enfim, minha grandíssima estatura
Neste remoto Cabo converteram
Os Deuses; e, por mais dobradas mágoas,
Me anda Thetis cercando destas águas" (V.56, 59).

28. Joshua St. Pierre, "The Construction of the Disabled Speaker: Locating Stuttering in Disability Studies," *CJDS* 1, no. 3 (August 2012), 6–11.
29. Adamastor is also possibly illiterate and/or has some sort of reading comprehension disorder. According to João R. Figueiredo, the giant could have avoided his fate had he only understood Ovid's *Metamorphoses*. Figueiredo, *A Autocomplacência da Mimese*, 63–71.
30. Gil and Macedo, *Viagens do Olhar*, 35.
31. Bacon's translation softens the Portuguese quite a bit, and as such I have altered it—as noted above—in order to more accurately capture the feeling of Camões' text:

Cessem do sábio Grego e do Troiano
As navegações grandes que fizeram;
Cale-se de Alexandro e de Trajano
A fama das vitórias que tiveram;
Que eu canto o peito ilustre Lusitano,
A quem Neptuno e Marte obedeceram.
Cesse tudo o que a Musa antiga canta,
Que outro valor mais alto se alevanta (I.3).

32. Gilles Deleuze, "He Stuttered," *Essays Critical and Clinical*, trans. Daniel W. Smith and Michael A. Greco (Minneapolis: University of Minnesota Press, 1997), 107.

WORKS CITED

Alves, Hélio J.S. *Camões, Corte-Real e o Sistema da Epopeia Quinhentista.* Diss. University of Coimbra, 2001.

Banks, Jared. "Adamastorying Mozambique: Ualalapi and Os Lusíadas." *Luso-Brazilian Review* 37, no. 1 (2000): 1–16.

Blackmore, Josiah. *Manifest Perdition: Shipwreck Narrative and the Disruption of Empire.* Minneapolis and London: University of Minnesota Press, 2002.

Camões, Luís Vaz de. *Os Lusíadas.* Porto: Porto Editora, 2000.

Camões, Luís Vaz de. *The Lusiads.* Trans. Leonard Bacon. New York: Hispanic Society of America, 1950.

Curtius, Robert Ernst. *European Literature and the Latin Middle Ages.* Princeton, NJ: Princeton University Press, 1953.

Deleuze, Gilles. "He Stuttered." *Essays Critical and Clinical.* Trans. Daniel W. Smith and Michael A. Greco. Minneapolis: University of Minnesota Press, 1997, 107–114.

Figueiredo, João R. *A Autocomplacência da Mimese: Uma Defesa da Poesia, Os Lusíadas e a Vida de Frei Bertolameu dos Mártires.* Coimbra: Angelus Novus, 2003.

Gil, Fernando and Helder Macedo. *Viagens do Olhar: Retrospecção, Visão e Profecia no Renascimento Português.* Porto: Campo das Letras, 1998.

Helliesen, George G. *Therapy for the Severe Older Adolescent and Adult Stutterer: A Program for Change.* Newport News, VA: Apollo Press, 2006.

Klobucka, Anna. "Lusotropical Romance: Camões, Gilberto Freyre, and the Isle of Love." *Portuguese Literary & Cultural Studies 9: Post-Imperial Camões* (Fall 2002): 121–138.

Jiménez-Sandoval, Saúl. "Love and Empire in Os Lusíadas." *Portuguese Literary & Cultural Studies 7: A Repertoire of Contemporary Portuguese Poetry* (Fall 2001): 239–254.

Johnson, Gerald F. "A Clinical Study of Porky Pig Cartoons." *Journal of Fluency Disorders* 12 (1987): 235–238.

Lipking, Lawrence. "The Genius of the Shore: Lycidas, Adamastor, and the Poetics of Nationalism." *PMLA* 111, no. 2 (Mar. 1996): 205–221.

Lobanov-Rostovsky, Sergei. "Taming the Basilisk." In *The Body in Parts: Fantasies of Corporeality in Early Modern Europe,* ed. David Hillman and Carla Mazzio. New York: Routledge, 1997.

Martz, Louis L. "Camoens and Milton." *Ocidente* 83 (1972): 45–59.

Monteiro, George. "The Adamastor Story." *The Presence of Camões: Influences on the Literature of England, America, and Southern Africa.* Lexington: The University of Kentucky Press, 1996, 120–131.

Pierce, Frank. "Camões' Adamastor." *Hispanic Studies in Honour of Joseph Manson.* Oxford: Dolphin, 1972, 207–215.

Quint, David. *Epic and Empire.* Princeton, NJ: Princeton University Press, 1993. Print.Rothwell, Phillip. *A Canon of Empty Fathers: Paternity in Portuguese Narrative.* Lewisburg, PA: Bucknell University Press, 2007.

Shell, Marc. *Stutter.* London: Harvard University Press, 2005.

Silverman, Franklin H. "The 'Monster' Study." *Journal of Fluency Disorders* 13, no. 3 (June 1988): 225–231.

St. Pierre, Joshua. "The Construction of the Disabled Speaker: Locating Stuttering in Disability Studies." *CJDS* 1, no. 3 (August 2012): 1–21.

5 "Stuttistics"

On Speech Disorders in *Finnegans Wake*

Chris Eagle

Searching for disordered speech in *Finnegans Wake* is a bit like looking for the hay in the proverbial haystack rather than the needle. Due to the sheer number of neologisms, portmanteau words, polyglot puns, nonsense refrains, and borrowings from over sixty different languages which James Joyce incorporated into his final work, it could be argued that disordered speech forms the very linguistic ground of Wakese and is therefore in a sense not disordered at all. Yet despite Joyce's systematic blurring of the distinction between "however basically English" (116.26) and the "meddlied muddlingisms" (303.20) of his "artificial tongue with a natural curl" (169.15), it is still the case that several clinically recognizable speech disorders—such as stuttering, interdental and bilabial lisping, slurring, parapraxis, and perseveration—are both present in *Finnegans Wake* and distinguishable within the book from other forms of wordplay.[1] The fact that the sleeping couple at the center of the narrative are each marked by speech impediments (HCE stutters and ALP lisps) is something that until recently has received very little attention in Joyce studies. David Spurr's recent article "Stuttering Joyce" offers the first substantial examination of the motif of stuttering from *Dubliners* through *Finnegans Wake*. For Spurr, stuttering is one of many "phonetic anomalies" that "have the effect of staging precisely the material production of the utterance which is so important to Joyce's language."[2] While Spurr's article provides an extremely lucid study of these "phonetic anomalies" across Joyce's corpus, a more systematic study of the role speech pathology plays in *Finnegans Wake* has yet to be pursued. Any such study needs to take into account not only the *performative* aspects of the stutter as a 'motif' or 'figure' for poetic language, but also the *portrayals* of disordered speech in the characters of HCE and the lisp of ALP. There would seem to be two main stumbling blocks for such a study. First of all, there is the longstanding debate amongst Joyce scholars as to the status of HCE and ALP as characters in any traditional novelistic sense. Obviously, their archetypal nature poses an added challenge in any attempt to read their speech disorders in standard clinical terms. Is it possible, for example, to offer a psychogenic analysis of the cause of HCE's stutter, when the issue of whether he is a traditional character with discernible psychological drives remains in question? Can we even call *Finnegans Wake* a narrative 'about' stuttering in the same way that we would with novels like *Billy Budd* or *One Flew Over the Cuckoo's Nest*? A second difficulty in determining the presence of distinct speech pathologies in *Finnegans Wake* is the tendency amongst poststructuralist readers of Joyce to interpret all forms of verbal experimentation in the *Wake* as fundamentally ludic in nature. For this reason, the *Wake*'s many stutters, lisps, slurs, and perseverations are subsumed, in many cases understandably so, under the broader aesthetic heading of Joycean wordplay.

This affinity between the aesthetic and the clinical, between controlled literary experimentation and uncontrollable pathological speech, is not restricted to the case of Joyce, however, but can be located throughout much avant-garde modernist writing. One need only think of the morphological similarities between works of Dadaist sound poetry or the Russian Trans-Sense movement and the speech of those aphasics suffering from the condition known as neologistic jargonaphasia. Or the syntactical similarities to be found between the repeating rhythms of Gertrude Stein and the perseverative speech of certain expressive aphasics. In any case, the fact that so much modernist writing was self-consciously modeled after pathological forms of speech did not escape critics of the time. Russian Formalists like Boris Eichenbaum and Victor Shklovksy often referred to the experimental works of poets like Majakovski and Khlebnikov in terms of a breakdown of language in which inarticulateness and awkward stammering rhythms were valorized on aesthetic grounds for their power to revitalize exhausted literary forms. In 1923, Eichenbaum wrote in reference to the Trans-sense movement that, "it became necessary to create a new, *inarticulate, uncouth speech*, to emancipate the tradition of poetic diction from the shackles of Symbolism" (emphasis added).[3] Moreover, what characterized the aesthetic of defamiliarization, for Shklovksy, was a "difficult, roughened, *impeded language*" (emphasis added).[4] In his 1926 work *The Art of Being Ruled*, Wyndham Lewis applied the same terminology, albeit perjoratively, to both Gertrude Stein and James Joyce. Together, their works exemplify for him a certain "*willed* sickness" endemic to experimental modernism, a "campaign against language and the articulate" in which sound is separated from sense, at the service of musicality, but at the expense of the intellect.[5] What results, argues Lewis, is "a literary system that consists in a sort of gargantuan mental stutter" whereby the mind is said to be attacked by its own instrument.[6]

More recently, critics and theorists like David Lodge and Gilles Deleuze have continued to understand modernist experimentation as a kind of controlled pathology, one in which the linguistic features of conditions like aphasia and stuttering are harnessed into a freely creative playing with language. In his influential essay "Metaphor and Metonymy in Modern Fiction," Lodge applies ideas derived from Roman Jakobson's study of aphasic speech to the altering styles of Gertrude Stein among others. In early works like *The Making of Americans*, Lodge writes that, "Stein was at this time deliberately and programmatically cultivating a kind of writing corresponding to the Similarity Disorder, or Selection Deficiency, type of aphasia."[7] In the later poems of *Tender Buttons*, Lodge argues that Stein's writing shifted from one pathology to another, and "the result sometimes resembles the speech of aphasics suffering from Jakobson's second disorder, contiguity disorder or contextual deficiency, where 'syntactical rules organizing words into a higher unit are lost' and sentences degenerate into 'a mere word-heap'."[8] An even more relevant example of this approach, for this chapter, is Deleuze's essay "He Stuttered," in which he offers (much like Eichenbaum) an emancipatory vision of the creative potentialities in stuttering to "make a language take flight."[9] Deleuze opens the essay by laying out three different possibilities for the incorporation of stuttering effects into literary works. The first is to transcribe stuttered speech directly into the written text. The second is to describe the stutter without ever actually transcribing it. In his words, "to do it" or "to say it without doing it."[10] With the third possibility, what he calls "when saying is doing," the writer need not portray a stuttering character at all since, "It is no longer the character who stutters in speech; it is the writer who becomes *a stutterer in language.*"[11] In this stylistic process, which Deleuze terms "creative stuttering," a "perpetual disequilibrium" is said to take place whereby "the language itself will begin to vibrate and stutter, but without being confused with speech."[12] As examples of this final and more radical possibility, Deleuze cites the styles of writers like Kafka, Beckett, Artaud, and Melville, among others.

It is safe to say that Joyce's name is conspicuous in its absence from Deleuze's list of creative stutterers, and in this chapter, I will address the extent to which Deleuze's three categories might apply to *Finnegans Wake*. This will require first an analysis of those two scenes in which H.C.E.'s stutter is most foregrounded in characterological terms: the well-known encounter with the Cad from Book I Chapter 2, and the oration offered by H.C.E. in his own defense at the Inquest from Book III Chapter 3. Using genetic methods, I will then clarify the chronology of the process by which stuttering words were introduced into the *Wake* from draft to draft. I will also elaborate on three well-known sources behind Joyce's decision to place a stutterer at the center of his final work. Those sources are the speech impediments of Lewis Carroll and Charles Stewart Parnell, and Giambattista Vico's theory that language originated in a primitive act of onomatopoeic stammering. Finally, I will compare the stutter of the husband to the lisping of his wife, to demonstrate yet another way in which Joyce's often gendered ideas about language function on the phonetic level as well.

What complicates any discussion of *Finnegans Wake* as a narrative about a man who stutters, to begin with, is Joyce's uniquely archetypal approach to his protagonist. As his primary acronym ("Here Comes Everybody") suggests, HCE is a universal, all-encompassing patriarch, a concatenation of all heroes of all eras. He is "Bygmester Finnegan of the Stuttering Hand" (4.18). He is "Twotongue Common." (385.4). He is the "seasea stamoror" (547.25), the "fafafather of all schemes" (45.13), the "stotterer . . . biggermaster Omnibil" (337.18–9), whose sleeping giant body stretches out to the size of the city he represents. At the same time, HCE is an ordinary family man, a Protestant publican of Scandinavian descent whose "speech thicklish" (38.17) erupts during moments of guilty nervousness into a pronounced "doubling stutter" (197.5). Those two scenes in which "the knots made in his tongue" (288.7) are most pronounced (his encounter with the Cad and his self-defense at the Inquest) form part of the central plotline of the *Wake*, begun in Book I Chapter 1 with the revelation that HCE has committed some mysterious transgression in the Park for which he spends the rest of the narrative trying to exonerate himself. His speech disorder is therefore directly associated with sin, and since the transgression in question occurs in a place called Edenborough, it is even more precisely linked to the Biblical Fall of original sin. Thus, HCE is often understood as an Adamic figure as well, as someone who "stutters fore he falls" (139.9), or as a refashioning of Humpty Dumpty, who "stottered from the latter" (6.9–10) and spends the rest of the book piecing his fragmented self back together again.

Joyce's highly mythic account of HCE nevertheless still bears some resemblance to more conventional narratives about stuttering, through its suggestion that feelings of private shame or public humiliation can trigger the condition. The scene of private shame in question occurs sometime after his alleged crime when HCE is "billowing across the wide expanse of our greatest park" (35.7–8) and meets the pipe-smoking man known as the Cad. The Cad asks HCE a simple question: "could he tell him how much a clock it was that the clock struck had he any idea by cock's luck as his watch was bradys. Hesitency was clearly to evitated. Execration as cleverly to be honnisoid" (35.18–21). Misunderstanding the Cad's intentions, HCE fears for his safety and proceeds to defend himself both physically and verbally, pulling out a weapon and offering up a lengthy assertion of his innocence. It is worth noting that this moment of misunderstanding closely parallels that scene from Chapter 14 of *Billy Budd* in which Billy is approached by the Afterguardsman, whose mutinous proposition triggers one of the more severe instances of Billy's own stutter. In *Epistemology of the Closet*, Eve Kosofsky Sedgwick reads a homoerotic subtext into the Afterguardsman's "obscure suggestions," and many Joyceans have read the encounter with the Cad in similar terms.[13] Mishearing the Cad's simple request for the time, perhaps reading sexual innuendo into the mention of "cock's luck," HCE is overtaken by a sort of homosexual panic and fears being mugged in not one but two senses: first, that he might be "hurled into eternity right then" (robbed and killed), and second, that he might be mugged in the homoerotic sense, or as he puts it, "plugged by a softnosed bullet" (35.25–26). What follows is one of the most condensed moments of disordered speech in all of the *Wake,* during which HCE stammers out an unexpected protest of his innocence:

Shsh shake, co-comeraid! Me only, them five ones, he is equal combat. I have won straight. Hency my nonation wide hotel and creamery establishments which for the honours of our mewmew mutual daughters, credit me, I am woowoo willing to take my stand, sir, upon the monument, that sign of our ruru redemption, any hygienic day to this hour and to make my hoath to my sinnfinners [. . .] that there is not one tittle of truth, allow me to tell you, in that purest of fibfib fabrications. (36.20–34)

Later on in Chapter 5 of Book I, Joyce provides us with a helpful term— "Sexophonologistic Schizophrenesis" (123.18)—for understanding the implied psychosexual nature of HCE's speech impediment in this scene. The encounter with the Cad, it is often noted, is the first instance of a pattern reenacted throughout the *Wake* where an older man is confronted and feels threatened by a younger one. For all of these reasons, it seems plausible to read this aspect of HCE in relatively straightforward characterological terms. To read this moment, in other words, as a conventional portrayal of a man who stutters due to fear and guilt. That being said, an analysis of the actual stuttered words in this scene reveals not a phonologically accurate transcription but rather a more aesthetic intention on Joyce's part to exploit the pathology's potential for wordplay. Specifically, the condition's potential for acoustic effects as well as puns (onomatopoeia and paronomasia).

PHRASE	PAGE
compompounded	36.02
hakusay accusation	36.04
shsh shake	36.20
co-comeraid	36.20
nonation	36.22
mewmew mutual	36.23
woowoo willing	36.23
ruru redemption	36.25
fibfib fabrications	36.34
ff, flitmansfluh	37.20
hahands	38.33
alcoh alcoho alcoherently	40.05
ex-ex-executive	42.08
fafafather	45.15

Considering that the most paradigmatic form of stuttering is the repetition of the onset syllable or first consonantal sound of the given word, many of these examples cannot be called accurate transcriptions at all. An apparently stuttered word like "ex-ex-executive," for instance, does not actually fall along syllable breaks. Moreover, "ex-" is a morphological unit with a distinct meaning (as in "former"), making the word "ex-ex-executive" signify something like a former-former-executive. The same process of conflating phonological and morphological levels together, through which the stutter is made to mean something, can be found in other expressions from this scene such as "fib fib fabrications" and "woo woo willing." Although the "woo" in "woowoo willing" comes slightly closer to approximating the sound of an actual stumbling on the word (wuh-wuh-willing), here again the repeated element is a meaningful unit in its own right. If we take "woo" in the sense of to woo someone, then we can infer a distinct meaning for this peculiar expression as well. To be "woowoo willing" would mean simply to be receptive to being wooed, and thus would not be a stutter at all, but simply another playful coinage.

One finds the same mixture of clinical and aesthetic intentions in the Inquest scene from Book III Chapter 3, where Joyce once again makes the stutter signify by way of this process of substituting morphemes for phonemes. Book III is often referred to as the Book of Shaun since uncovering the son's nature or identity is its overarching theme. On the one hand, answering the question of who Shaun is means finding the part of him that is his father. For this very reason, the Four Old Men in charge of the Inquest instruct Shaun to "identify yourself with the him in you" (496.25). On the other hand, Shaun's struggle for identity equally involves an overcoming of the Father. The result of this Oedipal tension is that identities become particularly unstable in this part of the *Wake,* with Shaun changing names from Jaun to Haun to Yawn, and HCE shifting roles from the dreamer dreaming about his son to the one at the center of the dream, defending himself before the Four Old Men. Needless to say, this instability raises the characterological question of whether HCE's identity is ever sufficiently fixed to analyze him as a character who stutters. Over the course of Book III, the protagonist shifts from son to father to some amalgamation of the two, and Shaun even exhibits his father's speech disorder at certain points as well. In this respect, Book III and the Inquest scene in particular can be said to reenact the Cad scene in more ways than one. Like the encounter with the Cad, Book III stages yet another confrontation between an older and a younger man, this time father and son, and the Inquest itself further resembles the Cad Scene in that HCE offers yet another longwinded and stutter-filled apologia in response to his perceived guilt. Following a lengthy and pompous process of "crossexanimation" (87.34) of one witness after another by the Four Old Men, H.C.E. is finally summoned to rise and speak in his own defense:

—Amtsadam, sir, to you! Eternest cittas, heil! Here we are again! I am bubub brought up under a camel act of dynasties long out of print [. . .] I am known throughout the world [. . .] by saints and sinners eyeeye alike as a cleanliving man and, as a matter of fict, by my halfwife, I think how our public at large appreciates it most highly from me that I am as cleanliving as could be and that my game was a fair average since I perpetually kept my ouija ouija wicket up. On my verawife I never was nor can afford to be guilty of crim crig con of malfeasance trespass against parson with the person of a youthful gigirl frifrif friend" (532.6–20).

This oration represents by far the thickest collection of stuttered speech in all of *Finnegans Wake*. In a matter of only a few pages, one finds no less than eighteen examples, listed in the following chart.

PHRASE	PAGE
bubub brought up	532.07
eyeye alike	532.14
crim crig con of malfeasance	532.19
ouija ouija wicket	532.18
gigirl frifrif friend	535.20
popo possess	532.30
kickkick keenly	532.36
pu pure	533.03
fufuf fingers	533.11
peepee period	533.26
buji buji beloved	533.28
am amp amp amplify	533.33
babad	534.10
dudud dirtynine	534.12
pupup publication	534.17
caca cad	534.26
lulul lying	534.33
glueglue gluecose	537.13
eggseggs excessively	537.28
choochoo chucklesome	538.19

In spite of Joyce's well-known antipathy to Freud, an overdetermined Freudian reading has dominated most commentaries on this scene, where the stutter is presumed to be triggered by HCE's unresolved guilt complex. In his *Reader's Guide To Finnegans Wake*, William Tindall, for one, notes "the guilt that *makes him* stutter" in the Cad Scene, and asserts that during the Inquest, "Earwicker shares, *as his stutter shows*, Adams's guilt" (emphasis added).[14] The many scatological references in HCE's oration would seem to further reinforce a psychoanalytic reading. Mentions of "pee pee," "po po," and "caca" exhibit not only a stutter but also something closer to the psychopathology Freud termed "parapraxis," more commonly known as the Freudian slip. For the most part though, stuttered words in this passage (e.g. "eyeeye alike," "ouija ouija wicket," or "kickkick keenly") follow the same double process from the Cad scene, where otherwise meaningful morphemes act simultaneously as puns and approximate phonetic renderings of stammering speech.

In recent years, genetic studies of the drafts, faircopies, typescripts, proofs, notebooks, and letters surviving from *Work in Progress* have greatly clarified the germination of HCE as a character, from a King Mark figure in Joyce's planned rewriting of the Tristan and Isolde story to a less determinate Father figure, known simply as "Pop," who is hounded by rumors that he once exposed himself to two girls in the park.[15] The question of when exactly Joyce decided to give HCE a stutter remains much hazier, however, and the *Notebooks* (still in the process of publication) have so far proved relatively unhelpful in dating this decision. Joyce writes the word "stammer" in one of his notebooks as early as 1924, but not in relation to any specific character.[16] In another notebook from 1931, he makes the notation "rH a stutterer," which would seem to allude to HCE, but this comes long after the introduction of stuttering into the text.[17] The Inquest and Cad scenes are fortunately helpful in this regard, since they are two of the earlier drafted sections in the extremely long genesis of *Finnegans Wake*. Thanks to the work of genetic critics like Geert Lernout, as well as the recent guide to the compositional history of the *Wake* edited by Luca Crispi and Sam Slote (*How Joyce Wrote Finnegans Wake*), we know that Chapters 2–4 of Part I were drafted collectively in 1923, and based on Joyce's letters, we can be further certain that the initial drafting of the encounter with the Cad happened sometime between September and November of that same year.[18] The first draft of HCE's response to the Cad shows no traces as yet of speech trouble. Moreover, like all of the first-draft versions of *Work in Progress*, it lacks the dense opacity of Wakese at this early stage:

I am prepared to ~~stand~~ take my stand ~~on~~ upon the monument any *hygienic* day at this hour and to declare ~~before~~ upon the open bible before the Great Taskmaster's eye & in the presence of the deity *my immediate neighbour* and my fellows [*in every corner on this globe in general*] & *to every **each living** soul acquainted with the British tongue* that there is not *one* tittle of truth in that purest of fabrications.[19]

This section of the *Wake* would be revised and expanded under the title *Continuation of A Work in Progress* for publication in the journal *Transition* in April 1927. It is during this round of revisions that the majority of stuttered words are added by Joyce to the typescripts and proofs. In some cases, Joyce adds the whole stuttered phrase in by hand at once. For instance, "Shsh-Shake co-comrade" ("comrade" is later changed to "comeraid") and "mewmew mutual daughters" are both whole units Joyce added by hand. But just as often, one finds Joyce affixing stutters to previously unstuttered words. For example, "woowoo" is added by hand to the word "willing," "hakusay" is inserted before "accusation," and "fibfib" is added to "fabrications."

Beginning around mid-1924, with the majority of Book I drafted, Joyce spent the next three years drafting what would become Book III. The Inquest scene was completed by the Spring of 1925, and it would later be published under the title *Haveth Childers Everywhere* in April 1930. The first draft version of this scene also contains no traces whatsoever of stuttering:

—Sir, to you! *I am brought up under an old act of Edward the First, but* I am known throughout the world *wherever good English is spoken* as a cleanliving man and I think ~~my~~ our public at large appreciates it most highly *of me* that I am cleanliving & as a matter of fact I possess the sweetest little wife on the globe *who won the consolation prize in the dreams of women ~~competition~~ handicap by 2 breasts.*[20]

The crucial difference in the genesis of this scene is that the addition of stuttering words to it is a matter of months not years. Almost all the stutters from the Inquest appear already in their final form as early as the fair copy from January 1925. The presence of phrases like "ouija ouija wicket," "popo possess," and "peepee period" at this stage makes it certain that already by early 1925, Joyce was not only set upon HCE being someone who stutters, but he had also developed his technique of punning through the stutter.[21] A genetic study of stutter words in other sections of the *Wake* further reveals that once Joyce had decided to make stuttering a key component of the *Wake* (circa January 1925), it became a general policy of sorts to mix stutters in throughout the text, something we find him doing at varying stages of revision from early 1925 until the very last galley proofs in 1939.[22]

The basic plotline of a man who speaks with a severe stutter and whose reputation has been tarnished by rumors of sexual impropriety suggests two obvious historical precursors for HCE. Both Lewis Carroll and Charles Stewart Parnell were men whose ambitions in the public realm were hampered by their acute speech impediments. Moreover, both Carroll and Parnell were tied to acts of sexual impropriety, the former being a private affair of an older man's attraction to young girls, the latter a much more publicized sex scandal of marital infidelity. It is easy to see the correspondences here between the biographies of Caroll and Parnell and those two key moments of stuttering in the *Wake*, the Cad and Inquest scenes. In the first case, HCE experiences a more private shame over a rumored indiscretion with two young girls, and in the second, HCE is placed in the impossible position of vocally defending his "clean character" to his own people in the public forum.

In terms of why Joyce chose to make HCE a stutterer, it would perhaps make for a more interesting textual history if this decision had coincided with Joyce's discovery of Lewis Carroll in 1928. In a letter to Harriet Shaw Weaver from March 28 of that year, Joyce writes: "I have been reading about the author of 'Alice.' A few things about him are rather curious. He was born a few miles from Warrington (Daresbury), and he had a strong stutter and when he wrote he inverted his name like Tristan and Swift. His name was Charles Lutwidge of which he made Lewis (i.e. Ludwig) Carroll (i.e. Carolus)."[23] As Joyce learned, Charles Lutwidge Dodgson (aka Lewis Carroll) came from a family of stammerers. Six of his seven sisters had the condition to varying degrees, along with his brother Edwin. It was long believed that Dodgson's "hesitation," as he always called it, was limited to his interaction with adults, and that his fondness for young girls stemmed in part from his ability to speak fluently when alone with them, however, Isa Bowman's report of his frequent stammering around her has called this theory into doubt.[24] Of course, we know that Joyce had already decided to integrate stuttering into the *Wake* well before he learned about Carroll's speech trouble. Still, we can be certain that Joyce identified more similarities than just the penchant for neologism between Carroll's writing and his own at this stage. As Adeline Glasheen writes in her *Third Census of Finnegans Wake,* Carroll represented for Joyce "the man and artist who responds to the feminine with sentimental, self-serving lust and sexual stinginess," and from 1928 onwards, Joyce adds references to Carroll that gesture specifically towards this coincidence of stuttering and sexual impropriety between the author of *Alice in Wonderland* and his own "fafafather" figure, HCE.[25] Several references to the Dodo bird, long believed to be Carroll's self-caricature of his inability to pronounce his own name, are added to the *Wake* in the 1930s, for example, when Kitty the Bead is summoned as a witness during the Inquest and likens massaging HCE's muscles to the stretching of "do dodo doughdy dough" with a rolling pin (531.7). Much earlier, in Book II Chapter 1, HCE is accused of plying "lilithe maidinettes" with "candid zuckers" (241.2–3), that is, seducing little girls with candy. During the Carrollesque teaparty that follows, HCE is more directly associated with the stuttering Victorian as the "Old grand tutut toucher up of young poetographies" (242.18), a rewording of a remark once made by Lewis Carroll to Isa Bowman about his hobby of photographing young girls.[26]

Compared to Joyce's relatively late interest in the "glass darkly speech" (355.9) of Lewis Carroll, his preoccupation with the story of Charles Stewart Parnell was both lifelong and more deeply personal. The observation that the persona of Parnell formed the early basis for HCE (specifically, as a great stuttering statesman whose downfall is caused by a sexual scandal), has already been made by several critics including Richard Ellmann among others.[27] In the newspaper article Joyce wrote in 1912 for the *Piccolo della Sera*, translated as "The Shade of Parnell," the young Joyce likens the Irish statesman to another great stuttering leader. Parnell, writes Joyce, "like another Moses, led a turbulent and unstable people from the house of shame to the verge of the Promised Land."[28] This seemingly oxymoronic role of the stuttering leader occupied by Parnell is more common throughout History than one might expect. Lawgivers like Moses and the Iroquois leader Dekanawida both relied on 'interpreters' to deliver the law due to their difficulties with speech. Moses called upon his brother Aaron to act as his divine spokesman, and it is Hiawatha who is said to have delivered the speeches for Dekanawida that led to the peaceful establishment of the Iroquois Confederacy. There is also the well-known case of the Greek orator Demosthenes, who is believed to have overcome his severe stutter by shouting with pebbles in his mouth, so as to strengthen the muscles of articulation. Parnell's own difficulties with public speaking only added to the mythology of the man for the young Joyce. In "The Shade of Parnell," Joyce marvels at the ability of this Irish Moses to rally his people despite his "speech defect," "his short and fragmentary speeches," and most fatal of all, his "distinct English accent."[29]

During the composition of *Work in Progress,* Joyce is known to have relied on St. John Ervine's 1925 biography *Life of Parnell* as one of his primary sources. According to Ervine, Parnell acquired the speech disorder as a boy by mimicking the stammer of his older brother John, and it produced such "agonies of nervousness" for the adult Parnell that he would lacerate his own palms with his fingernails whenever delivering a speech.[30] In another letter to Weaver from June 1926, Joyce writes: "I should like you to read St John Irvine's *Life of Parnell* to begin with. It is not good but you ought to know some of the facts. For instance the word 'hesitency.'"[31] Joyce's mention of 'hesitency' of course refers to the Pigott forgery plot, in which Parnell's enemies forged a letter in his name endorsing the Phoenix Park murders. The plot was eventually exposed due to Pigott's habit of misspelling the word hesitancy. There is another curious coincidence here, between the "hesitation" of Lewis Carroll and the "hesitancy" of Parnell. Throughout the *Wake*, Joyce combines these two cognates into a recurring trope for HCE's guilt-ridden and hesitant speech patterns. In the Cad scene, for example, HCE seems to be reminding himself that "Hesitency was clearly to be evitated" (35.21) before launching into his stutter-filled apologia. During Chapter 4, in a scene that is often said to echo the Cad encounter, HCE is locked in a struggle with a figure known as the "attackler" (81.18). When he tries to speak to the attackler, he again stutters "for he was hesitency carried to excelcism" (82.30–31). In this way, Joyce repeatedly puns on "his hes hecitency Hec" (119.18), with over twenty "variously inflected, differently pronounced, otherwise spelled, changeably meaning vocable scriptsigns" to describe the hesitant speech of HCE (118.26–28).

A third and final source for HCE's "vociferated echoating" (404.7), more mythopoeic than biographical, is the theory of the origin of language put forward by Vico in his *New Science*. In Vico's account of the period he calls "the childhood of the world," the first act of primitive language would not have occurred until two centuries after the Great Flood, once the flood waters had evaporated into the atmosphere, generating violent lightning storms that terrified the mute giants then walking the Earth. To their crudely poetic imaginations, the sounds of the thunder overhead represented the exclamations of a Father God (Jupiter or Jove), which they mimicked through onomatopoeic grunts and shouts. The exact sound the giants uttered over and over, according to Vico, had to be the consonant cluster "*pa-*" (and later "*pape*"), which for him reveals the true etymology of father-words across most Western languages. Language thus begins for Vico in a manner not unlike Joyce's "doubling stutter," that is to say, through an act of onomatopoeic stammering. The primitive language that grows from this, Vico believes, must initially have been limited by the rigidity of the giants' vocal organs, since prior to their mimicry of thunder, they would have been entirely mute. It was therefore only through singing that the giants were able to progress from mutism to stammering to full fluency:

> People were originally mute. Hence, like mute people, they must have uttered crude vowels by singing; and like stammerers, they must have articulated consonants by singing [. . . .] The reason for this is that vowels are easy to pronounce, and consonants difficult. The first people, being dull-witted, were only moved to utter sounds when they felt violent emotions, which they naturally expressed in a very loud voice.[32]

Vico's ideas about the gradual development of consonants and vowels also help to explain the entirely opposite verbal patterns of HCE and ALP. Like her husband, ALP also speaks with a clinically recognizable and rather common speech disorder, namely, lisping. When ALP first addresses HCE in his position as "Bygmester Finnegan, of the Stuttering Hand" (4.18), we are told that, "with lipth she lithpeth to him all to time of thuch and thuch and thow on thow" (23.23–24). When one considers the altogether different phonetic features of stutters and lisps, it is apparent that Joyce's rendering of these two conditions is inflected through his deeply gendered sense of language. HCE's stutter is described at various points as a "speech thicklish," characterized by the harsh cacophony of his "masculine monosyllables"

(190.35). In contrast to the "disemvowelled" nature of HCE's "thick spch spck" (515.12, 23.4*)*, the speech of ALP is always delivered "with a soft-rolling lisp of a lapel to it" (404.23). It is characterized, in other words, by a softening or, to Joyce's mind, a feminizing of consonants.

Speech pathologists usually divide this other speech disorder of the *Wake* into the two categories of bilabial or interdental lisping. In bilabial lisping, approximant or 'liquid' consonants such as /l/ or /r/ are replaced with the bilabial /w/. That character in the *Wake* whose speech is most strongly associated with bilabial lisping is Sylvia Silence, the girl detective who makes her first appearance during the trial scene in I.3. Relaxing in her easy chair, Sylvia reflects (in a voice reminiscent of the character Elmer Fudd from *Looney Tunes*) on the situation of H.C.E.'s possible crime: "Have you evew thought, wepowtew, that sheew gweatness was his twadgedy? Nevewtheless accowding to my considewed attitudes fow this act he should pay the full penalty" (61.6–9). The second category of interdental lisping, where fricatives like /s/ or /z/ are replaced with a theta sound, represents the vast majority of lisping effects in the *Wake*. The theta sound is already linked to ALP as an onomatopoeic sign of her riverlike nature as early as 1924. In the first drafts of Book I Chapter 8, composed in February of that year, Joyce writes the famous refrain: "Beside the rivering waters of, hither and thither waters of. Night!"[33] As the personification of the River Liffey, ALP is constantly "babbling, bubbling, chattering to herself, deloothering the fields on their elbows leaning with the sloothering slide of her" (195.1–3). It is not until late 1926, however, that Joyce attaches a clinical dimension to the mellifluous sound of Anna's hither and thithering waters. In the first draft of page 23, he writes: "with lipth she ~~lispeth~~ lithpeth to him ever and ever of thow and thow all the time of thuch and thuch and thow and thow."[34] In the climax of Book IV, when ALP announces her presence as the very voice of the River itself, these two motifs of rushing water and lisping are more explicitly combined: "Lsp! I am leafy speafing. Lpf! Folty and folty all the nights have fallen on to long my hair. Not a sound, falling. Lispn!" (619.20–22).[35] In this case, it is easier to understand how the basic clinical fact that "Annshee lispes privily" (571.26) has been treated as secondary to the aesthetic intentions behind ALP's "leafy speafing." Lisping effects are present in many of the *Wake*'s most lyrical, most childlike, and most silly moments. Whenever children speak in the *Wake*, some degree of lisping is always present, as in the first of the twelve riddles from Book I Chapter 6, where Finn Maccool is said to "lusteth ath he listeth the cleah whithpeh of a themise" (138.10). And we hear lisping's potential for musicality in phrases like "the siss of the whisp of the sigh of the softzing" (158.6), or its comedic value in virtually unpronounceable phrases like "mhuith peisth mhuise" (91.4).[36]

Although Wakese has long been described in aesthetic terms as playful, lyrical, experimental, and so on, relatively little attention has been paid to the clinical roots of these aesthetic features, not only in stuttering and lisping, but in related disorders of language such as perseveration and jargonaphasia. It remains finally to be asked whether Deleuze's model of creative stuttering might help to clarify this relation between clinical portrayal and aesthetic performance of speech disorders in *Finnegans Wake*.[37] In "Stuttering Joyce," David Spurr alludes briefly to Deleuze's use of the stutter "as a figure of poetic language," but Spurr does not address if or how Deleuze's categories apply to the *Wake*. Instead, he argues that the *Wake* is better understood as an example of what Maurice Blanchot calls the "parole de fragment." As Spurr describes it, this means "the word as fragment which releases a liberating force from within the woven substance of language."[38] "Joyce's method in *Finnegans Wake*," adds Spurr, "will be to apply this dislocating force to the language of myth in an attempt to get at the physical and emotional instincts that constitute the ground of mythic thought."[39] So the question I posed at the outset of this chapter remains to be asked: whether the *Wake* fits solely into Deleuze's first two categories, with its portrayal of a stuttering husband and a lisping wife, along with its transcriptions of their disordered speech, or whether the style of the *Wake* can also be said to deploy a metaphorical kind of stuttering on the level of language itself.[40]

Arguments for and against Wakese as the embodiment of creative stuttering would both seem to relate to the role that borrowings from foreign languages play in the *Wake*. In his essay, Deleuze is careful to point out that the perpetual disequilibrium of creative stuttering is never simply a matter of the mixing of languages, almost as though he had the *Wake* in mind: "This is not a situation of bilingualism or multilingualism. We can easily conceive of two languages mixing with each other, with incessant transitions from one to the other."[41] Rather than mixing languages on the level of speech, the creative stutterer instead works as though he were a foreigner in his native tongue, "carving out a non-preexistent foreign language *within* his own language."[42] Deleuze's examples of this, for the most part, involve syntactic deformations that more subtly disrupt the equilibrium of the substrate language, producing what he describes as a minor use of the major language. Ironically, from this vantage point, Joyce's elaborate project of combining approximately 60 different languages would appear to make the *Wake* less disruptive than the prose styles of a Kafka or a Celine or a Beckett, since the linguistic substrate of the *Wake* is arguably never stable enough in the first place to be destabilized.

At the same time, Deleuze also points out that the primary means by which language is made to stutter in literature is through the violation of the semiotic principle of disjunction (or selection), and it is here that the *Wake* would appear to be the ultimate example of creative stuttering. Again almost as though he had the *Wake* in mind, Deleuze writes: "As long as language is considered as a system in equilibrium, the disjunctions are necessarily exclusive (we do not say 'passion,' 'ration,' 'nation' at the same time but must choose between them)."[43] But of course the *Wake* does in fact say passion and ration and nation at the same time all the time. Wakese constantly violates this fundamental semiotic principle, and it does so both inter- and intra-linguistically: through its many portmanteau words, which combine meaningful units within a given language (e.g. chaosmos), and its many polyglot coinages, which exist in a sense across languages.[44]

The result of this is that the typically Wakean word is a "word as cunningly hidden in its maze of confused drapery as a fieldmouse in a nest of coloured ribbons" (120.5). As readers, we are dropped into a semantic field where, "We are once amore as babes awondering in a wold made fresh where with the hen in the storyaboot we start from scratch" (336.16), that is to say, the various strategies by which Joyce impedes our normal reading process render us as hermeneutically helpless and innocent as "babes awondering." With the unprecedented amount of attention Joyce forces us to pay to his "fermented words" (184.26) as independent semantic units, an altogether different model for creative stuttering emerges in the *Wake*, a readerly stuttering where we are forced to hesitate, to "stotter from the latter," word by word, letter by letter.

ACKNOWLEDGMENTS

I would like to thank Dirk Van Hulle and Geert Lernout of the Centre for Manuscript Genetics in Antwerp for their insights and suggestions during the research and writing of this article.

NOTES

1. James Joyce, *Finnegans Wake* (London: Penguin, 1998). All subsequent citations from this edition are included within parentheses within the text.
2. David Spurr, "Stuttering Joyce," *European Joyce Studies* 20 (July 2011), 21.
3. Boris Eichenbaum, *Anna Akhmatova* (Petrograd 1923), 66. Cited in Victor Erlich, *Russian Formalism History—Doctrine* (Hague: Mouton & Co. Publishers, 1955), 256.
4. Victor Shklovsky, "Art as Technique," in *Russian Formalist Criticism: Four Essays*, ed. Lee T. Lemon and Marion J. Reis (London: University of Nebraska Press, 1965), 22.
5. Wyndham Lewis, *The Art of Being Ruled* (New York: Haskell House Publishers, Ltd, 1972), 400, 396.
6. Lewis, *The Art of Being Ruled*, 400.
7. David Lodge, "The Language of Modernist Fiction: Metaphor and Metonymy," in *Modernism 1890—1930*, ed. Malcolm Bradbury and James McFarlane (New York: Penguin Books, 1976), 83.
8. Lodge, "The Language of Modernist Fiction: Metaphor and Metonymy," 84.
9. See Gilles Deleuze, "He Stuttered," *Essays Critical and Clinical* (Minneapolis: University of Minnesota Press, 1997), 109
10. Deleuze, "He Stuttered," 107.

11. Deleuze, "He Stuttered," 107.
12. Deleuze, "He Stuttered," 108.
13. See Eve Kosofsky Sedgwick, *Epistemology of the Closet* (Berkeley: University of California Press, 2008), 103.
14. William York Tindall, *A Reader's Guide to "Finnegans Wake"* (Syracuse: Syracuse University Press, 1972), 59, 272.
15. See *How Joyce Wrote Finnegans Wake: A Chapter-by-Chapter Genetic Guide*, ed. Sam Slote and Luca Crispi (Madison: University of Wisconsin Press, 2008), 9.
16. James Joyce, *Finnegans Wake: A Fascimile of Buffalo Notebooks VI.B.13–16*, prefaced and arr. David Hayman (New York: Garland Pub., 1978), VI.B.16.143.
17. James Joyce, *Finnegans Wake: A Fascimile of Buffalo Notebooks VI.B.29–32*, prefaced and arr. Danis Rose (New York: Garland Pub., 1978), VI.B.31.204.
18. Slote and Crispi, *How Joyce Wrote Finnegans Wake*, 13.
19. James Joyce, *A First-Draft Version of Finnegans Wake*, edited and annotated by David Hayman (Austin: University of Texas Press, 1963), 64.
20. Joyce, *A First-Draft Version of Finnegans Wake*, 245.
21. In August 1929, Joyce revisited these pages, at which point he added another layer of stutters to the scene. The "girl" in "girl frifrif friends" is changed by hand on the fair copy to "gigirl." He also adds another "amp" to "am amp amplify" on the typescript. The phrase "my babad" changes from "bad" in the Third Draft (1924) to "baad" in the fair copy (1925) and is only made into a stutter in the typescript (1930) when Joyce adds an additional "b" by hand.
22. In his article "Hesitancy in Joyce and Beckett's Manuscripts," *Texas Studies in Literature and Language* 51, no. 1 (Spring 2009), Dirk Van Hulle lays out the genetic history of the motif of hesitant speech in *Finnegans Wake*, with specific reference to its relation to the stuttering of HCE. Relatedly, Van Hulle points out the role Wyndham Lewis' criticism of Joyce and Stein as literary 'stammerers' in *The Art of Being Ruled* may have played the development of the theme of stuttering in *Finnegans Wake*. As I have shown, stuttering was already an overt leitmotif of the *Wake* at least a year before the publication of *The Art of Being Ruled*, however, as Van Hulle rightly notes, "Lewis may not have been the direct source of the 'hesitency' and the stuttering motifs, but Joyce's reaction to *The Art of Being Ruled* and *Time and Western Man* most probably accelerated the process of his combining them and turning this complex of references into a major leitmotif because it gave the stammering a certain depth in terms of poetics." Van Hulle, "Hesitancy in Joyce and Beckett's Manuscripts," 20.
23. James Joyce, *James Joyce Letters* ed. Gilbert, Stuart and Richard Ellmann, 3 vols. (New York: Viking, 1966), III.174.
24. See Isa Bowman, *Story of My Life* (New York: Dutton, 1899), 10. Dodgson spent many years in the care of two of the most preeminent speech therapists of his day, James Hunt and Henry Rivers, but he never fully overcame the condition, and his difficulties with public speaking would forever limit his ability to fulfill his duties as an ordained Deacon in the Anglican Church.
25. Adeline Glasheen, *Third Census of Finnegans Wake* (Los Angeles: University of California Press, 1977), 51.
26. See Bowman, for account of Carroll's distaste for "modern professional photographers [who] spoilt all their pictures by touching them up," *Story of My Life*, 16.
27. Richard Ellmann, *James Joyce* (Oxford, Oxford University Press, 1983), 320.

28. James Joyce, *Critical Writings*, ed. Ellsworth Mason and Richard Ellmann (New York: Cornell University Press, 1989), 225.
29. Joyce, *Critical Writings*, 225.
30. See St. John Greer Ervine, *Parnell* (London: E. Benn Limited, 1925), 97.
31. Joyce, *Letters*, I.241.
32. See Giambattista Vico, *New Science: Principles of the New Science Concerning the Common Nature of Nations,* trans. David Marsh (New York: Penguin Books, 1999), 189.
33. Joyce, *Finnegans Wake Notebooks VI.B.13–16*, 47471b 90.
34. Joyce, *A First-Draft Version of Finnegans Wake*, 59.
35. Later on, when Anna turns into the old and tired Liffey, the tone of her thetas turns from comic to elegiac, even bitter, as she passes into the sea: "they are becoming lothed to me. I am lothing their little warm tricks. And lothing their mean cosy turns . . . I'm loothing them that's here and all I lothe" (627.17–33).
36. The presence of child-speak in the *Wake* also has a well-known Viconian element to it. In his *New Science*, Vico likens the primitive progression from mutism to fluency with the developmental speech of children: "The earliest people had rigid vocal organs, and knew very few words. Even today, when children have supple vocal organs, and are born amid a wealth of words, they still find consonants hard to pronounce." Vico, *New Science*, 190. This sense of language in "the childhood of the world" results in the *Wake* in the further association between ALP's "leafy speafing" and the childish lisping of Shaun and Issy. Not only does Shaun emulate the stuttering speech of his Father at points in Book III, but he and his "sissibis dearest" are also prone "to thalk thildish" like their mother, for example during Shaun's Watches, "whesen with other lipth I nakest open my thight when just woken by his toccatootletoo my first morning. So now, to thalk thildish, thome, theated with Mag at the oilthan we are doing to thay one little player before doing to deed" (461.26–30). The theta sound evidently had a childish ring to Joyce as early as *A Portrait of the Artist*, based on the description of young Stephen's lisping out of a song for his parents: "*O the green wothe botheth.*" James Joyce, *A Portrait of the Artist* (New York: Viking Press, 1964), 1.
37. In his article "Stuttering Joyce," David Spurr summarizes Deleuze's figurative reading of the stutter as a trope for poetic language.
38. Spurr, "Stuttering Joyce," 121.
39. Spurr, "Stuttering Joyce," 125.
40. In his essay, Deleuze acknowledges that creative stuttering bears on the form of content in addition to the form of expression, and beyond HCE and ALP's respective speech disorders, the various perturbations of normal communicative language in the *Wake*—from the slurring of words in the sleep state, to the perseverative nonsense refrains of the Four Old Men, to the verbal tic of speaking in words ending in the suffix -ation exhibited by the Twelve Jurors, to the radio static of Book III, to the hyperbolically stuttered 100-lettter thunder words—all would seem to point to Joyce's attempt to make language stutter or tremble on a thematic level.
41. Deleuze, "He Stuttered," 109.
42. Deleuze, "He Stuttered," 110.
43. Deleuze, "He Stuttered," 110.
44. See Jacques Derrida, "Des Tours de Babel," in *Difference in Translation*, ed. and trans. Joseph F. Graham (Ithaca and London: Cornell University Press, 1985). Also see Laurent Milesi, "Finnegans Wake: The Obliquity of Translations" in *Joyce in the Hibernian Metropolis*, ed. Morris Beja and David Norris (Ohio State University Press, 1997).

WORKS CITED

Bowman, Isa. *Story of My Life*. New York: Dutton, 1899.

Deleuze, Gilles. "He Stuttered." *Essays Critical and Clinical*. Minneapolis: University of Minnesota Press, 1997.

Derrida, Jacques. "Des Tours de Babel." In *Difference in Translation*. Edited and translated by Joseph F. Graham. Ithaca and London: Cornell University Press, 1985.

Eichenbaum, Boris. *Anna Akhmatova*. Petrograd, 1923.

Ellmann, Richard. *James Joyce*. Oxford, Oxford University Press, 1983.

Erlich, Victor. *Russian Formalism History—Doctrine*. Hague: Mouton & Co. Publishers, 1955.

Ervine, St. John Greer. *Parnell*. London: E. Benn Limited, 1925.

Glasheen, Adeline. *Third Census of Finnegans Wake*. Los Angeles: University of California Press, 1977.

Joyce, James. *A Portrait of the Artist as a Young Man*. New York: Viking Press, 1964.

Joyce, James. *A First-Draft Version of Finnegans Wake*. Edited and annotated by David Hayman. Austin: University of Texas Press, 1963.

Joyce, James. *Critical Writings*. Edited by Ellsworth Mason and Richard Ellmann. New York: Cornell University Press, 1989.

Joyce, James. *Finnegans Wake*. London: Penguin, 1998.

Joyce, James. *Finnegans Wake: A Fascimile of Buffalo Notebooks VI.B.13–16*. Prefaced and arranged by David Hayman. New York: Garland Pub., 1978.

Joyce, James. *Finnegans Wake: A Fascimile of Buffalo Notebooks VI.B.29–32*. Prefaced and arranged by Danis Rose. New York: Garland, 1978.

Joyce, James. *James Joyce Letters*. Ed. Gilbert, Stuart and Richard Ellmann, 3 vols. New York: Viking, 1966.

Lewis, Wyndham. *The Art of Being Ruled*. New York: Haskell House Publishers, Ltd, 1972.

Lodge, David. "The Language of Modernist Fiction: Metaphor and Metonymy." In *Modernism 1890–1930*, edited by Malcolm Bradbury and James McFarlane. New York: Penguin Books, 1976.

Milesi, Laurent. "Finnegans Wake: The Obliquity of Trans-lations." In *Joyce in the Hibernian Metropolis*. Edited by Morris Beja and David Norris. Columbus: Ohio State University Press, 1997.

Sedgwick, Eve Kosofsky. *Epistemology of the Closet*. Berkeley: University of California Press, 2008.

Shklovsky, Victor. "Art as Technique." In *Russian Formalist Criticism: Four Essays*, edited by Lee T. Lemon and Marion J. Reis. London: University of Nebraska Press, 1965.

Slote, Sam, and Luca Crispi, eds. *How Joyce Wrote Finnegans Wake: A Chapter-by-Chapter Genetic Guide*. Madison: University of Wisconsin Press, 2008.

Spurr, David. "Stuttering Joyce." *European Joyce Studies* 20 (July 2011): 21–33.

Tindall, William York. *A Reader's Guide to "Finnegans Wake."* Syracuse: Syracuse University Press, 1972.

Van Hulle, Dirk. "Hesitancy in Joyce and Beckett's Manuscripts." *Texas Studies in Literature and Language* 51, no. 1 (Spring 2009), pp. 17–27.

Vico, Giambattista. *New Science: Principles of the New Science Concerning the Common Nature of Nations*. Translated by David Marsh. New York: Penguin Books, 1999.

6 Jackson's Parrot

Samuel Beckett, Aphasic Speech Automatisms, and Psychosomatic Language

Laura Salisbury and Chris Code

In June of 1845 a parrot, known simply as Poll, was ejected from a funeral. The bird had been taught to swear by the deceased, one Andrew Jackson, who also happened to be the 7th President of the United States. Poll was removed because as the preacher spoke to those gathered in the congregation, it began to squawk such unpretty interruptions that the work of the funeral could not proceed. An embarrassing situation, certainly, but there is little sense that the parrot was finally deemed to be at fault. Despite the seemingly inevitable suspicion that this uncanny bird may have been cannily up to something, whether they knew it or not it is likely that those in attendance would have taken a Cartesian view of the situation. In *Discourse on the Method* of 1649, René Descartes influentially determined that it was the capacity for propositional speech that separated the human from the animal, or from the mechanical that, in fact, animals simply were. Talking parrots proved no problem for Descartes's logic, for they were deemed simply to be fleshly machines that uttered in ways that were to be firmly distinguished from the speech proper to humanity. As Descartes puts it:

> we can see that magpies and parrots can utter words as we do, and yet they cannot speak as we do: that is, they cannot show that they are thinking what they are saying. On the other hand, men born deaf and dumb, and thus deprived of speech-organs as much as the beasts or even more so, normally invent their owns signs to make themselves understood by those who, being regularly in their company, have time to learn their language. This shows not merely that beasts have less reason than men, but that they have no reason at all [. . .] [I]t would be incredible that a superior specimen of the monkey or parrot species should not be able to speak as well as the most stupid child—or at least as well as a child with a defective brain—if their souls were not completely different in nature to ours.[1]

For Descartes, then, the capacity for propositional language remains a product of a rational soul annexed to the body rather than any simple precipitate of the corporeal organs. It is the faculty of speech that lifts the human both beyond the animal and beyond the limits of its own flesh.

Though hardly an expert, Samuel Beckett knew more than a little about Descartes's philosophy, and his early poem *Whoroscope* (1930) is coddled with obscure references to Descartes, alongside the description of a "pale abusive parakeet."[2] As is perhaps more well-known, a parrot also appears in *Molloy* (1947) that is as foul-mouthed as Jackson's Poll:

> He exclaimed from time to time, Fuck the son of a bitch, fuck the son of a bitch. He must have belonged to an American sailor, before he belonged to Lousse. Pets often change masters. He didn't say much else. I'm wrong, he also said Putain de merde [. . .] Lousse tried to make him say Pretty Polly! I think it was too late. He listened, his head on one side, pondered, and then said, Fuck the son of a bitch.[3]

It is, of course, in Beckett's *Malone Dies* (1947–48) that a pink and grey parrot called Polly belonging to a "Jackson" appears, although this bird does not swear; instead, the "dumb companion" is taught to utter the scholastic dictum "Nihil in intellectu, etc"—a phrase that might be translated as "nothing in the mind."[4] Ironically, given the fact that the subject of the paragraph is supposedly "conation" (what might be glossed as the part of the mind given over to will and volition), Malone notes that the animal is unable to get as far as "the celebrated restriction" that usually accompanies the phrase: "*quod non prius fuerat in sensu.*"[5] The joke is that the parrot is only able to utter that there is nothing in the mind at all, without the qualifier "that has not first been in the senses," and also without Leibniz's suggestion that the mind itself should be the exception to this rule.[6] If it is true that there is nothing in the mind that has not first been in the senses apart from the mind's own singularity, this parrot cannot articulate it; instead, it remains nailed to reproductions that, in the end, have never securely been in the mind, or not at least if Descartes is to be believed.

Daniel Albright has suggested that Jackson's parrot is "a kind of ideal recording device" and Beckett's obsession both with repetitions and forms of mechanical reproduction, with language loosened from the tightened intentionality of a rational mind and a self-identical speaking subject, echoes across the *oeuvre*.[7] Much of Beckett's work indeed seems precisely to be exploring the possibility of understanding language beyond the Cartesian philosophical frame—beyond its underpinning of the human as the animal that talks (*anthropos zoon logon echon*) and therefore the rational animal, as Aristotle has it.[8] But if this is so, there might be another Jackson who could be brought into illuminating contact with Beckett and both his avian and rather more human parrots. For it was the neurologist John Hughlings Jackson who, in 1874, first explored in both depth and detail a mode of involuntary parrot-ing in human speech: the phenomenon of "aphasic speech automatisms" or unwilled recurrent or recurring utterances in people who had undergone brain damage, most usually to the anterior left hemisphere. There is no empirical evidence that Beckett read Hughlings Jackson's work, although he was sufficiently influential to become known as "the father of English neurology" and emerges as the most important English aphasiologist of his time.[9] Beckett certainly did know something of aphasia (language processing impairments) and speech automatisms, having met during the war the poet Valery Larbaud whose stroke had left him with the rather melancholy utterance, "Bonsoir, les choses d'ici-bas" ("Farewell material things of the earth"), that emerged whenever he tried to speak.[10] But we believe that it is also possible to argue that Hughlings Jackson's post-Darwinian account of language as something that emerges from various levels of representation within the brain and from a central nervous system laid down over evolutionary time, is part of a general revolution in the conception of language with which Beckett's work finds itself in clear though complex dialogue. Hughlings Jackson brings to scientific visibility the fact that language cannot be understood as simply the expression of the most willed, most abstract, or "highest" qualities and strata of the mind; it must also be understood as formed within and produced by the more "automatic," "primitive," "emotional," parts of an evolutionarily developed brain. Reading Beckett's work alongside Hughlings Jackson's thus allows us to explore the ways in which Beckett persistently returns to a sense of language as the product of a fragile, material brain, which, though partially able to subserve subjective intention and rationality, is nevertheless always both in continuity with a material body and in cahoots with those automatic and involuntary aspects of human functioning that force any understanding of the self beyond the impervious boundaries of a Cartesian *cogito*.[11]

LANGUAGE OF THE BORDERMAN

Although Beckett seems interested in Descartes's work, he was never simply Cartesian in either his thinking or his writing, and certainly never seemed to imagine that language could usefully be detached from corporeality. As early as the 1930s, plagued by a sense that no one was interested in publishing his work and that he was not in full control of his artistic material, Beckett was able to imagine a strikingly embodied aesthetic that could actually take a bit of capital from this incompetence. In a letter to his friend Thomas MacGreevy in 1932, Beckett indeed speaks of wanting to produce a writing that would not be "facultatif," optional; instead, he imagines producing an ejaculatory form of expression that would be obligatory, reflexive even.[12] "I'm in mourning for the integrity of a pendu's [hanged man's] emission of semen [. . .] the integrity of the eyelids coming down before the brain knows of grit in the wind," he states.[13]

Afflicted with boils and cysts that he imagined he worked up out of his involuted self-involvement and mental distress, Beckett here associates all of his writing that does "not represent a necessity," with a style that somehow mirrored his ailments, calling it "the work of the abscess."[14] Peculiarly, though, the fact that Beckett's abscesses wept involuntarily and persistently refused to sit peaceably with him. His cognitive intentions, while clearly the instigator of terrible pains for him, paradoxically also seemed to figure a little hope—a precious, albeit abjected, sense of relief and release from an art that otherwise felt "all frigged up, in terram, faute d'orifice [for want of an orifice]."[15] Here, one sees Beckett turning his language towards modes of reflexive embodiment that might puncture the tightened skin of an artistic intention linked with cognition and the onanistic exercising of will. In *Dream of Fair to Middling Women*, which he was writing during the same period, Beckett muses, longingly, that though "[t]he night sky was stretched like a skin," there might be some possibility of "scal[ing] the inner wall, his head would tear a great rip in the taught sky, he would climb out above the deluge, into a quiet zone above the nightmare."[16] And seven months after the letter to MacGreevy he is indeed able to write of both the pains and possibilities of this way of going on: "It's an ill cyst that blows nobody any good. I find it more and more difficult to write and I think I write worse and worse in consequence. But I still have hopes of its all coming in a gush like a bloody flux."[17]

It was perhaps not until the *Trilogy* and *Texts for Nothing*, written in an extraordinary, compulsive burst of creative activity between 1947–1951, that Beckett was finally to find an appropriate artistic container for this aesthetic of spontaneous emission, as language is imaged as vomit, shit, slobber and tears that dribble or gush from his creatures. In *Text for Nothing VIII* (1951), an aesthetic that resonates with the earlier notion of a weeping abscess indeed mingles verbal outpouring with bodily fluids, words with tears, as the discrete qualities of determinable, intention-bound meaning seep towards disorganization:

> I confuse them, words and tears, my words are my tears, my eyes my mouth [. . .] it's forever the same murmur, flowing unbroken, like a single endless word and therefore meaningless, for it's the end that gives meaning to words.[18]

In *The Unnamable* (1949), anal incontinence had already become an analogue for the birth of language, subject and artwork, in a way that oddly and explicitly repeats those feared and longed-for emissions and explosions of the 1930s: "I'll let down my trousers and shit stories on them, stories, photographs, records, sites, lights, gods and fellow-creature [. . .] Be born, dear friends, be born, enter my arse, you'll just love my colic pains, it won't take long, I've the bloody flux."[19] And while the cockatoo in *Mercier and Camier* (1946) has a verbal constipation that matches its anal blockage, by the time *The Trilogy* is reached, parrots can and do utter.[20] The Unnamable is force-fed and vomits forth words of others that will never be fully at one with its intentional capacities, stating:

> It is they who dictate this torrent of balls, they who stuffed me full of these groans that choke me. And out it all pours unchanged, I have only to belch to be sure of hearing them, the same old sour teachings I can't change a tittle of. A parrot, that's what they're up against, a parrot.[21]

For better and for worse, writing and language pour out in both terror and relief as shit, vomit, slobber, pus and tears in a relentless logorrhea. *Nihil in intellectu* indeed.

It has often been noted that in the early 1930s Beckett was keen to hoard words, ideas, and symptoms of physical and psychological pathology. The reasons why Beckett seemingly felt compelled to do this come more clearly into focus, however, when a link is made between his gathering up of signs and symbols of states of mind and corporeality that have the frisson of compact with the compulsive, with so-called mindlessness, and the search for an aesthetic practice that could write itself beyond the frame of an artistic will "frigged up" with cognitive intentions. As Ulrika Maude has suggested, some of the earliest appearances of neurological and psychological pathologies in Beckett's work are to be found in the *Dream* Notebook of the very early 1930s.[22] There, Beckett transcribed from Max Nordau's 1892 treatise on *Degeneration* terms such as "Zwangs-Vorstellung (coercive idea, obsession)," "aboulia (absence of will)," "echolalia (word and sound repetition)," and "logorrhea."[23] But the link with aesthetic practice could never have been far from Beckett's mind. Nordau, who as a doctor had studied under the famous neurologist Jean-Martin Charcot and dedicated *Degeneration* to Cesare Lombroso (the psychiatrist who infamously sought to find the stigmata of mental and nervous degeneracy in the physiognomy of criminals), was, at one level, profoundly non-dualist. And yet, the terms of value with which Cartesian thought is freighted are smuggled back into his work as he praises manifestations of human culture that represent control of the "higher" faculties over the "lower." Indeed, he explicitly condemns as symptoms of pathology the modern art of the 1890s and its eschewal of the rationality associated with realism and modes of formal, figurative ordering. Disturbed by "lower" faculties that will not remain in their rightful place, modern artists are, by Nordau's account, afflicted by a moral and nervous lassitude that it takes a physician's eye to diagnose. "[T]he physician, especially if he ha[s] devoted himself to the special study of mental and nervous maladies, recognizes at a glance, in the *fin-de-siècle* disposition, in the tendencies of contemporary art and poetry, in the life and conduct of men who write mystic, symbolic and 'decadent' works, and in the attitude taken by their admirers [. . .] degeneration (degeneracy) and hysteria, of which the minor stages are designated as neurasthenia," he opines.[24] For Nordau, then, such artists and their work, alongside their audiences, are contaminated by expressions of mind that are degenerate because defective in cognition and conation—they are compulsive, willless. As Nordau puts it, and as Beckett transcribes, "Genius," at least of this sort, "is a disease of the nerves."[25]

Beckett surely hoped that his own unruly bodily systems might allow him to be counted among those whom he transcribed from Nordau as the "high degenerates, bordermen, mattoids, and graphomaniacs" of modern art.[26] He certainly suggested to MacGreevy, in what seems like both pride and despair, that he remained compelled to reject what was high-minded in his poetry to pursue the back passages of art: the "'Give us a wipe' class of guttersnippet continues to please me," he groans. For, as he goes on to note, "[o]ne has to buckle the wheel of one's poem somehow [. . .] or run the risk of Nordau's tolerance"—something which is seemingly more abject than being classed a dirty "degenerate."[27] Although it is clear that there is something disgusted in this self-recognition, the "guttersnippet" becomes a kind of contamination that also offers up hope of a cure. As thought, language, and will are forced into an alarmingly slippery continuity with the somatic, there is the sense of liberation in finding a language that might be detached from what is paralyzingly self-conscious. Still, for an unsuccessful artist who continually felt "Shatupon" by at best indifferent and at worst dismissive publishers and public, holing up with the "bordermen" is an act fraught with ambivalence.[28] His oddly compulsive method of parroting material from Nordau allows him to be positively identified with those modern artists compelled by obsessions, pathologies, bodily drives, "echolalia" and "coproplalia (mucktalk)"; but the abjection of the method insists.[29] For Beckett was, of course, to complain of feeling "soiled [. . .] with the old demon notesnatching," and later, when in Germany in 1937 and filling his diary with lists of dates and prosaic details of painters and paintings, the "mindlessness" of notation becomes even more explicitly ambivalent.[30] He affirms, at one moment, that "[w]hat I want is the straws, flotsam, etc., names, dates, births and deaths, because that is all I can know," and yet, only a short while later, he pitifully condemns himself as:

> pathologically limp and opinionless and consternated. The little trouble I give myself, this absurd diary with its lists of pictures, serves no purpose, is only the act of an obsessional neurotic. Counting pennies would do as well. An "open-mindedness" that is mindlessness, the sphincter of the mind limply forever open, the mind past the power of closing itself *to everything but its own content. I have never thought for myself.*[31]

Caught between the release and the abjection of mindlessness, Beckett indeed seems compelled to experience both the pleasures and pains of the "borderman."

Nordau spoke, in fact, of what "Maudsley and Ball call [. . .] 'Borderland dwellers'—dwellers on the borderland between reason and pronounced

madness"; but perhaps it is more suggestive to think of the border territory as that marked out between what is willed by a fully intending mind
and what is completely automatic—that place where mind and matter
seem explicitly to collude to produce acts, events, and experiences.[32] For
despite his clear interest in involuntary emissions, Beckett was never to
be engaged by the fluid transcriptions of unconscious states produced in
so-called "automatic writing." In 1930, while lecturing at Trinity College
Dublin, he affirmed that pure unconscious states should not be used in
literature as they "destroy the integrity of the real."[33] Rachel Burrows's
lecture notes record instead Beckett's approving remarks on the forms of
half-consciousness the author of *Degeneration* found so troubling: "Gide
interested in liminal consciousness (sneered at by Nordau)," Beckett told
his students.[34] These assertions are revealing because in his own aesthetic
work that followed, Beckett was insistently to imagine language in terms
of bodily functions that, though hardly expressions of an intending mind,
are rarely fully automatic. The body's oozings and excreta are, instead,
more accurately understood to be highly susceptible to the formation of
habits that can subserve a person's purposes, even as they always bear
within themselves the threat of an uncontrolled emission. Of course, the
fact that these bodily functions are plastic, malleable in relation to the
mind, produces problems for a *cogito*. The Beckett who read psychoanalytic work in detail, who feared he was an "obsessional neurotic,"
certainly lived out the terrible failure of Cartesian dualism in the irrup-
tions of the psychosomatic: he experienced the appalling tendency for
seemingly mental states to convert themselves into physical symptoms
and for physical problems to produce mental distress.[35] And yet, he came
to produce an aesthetic somehow aligned with his powerfully disrupted
peristalsis and what a doctor described as his "deep-seated septic cys-
tic system."[36] Although it is clear that he hopes that various forms of
somatic "incontinence," transformed into language, might cure his writing of its blockages, from its constipating intentions, what Beckett seems
truly compelled by is not a language that is completely mindless, but one
that bears witness to the compact between mind and body, intellection
and emotion, between the intention and the automaticity both in and of
words. It is precisely in this "borderland," we maintain, that Beckett's
psychosomatic language stakes its aesthetic claim.

FUNCTION RUNNING AWAY WITH ORGAN

If one were searching for representations of the automatic in Beckett's
work, one might well alight on *Not I* (1972), where the speaking subject is
reduced to a mouth, isolated in the blank blackness of the stage space, spitting and leaking language. Mouth experiences herself as subjected to the
jagging, gagging and glitched fastforwards and rewinds of mechanization,

and although her words emerge from the matter inside, from a "dull roar in the skull," their source is also somehow beyond her:

> all dead still but for the buzzing . . . when suddenly she realized . . . words were . . . [. . .] words were coming. . . . A voice she did not recognize . . . at first . . . so long since it had sounded . . . then she finally had to admit . . . could be none other . . . than her own . . . certain vowel sounds . . . she had never heard.[37]

This recognition, this sense of her experience, affirms, however, that language does not emerge with the absolute unfettered unconsciousness, just as the drafts of the manuscript prove decisively that the piece was not written automatically. Mouth's language is hardly synonymous with intention and volition, nor is it the precipitate of conation; nevertheless, the compulsive push and pull that produces words spilling over with subjective affect demonstrates that mind is far from absent from the scene.

In 1972, however, Beckett does seem to affirm a certain automatism within *Not I* by writing to Alan Schneider that there is a distinction to be made

> between mind & voice [. . .] Her speech a purely buccal phenomenon without mental control or understanding, only half heard. Function running away with organ [. . .] I hear it breathless, urgent, feverish, panting along, without undue concern with intelligibility. Addressed less to the understanding than the nerves of the audience which should in a sense *share her bewilderment*.[38]

But the nuances of this position come more clearly into focus if one realizes that, consciously or not, Beckett is parroting material here that he read nearly forty years earlier. In 1934–35, distressed to the point of incapacity by his psychosomatic symptoms, Beckett sought psychotherapy from Wilfred R. Bion and supplemented his analytic experience with readings on psychology and psychoanalysis. These further "notesnatchings" speak to his growing interest in the automatic and the seemingly mechanical aspects of psychology, in "behaviorism," for example; but Beckett also transcribes from Karin Stephen's *Psychoanalysis and Medicine: A Study of the Wish to Fall Ill*, not just "bewilderment," but the "*sheer terror* of being run away with by a bodily function" (emphasis added)—the dread that can accompany what emerges without volition.[39] Nearly forty years after first reading it, and perhaps surprisingly, Beckett finds himself echoing a psychoanalytic mode in his efforts to evoke a language that would bear witness to the slippery continuum between idea and matter, mind and body. This language is addressed to and perhaps more of "the nerves" than "mental control or understanding"; nevertheless, in its evocation of a form of nervous bewilderment, both character and audience find themselves pushed and pulled by affective states that refuse the relief and reflexive simplicity of any pure mindlessness.

Now, Stephen's book is distinctive in terms of psychoanalytic texts in its emphasis on specifically embodied symptoms that are nevertheless understood to be psychogenic in origin. By the 1930s, psychoanalysis as a discipline had moved away from its neurological beginnings, from Freud's early study of aphasia and his somewhat later sense of the material action of the nerves in the production of neurosis. Stephen's work, however, decisively takes psychoanalysis back to the body and to the mind's continuum with it—to the early Freud's emphasis on the conversion of mental states into embodied symptoms according to a mysterious, almost magical sense of the body's neurology functioning through various modes of representation and symbol formation.[40] While psychoanalysis's insistence upon physical symptoms as expressions of repressed ideas and stuttering, unexpressed affect worked to liberate patients from the stigma of biological "degeneracy," something perhaps also got lost in the more or less explicit disavowal of the neurological body and the mechanisms of conversion of *psyche* into *soma*, *soma* into *psyche*, that Freudian psychoanalysis finally performed.[41] Although Freud, the one time aphasiologist, never relinquished the idea that language was a function of a material body, his determination to listen to language, to hear the twists and turns of symbol formation in narrative rather than attempt to observe or map nerve action within a patient's unfolding psychosomatic system, does finally privilege the ideational in a way that tends to foreclose the complex role of the neurological in the psychoanalytic understanding of neurosis.

Karin Stephen is also silent about the neurology of the conversion of *psyche* into *soma*, and *vice versa*; nevertheless, she insists on its effects. She affirms that psychogenic symptoms are neurotic defenses that vent pent-up nervous energy and prevent anxiety from developing when earlier acts of repression begin to falter. Many such symptoms appear in relation to the repression that can attend the infant's first experiences of ingestion and excretion and the inevitable disappointment of its natural hopes for fulfilled desire and omnipotence. As Beckett transcribed: "All psychogenic illness proceeds form [sic] deadlock between infantile sexuality & fear, aggression & rage"; for if the desire and aggression that meets disappointment is not tolerated and contained by benign parental attention, the ensuing repression can produce an unconscious, seemingly involuntary, but hardly mindless hoarding and then expulsion of bodily fluids.[42] Beckett notes down the "[o]verwhelming quality of infantile excretory processes," which means that "they are both dreaded & desired by the subject." These processes:

> constitute a diffuse form of orgasm, taking control of the organism & carrying themselves through to a crisis independently of volition. This typical of sensation of excretion before sphincter control has been established. The child punished for lack of control may grow up dreading

loss of control on various planes, excretory, genital, etc., resulting in constipation, frigidity, etc. The sheer terror of being run away with by a bodily function.[43]

Stephen is quite clear that words frequently come to function as the instruments of this arm-twisting "deadlock": "[p]atients often equate a flow of words or a flood of tears with excretory gifts," while the "almost reflex inhibition" that results from this "sheer terror of being run away with by bodily function", "may produce disturbances of a variety of bodily function: speech may be checked, producing a stammer; the free evacuation of the bowels or bladder may be interfered with."[44]

These psychosomatic illnesses that Stephen describes that are driven by neuroses—by nervous matter working in concert with the mind to produce mental and somatic experience—remain under the sway of what Beckett transcribed from Ernest Jones's *Treatment of the Neuroses* during the same period as "*Zwang*." Laplanche and Pontalis gloss *Zwang* as denoting, in Freudian vocabulary, "a constraining internal force. It is most frequently employed in the context of obsessional neurosis, where it implies that the subject feels obliged by this force to act or think in a particular way, and that he struggles against it."[45] Jones describes and Beckett transcribes such obsessional, compulsive symptoms in these terms:

> **Obsessional neurosis** (Zwangsneurose): feeling of mustness. Symptoms: (1) Motor: Zwangshandlungen (avoiding cracks in pavement, etc) (2) Sensory: [sic] (3) Ideational: Zwangsvorstellungen. (4) Affective (obsessive emotions). Also tics (habit spasms). The Zwang may appear as paralysis of the will, e.g. paralysis at the most trifling dilemma.[46]

As we have seen, "Zwangs-Vorstellung (coercive idea, obsession)," held alongside "aboulia" (absence of will), both appear in the *Dream* notebook; but Beckett explicitly learns from Jones that this "feeling of 'mustness'" strips back the subject's capacity for intentional thought, as the "patient oscillates between the two conditions of not being able to act or think (when he wants to) and being obliged to act and think (when he doesn't want to)."[47] Seemingly recognizing himself as compelled by *Zwang*, Beckett writes to MacGreevy after his psychotherapy had come to perhaps a precipitate end: "As I write, think, move, speak, praise & blame, I see myself living up to the specimen that these 2 years have taught me I am. The word is not out before I am blushing for my automatism."[48] The automatic may offer some relief from the thinking subject but, for Beckett, psychoanalysis has seemingly taught him that what erupts in this manner has little of the relief of the knee jerk. The compulsive is not an escape from the mind; rather, it remains contaminated with and indeed driven by feeling, constellating within an affective, affected subject that remains sufficiently conscious to act as its own sometimes amused, sometimes melancholy, witness.

Although to contemporary eyes the discourses of psychoanalysis and neurology may seem incommensurable, their history tells a different story, and Beckett read across them both, persistently alighting on the places where the mind's material functioning and the body's capacity and tendency both to receive the impression and dramatize the expression of psychological states, are brought to consciousness. In what follows, we suggest that Beckett's determination that his art should use the emotional and the somatic to write language beyond any simple expression of intention and rationality can be historically contextualized and its nuances illuminated by placing it alongside aphasiological understandings of language that demonstrate that much of our speech activity is not under ongoing, moment-to-moment control. And by exploring the meeting within speech and language of the voluntary and the involuntary, the rational and the emotional, the conscious and the unconscious, the representational and the modal, we can perhaps better understand Beckett's vital attempt to write the linguistic self as an insistently psychosomatic entity.

OLD STYLE

In terms of the scientific understanding of language, 1861 marks a moment when the concept of language that subtended Cartesian dualist accounts of the relationship between mind and body underwent an authentic paradigm shift. 1861 is the year that Paul Broca delivered a paper in Paris detailing the case of a patient called Leborgne who had become known simply as "Tan." "Tan" had earned his name because, apart from a few oaths and swear words, the reiterated nonsense syllables of "*tan tan*" were the only ones he could utter, despite seemingly unimpaired intelligence and speech organs unaffected by paralysis.[49] Although his disability had been somewhat mysterious to his doctors, when his brain was examined by Broca at autopsy a determining cause for Leborgne's aphasia was found. His brain was revealed to have a lesion in the third frontal convolution of the left hemisphere caused by a cyst, and this area was consequently inferred by Broca to be the seat of "the faculty of articulated language."[50] The third frontal convolution is now known as Broca's area, with the broad severe form of aphasia that can include speech automatisms, nonfluency and syntactic impairments with relatively intact comprehension, given the name Broca's aphasia.[51] What Broca's work on aphasia seemed decisively to demonstrate was that, *contra* Descartes, those seemingly immaterial faculties of the human had a determinable material seat that was linked to their causation rather than simply marking their location. Becoming the first fully materialist model of language production to be accepted as scientific orthodoxy, Broca's contributions to aphasiology might thus be understood as inaugurating a crucial moment in the history of subjectivity. They mark the moment when key aspects of the psyche—its ability to speak, think, and form rational, abstract intentions—are shown scientifically to be dependent on an embodied, material organization.[52] This is also the moment that language comes to be understood as a properly psychosomatic entity.

A little later in the nineteenth century, the neurologist John Hughlings Jackson developed an idea that was to have a significant impact on aphasiology and subsequent developments in neurolingusitics. He determined that all language was more or less "propositional" in nature—dependent on context. From his observation and treatment of aphasic people, however, Hughlings Jackson also proposed the significant insight that a great deal of our spoken language is in fact produced automatically, and that this nonpropositional language arises from more primitive and ancient areas of the brain. Hughlings Jackson had turned his attention specifically to the striking phenomenon of "speech automatisms," or recurring utterances articulated mainly by people with Broca's aphasia either frequently or invariably when they try to speak. Although these automatisms sometimes consist of nonsense syllables (*nonlexical* speech automatisms such as "*tan tan*"), one finds very commonly *lexical* speech automatisms that are made up of recognizable words and syntactically correct structures (for example, Leborgne's other automatism, the oath "sacré nom de Dieu"). What Hughlings Jackson proposed, following the work of the evolutionary psychologist Herbert Spencer, was that language had evolved inseparably with the central nervous system. He suggested, in terms that can still be found in contemporary neurology, that language is represented at different anatomico-structural levels in the brain, with expression by older levels lower down the hierarchy inhibited by younger controlling mechanisms higher up the nervous system—the highest level being the neocortex.[53] It was on the basis of this evolutionarily subtended model that Hughlings Jackson inferred that the kinds of phrases such as oaths and swear words that are preserved as speech automatisms after brain damage suggest "a loss of intellectual (the more voluntary) language, with persistence of emotional (the more automatic) language."[54]

Hughlings Jackson concluded that the nonpropositional speech he observed in aphasic speech automatisms is preserved because it is produced at lower levels in the brain and somewhat automatically. Nonpropositional speech includes cursing, swearing, rote learnt activities such as automatic counting, nursery rhymes and prayers, clichés, and idioms such as "now and then" or "by the way." The linguistic elements within such speech are not newly or individually generated in each utterance, unlike in propositional speech where original ideas are encoded into newly constructed and novel utterances. Using terms and models that are still to be found in the contemporary neurological model, Hughlings Jackson suggested that if propositional, or referential, speech is under conscious control and nonpropositional speech is the product of phylogenically earlier, less evolutionarily developed, processes, when higher areas of brain function (such as Broca's area) are damaged to the degree that they fail to inhibit the behavior of the lower levels, the result can be the automatic production of emotionally charged utterances. He describes the nonpropositional quali-ties of oaths in these terms:

> Although oaths differ from mere alterations of tone, in that they consist of *articulate words*, they are generally used in talking, not to express ideas, but to make up by vigour in delivery what is wanting in precision of expression. They may, indeed, be considered as phrases that emotion has filched from the intellect, to express itself in more definite terms than it could do by mere violence of tone or manner.[55]

For Hughlings Jackson, speech automatisms, like the oaths they retain, "in spite of their propositional structure, [have] no propositional function. No man intends to say, nor is believed by others to say, anything when he swears to his own eyes" (i.e., "Cor Blimey" from "God blind me").[56] Consequently, for Hughlings Jackson, such ejaculations "take low rank in language, little above that of other bodily starts."[57] And yet, though such ejaculations are in some senses reflexive, the emotional qualities Hughlings Jackson emphasizes demonstrate clearly that such seemingly automatic lan-guage is hardly mechanical, for it is frequently and vitally concerned with the social and emotional aspects of communication. Even so, for Hughlings Jackson, and in terms that Nordau echoes, brain damage represents a kind of evolution in reverse: a "reduction to a more automatic condition: in each [case of aphasia] there is Dissolution, using this term as Spencer does, as the opposite of Evolution," he states.[58]

Placed alongside the historical and disciplinary context of this embodied neurological understanding of language, we can perhaps understand a little more of the force of Beckett's irony in the Unnamable's demands for reflex-ive, rote learning from Mahood, just before evolution in reverse takes him back to Worm and language as slobber—reflex-driven matter:

> Pupil Mahood, repeat after me, Man is a higher mammal. I couldn't. Always talking about mammals, in this menagerie. Frankly, between ourselves, what the hell could it matter to pupil Mahood, that man was this rather than that? Presumably nothing has been lost in any case, since here it all comes slobbering out again.[59]

Ulrika Maude has also firmly demonstrated Beckett's characters' propensity for ticcing obscenities, for the coprolalic "mucktalk" found in Tourette's syndrome, or the verbal manifestation of base urges over which the indi-vidual has no control produced by the disinhibition of material most likely associated with the phylogenically earlier basal ganglia of the brain.[60] But Beckett's insistent, albeit untheorized, concern with precisely the forms of language so oddly preserved in speech automatisms is perhaps even more clearly to be found in his stylistic obsession with the complex manipulation of idiom and cliché. As Elizabeth Barry has meticulously shown, in Beckett's texts smithereens of readymade language work as expressions of a kind of "collective memory" that precisely interfere with an idea of art as the willed recollection and then expression of individual subjective experience.[61] As she puts it, Beckett's persistent stylistic return to cliché, aligned with the *Trilogy's* thematic account of language as the eruption of improperly digested sustenance—vomit and the "bloody flux"—shows how language has the capacity to be "regurgitated automatically without being assimilated to the self."[62] Similarly, Winnie in *Happy Days* (1961), though certainly capable of uttering more than "automatisms," nevertheless remains strikingly nailed to the same nonpropositional language that finds itself preserved in aphasic speech automatisms—rhymes, prayers, clichés and idioms. The very first lines of the play set this language in operation, as Winnie, in evening dress though buried in a mound up to her waist, intones: "Another heavenly day [. . .] *Lips move in inaudible prayer* [. . .] For Jesus Christ sake Amen [. . .] World without end Amen."[63] Surrounded by "old things," by the detritus of a life she can no longer inhabit, she remains incapable of finding a new style of speaking that might suit her situation. Instead, sensing the merest flicker of comfort within it, she rests on the language of half-remembered clichés ("what are those wonderful lines") and the "old style" to which she persistently returns and upon which, through which, she lies.[64] Although Winnie is presumably speaking historically when she refers to the "old style," it is highly suggestive that Billie Whitelaw, when attempting to find a voice in which the later play *Not I* could be uttered, spoke of an intuitive need to return to the regional accent of her childhood—one might say an ontogenic "old style"—rather than the received pronunciation she acquired later at drama school.[65] Aphasiologists have suggested that the remarkably restricted semantic range of lexical speech automatisms may indicate a common limbic basal neurogenic location for this nonpropositional language; and what aphasiology thus allows us to map in Beckett's work is the extraordinarily persistent desire to invoke forms of language that seem both phylogenically and ontogenically to precede the propositional language we associate with a the "higher" functioning of an intentional consciousness.[66]

The final link we wish to draw between aphasic speech automatisms and Beckett's mature style is the propensity for using the most commonly observed aphasic lexical automatism—pronoun plus modal or auxiliary verb constructions. Lexical speech automatisms of this sort rarely break syntactical rules, but they are commonly emotionally toned and incomplete or interrupted before any main verb can be evoked (I can't . . . I want to).[67] Now, the evacuation of main verbs, alongside the suggestive figuration of what is left as bodily discharge, oddly insists in Beckett's texts, functioning as a stigmata of linguistic incompetence. In *Rough for Theatre II* (written in French in the late 1950s and translated in the 1970s), the bureaucrat reading the report of a potential suicide's life shouts:

B: Shit! Where's the verb?
A: What verb?
B: The main!
A: I give up.
B: Hold on till I find the verb and to hell with all this drivel in the middle.
      [*Reading.*] " . . . were I but . . . could I but . . ."–Jesus!–" . . . though
      it be . . . be it but"–Christ!–ah! I have it–" . . . I was unfortunately
      incapable . . ." Done it![68]

In *Text for Nothing II*, a similar evacuation of main verbs is invoked, only
here there seems to be a more or less explicit link with a sense of damaged
matter in the head, the skull: "it must be in the head, slowly in the head the
ragdoll rotting, perhaps we're in a head [. . .] ivory dungeon. The words
too, slow, slow, the subject dies before it comes to the verb."[69]

The most ubiquitous feature of aphasia with which these examples seem
to resonate is *anomia*: the failure to access a lexical item, but most commonly nouns or verbs.[70] As Hughlings Jackson has shown, however, not
all language is affected equally. While representational language is severely
impaired in aphasia, what have been termed "modal" structures remain
more easily accessible. Of course, within non-pathological speech modal
verb constructions commonly mark out the territory of subjective possibility: I must, I shall, I will, I should, I would, I can, I could, I may, I might.
And in a general sense the *Trilogy* finds itself definitively within the terrain
of such modal verbs: probability, ability, obligation and advice, permission, habits. Towards the end of *The Unnamable*, the pronoun plus modal/
auxillary verb construction indeed begins insistently to appear, though,
crucially, in a negative form. As the desperate, futile attempts to articulate a voice which isn't simply the voice of others, or otherwise give up on
speaking completely, are ratcheted up, "I" (the most common word in the
largest corpus of aphasic speech automatisms compiled in English) begins
to cascade down the page, with comma splices invoking a sense of both
interruption and urgent propulsion:

> I must understand, I'm doing my best, I can't understand, I stop doing
> my best, I can't do my best, I can't go on, poor devil, neither can they, let
> them say what they want, give me something to do, something doable
> to do, poor devils, they can't, they don't know, they're like me.[71]

Propositional, referential language seems on its way to disappearance, to be
replaced with a rhythmic flow of modalizing:

> you must say words, as long as there are any, until they find me, until
> they say me, strange pain, strange sin, you must go on, perhaps it's
> done already, perhaps they have said me already, perhaps they have
> carried me to the threshold of my story, before the door that opens on

my story, that would surprise me, if it opens, it will be I, it will be the silence, where I am, I don't know, I'll never know, in the silence you don't know, you must go on, I can't go on, I'll go on.[72]

Here, though, as in the aphasic speech automatism, the modal verb appears in a form that precisely suggests incapacity and uncontrolled, compulsive necessity, rather than possibility.

One of the things an understanding of aphasia allows us to tease out in Beckett's texts is that although the modal language that begins to dominate towards the end of *The Unnamable* may not be the language of a *cogito*, it nevertheless retains a sufficient link with consciousness to disallow any ecstatic, unfettered, automaticity. For modalizing language constellates precisely around subjective attitude and social demands, and although aphasic speech automatisms may be more automatic than not, they are always formed in dialogue with capacities and articulations of consciousness that are retained. Indeed, this non-propositional language emerges because of a failure of the aphasic person's "executive functions" (which include attention, shifting between mental sets or tasks, updating/monitoring of contents of working memory, and awareness and inhibition of prepotent responses) and disinhibition of the "lower" strata of language that ensues. Consequently, not only are emotional functions preserved, they can also appear to be heightened with the loss of inhibition.[62] Aphasia seems, in fact, to be a disorder that often leaves the capacity of the self to feel and gauge its losses within consciousness agonizingly untouched, with speech automatisms seeming to appear with greatest potency precisely when aphasic people are asked to deploy their impaired executive functions in speaking.[73] The sense of incapacity, inability and frustration produced by a sense of demand—a demand for answers, or for referential and propositional speech, that Beckett also persistently dramatizes—indeed seems to release this automatic, modalizing language. When left hemisphere damage removes any possibility of propositionising, modalizing language, which appears to be produced by both right and left hemispheres, begins to utter in anxious compensation. Not only is this the only language to which most people with aphasic speech automatisms have access, it is the language that begs to be expressed as a reaction to the failure to access propositional speech.[74] Clinical work with aphasic patients indeed seems to suggest that the frustrated incapacity of "I can't" is precisely linked to the production of words under "I must" conditions—conditions that release, even propel, them.

Beckett famously asserted to Lawrence Harvey the sense of compulsion that seemed to subtend his artistic production: "I write because I have to [. . .] What do you do when 'I can't' meets 'I must?'"[75] Beckett's texts indeed seem to dramatize a compulsive back and forth in this border territory triangulated between the unreachability of full linguistic propositionality and an absolute automaticity or indeed a silence that can never finally be achieved. The words that insist in this borderland instead refract what remains of the speaking self through both the idea and the sense of a subjectivity it can no longer inhabit, and an unfettered unconsciousness it knows it cannot attain. So in his search for words that could be held in this territory Beckett turns, albeit in an untheorized fashion, to a modalizing language imaged as a body language of slobber, pus, shit, tears and vomit. Although this is a language that necessarily sticks in the craw of the idea of speech as an unsullied expression of cognition and intention, it is a language that uses both the "understanding" and the "nerves" of a reader and audience to stage the fact that *zoon logon echon* is never fully conterminous with the rational animal.

BETWEEN CAN'T AND MUST

As he came towards the end of his life, Beckett struck up a friendship with a writer called Lawrence Shainberg who was exploring neurological dysfunction in his work. And it was in his conversation with Shainberg that Beckett himself makes a link between a writing compulsively held between "can't and must" and neurological dysfunction. As Shainberg recounts, Beckett affirmed:

> "With diminished concentration, loss of memory, obscured intelligence—what you, for example, might call 'brain damage'—the more chance there is for saying something closest to what one really is. Even though everything seems inexpressible, there remains the need to express [. . .]." Of course, he knew that this was not a new project for him, only a more extreme version of the one he'd always set himself [. . .] It was always here, in "the clash," as he put it to me once, "between can't and must" that he took his stand.[76]

Although these conversations took place towards the end of Beckett's life, they seem to gesture backwards. For one can hear in them what Beckett described to Georges Duthuit, during the time he was writing *The Unnamable,* as the need to find a "non-relational," a disconnected, art. He states that the artist should be "at ease enough with the great tornadoes of intuition, to grasp that the break with the outside world entails a break with the inside world, that there are no replacement relations for naïve relations." Art must indeed, in Beckett's terms, instantiate "the impossibility of reconnecting," and he goes on to affirm that "to want the brain to function is the height of crassness."[77] The idea that Beckett might somehow be using a mode related to neurological dysfunction and disconnection comes even more clearly into focus in his suggestive remark to Shainberg that the writing he developed during the *Trilogy* emerged from an affectively charged encounter with Parkinson's disease. Shainberg recounts:

> speaking of *Molloy* and the work that followed it, he told me that, returning to Dublin after the war, he'd found that his mother had

contracted Parkinson's Disease. "Her face was a mask, completely unrecognizable. Looking at her, I had a sudden realization that all the work I'd done before was on the wrong track. I guess you'd have to call it a revelation. Strong word, I know, but so it was. I simply understood that there was no sense adding to the store of information, gathering knowledge. The whole attempt at knowledge, it seemed to me, had come to nothing. It was all haywire. What I had to do was investigate not-knowing, not-perceiving, the whole world of incompleteness."[78]

In the face of neurological damage, Beckett does not turn away from language; rather, he turns towards a new kind of work that disarticulates language's seemingly immutable connection with knowledge, intention, propositionality and the rational self-expression of a *cogito*. In another interview, Beckett again affirmed his orientation towards "the whole world of incompleteness," stating: "I'm no intellectual. All I am is feeling. 'Molloy' and the others came to me the day I became aware of my own folly. Only then did I begin to write the things I feel."[79] And perhaps by noting the suggestive symmetry between the language preserved in the aphasic speech automatism and some of the central features of Beckett's postwar work, we can gain some understanding of how and where, in neurological terms, Beckett was to find his compulsive, decidedly un-Romantic, language of feeling, and how and where it continues to rattle and resonate within readers and audiences.

The aphasiologist Théophile Alajouanine, when writing in the 1940s of the aphasic poet Valery Larbaud whom Beckett met during his illness, is clear that Larbaud's inability to speak and write propositional language fundamentally disarticulates the possibility of the author's literary production. For Alajouanine, aphasia "abolished the possibility of literary artistic realization" for Larbaud, although he goes on to add this qualifier, "at least the one he was used to for he did not employ that conventional agrammatism of some of the young literary schools."[80] Presumably, Alajouanine means that Larbaud never had, so never could, write like a Joyce (whose *Ulysses* he translated), a Surrealist, or one of Nordau's "degenerates." As far as Alajouanine is concerned, "[t]he aphasic patient, with his involuntary use of ready-made sentences unadapted to what he wants to express, shows in some way a negative picture of literary art."[81] But Beckett, who was well-versed in modernism's attachment both to agrammatism and to "readymades" is no longer seeking "naive relations" in his art; he does not wish for the brain and the writing hand simply to function with the "crassness" of the normative. Perhaps in his search for a non-relational art of "not-knowing," of "incompleteness,'" Beckett was to intuit, through its affect, something of the functional dissociation between propositional-referential and modalizing language that neurolinguistic understandings of language have revealed, invoking such disturbance as a method that might precisely enable his aesthetic bound to buckling the wheel of the word.

Staked to and compelled by the affective space between "I can't" and "I must" of modalizing utterances spewed, spat, dribbled and shat out, Beckett seems to find a language that beggars the putative power of knowledge and intentional capacity, while retaining a sense of an affective life that hopes for expression and to speak for itself even amidst its decomposition. The Samuel Beckett who returned obsessively to the glitches and discontinuities in and of translation, to the impossibility of smooth conversions between media, the Beckett who compulsively refused the naive relations between languages, genres, and, perhaps most fundamentally, between mind and body—breaking up and breaking down the imagined simplicity of the continuum between them—seems indeed to offer us the beginnings of a mode of reading and experiencing through which we might be able both to comprehend and to feel how language drives the torsions and vicissitudes of our psychosomatic lives.

NOTES

1. René Descartes, *Discourse on the Method*, in *Descartes: Selected Philosophical Writings*, trans. John Cottingham, Robert Stoothoff and Dugald Murdoch (Cambridge: Cambridge University Press, 1988), 45.
2. Matthew Feldman, *Beckett's Books: A Cultural History of Samuel Beckett's "Interwar Notes"* (London: Continuum, 2006), 46–57; Samuel Beckett, *Poems: 1930–1989* (London: John Calder, 2002), 5
3. Samuel Beckett, *Molloy*, (London: Faber, 2009) 35–36.
4. Samuel Beckett, *Malone Dies* (London: Faber, 2010), 44.
5. Beckett, *Malone Dies*, 44.
6. Beckett noted down the dictum from Wilhelm Windelband's *A History of Philosophy* in his 'Whoroscope Notebook' (1932–37), but included Leibniz's response to Locke's empiricism: *'nisi ipse intellectus'* [except the mind itself].
7. Daniel Albright, *Beckett and Aesthetics* (Cambridge: Cambridge University Press, 2003), 91.
8. Aristotle, *The Complete Works of Aristotle: Volumes 1 & 2: Revised Oxford Translation*, ed. Jonathan Barnes (Princeton: Princeton University Press, 1984), 1253.
9. See Macdonald Critchley, *John Hughlings Jackson: The Father of English Neurology* (Oxford: Oxford University Press, 1998).
10. James Knowlson, *Damned to Fame: The Life of Samuel Beckett* (London: Jonathan Cape, 1996), 298–99, offers and account of the meeting between Beckett and Larbaud, while Francois Boller gives further details of Larbaud's aphasia in his chapter "Valery Larbaud," in Julien Bogousslavsky and Francois Boller (eds), *Neurological Disorders in Famous Artists: Part 2* (Basel: Karger, 2005), 85. The translation of Larbaud's automatism is Boller's, although he concedes that it "has a literary flavour, which is difficult to translate." The phrase is idiomatic, in a rather archaic and figurative way.
11. A number of critics have explored the link between Beckett's work and neurological understandings of language subtended by studies of aphasia. See Michel Beausang, "*Watt*; Logique, démence, aphasie," in *Beckett avant Beckett: essays sur le jeune Beckett, 1930–1945*, ed. Jean-Michel Rabaté (Paris: Presses de l'Ecole Normale Supérieure, 1984), 153–172; Laura Salisbury, "'What Is the Word': Beckett's Aphasic Modernism," *Journal of*

Beckett Studies 17, nos. 1–2 (2008), 78–126; Gabriela Garcia Hubard, "En traversant l'aphasie," *Samuel Beckett Today/Aujourd'hui* 20 (2008), 335–345; Natália Laranjinha, "L'Écriture aphasique de Samuel Beckett," *Samuel Beckett Today/Aujourd'hui* 22 (2010), 449–462.

12. *The Letters of Samuel Beckett Vol. I: 1929–40*, ed. Martha Dow Fehsenfeld and Lois More Overbeck (Cambridge: Cambridge University Press, 2009), 133.
13. Beckett, *Letters: Vol I*, 134–135.
14. Beckett, *Letters: Vol I*, 133, 134.
15. Beckett, *Letters: Vol I*, 134. LS believes that the editors of the published version of this letter have mistranscribed "frigged" as "trigged," and "in terram" as "in terrain."
16. Samuel Beckett, *Dream of Fair to Middling Women* (London: Calder, 1993), 27.
17. Beckett, *Letters: Vol I*, 159.
18. Samuel Beckett, *Texts for Nothing* (London: John Calder, 1999), 40.
19. Samuel Beckett, *The Unnamable* (London: Faber, 2010), 97.
20. Samuel Beckett, *Mercier and Camier* (London: Calder and Boyars, 1974), 27.
21. Beckett, *The Unnamable*, 49.
22. Ulrika Maude, "'A Stirring Beyond Coming and Going': Beckett and Tourette's," *Journal of Beckett Studies* 17, nos. 1–2 (2008), 158, 160.
23. *Beckett's Dream Notebook*, ed. John Pilling (Reading: Beckett International Foundation, 1999), 89, 89, 91, 92.
24. Max Nordau, *Degeneration* (London: William Heinemann, 1895), 15.
25. Pilling, ed., *Beckett's Dream Notebook*, 90.
26. Pilling, ed., *Beckett's Dream Notebook*, 89.
27. Beckett *Letters: Vol I*, 87.
28. In a letter of 1934, Beckett called Chatto and Windus, who were rather desultorily publishing *More Pricks than Kicks*, "Shatupon & Windup," *Letters: Vol I*, 212.
29. Pilling, ed., *Beckett's Dream Notebook*, 91, 97.
30. Undated letter to Thomas MacGreevy probably written in early August 1931. Quoted by Pilling in *Beckett's Dream Notebook*, xiii.
31. Knowlson, *Damned to Fame*, 244, 252.
32. Nordau, *Degeneration*, 18.
33. Rachel Burrows, in Brigitte Le Juez, *Beckett Before Beckett: Beckett's Lectures on French Literature* (London: Souvenir Press, 2008), 53.
34. Pilling, ed., *Beckett's Dream Notebook*, 91.
35. In 1935, Beckett writes to MacGreevy, in relation to the latter's mother's illness, "[t]he discrepancy between mind and body is terrible," *Letters: Vol I*, 273.
36. Beckett, *Letters: Vol I*, 144.
37. Samuel Beckett, *The Complete Dramatic Works* (London: Faber, 1990), 379.
38. *No Author Better Served: The Correspondence of Samuel Beckett and Alan Schneider*, ed. Maurice Harmon (Cambridge, MA: Harvard University Press, 1998), 283.
39. TCD MS 10971/7/2, in Matthew Feldman, "Sourcing 'Aporetics': An Empirical Study on Philosophical Influences on the Development of Samuel Beckett's Writing" (Ph.D. thesis, Oxford Brookes University, 2004), 310.
40. For an account of the relationship between the aphasiological, neurological and psychoanalytic Freud and the importance of language in his thought see John Forrester, *Language and the Origins of Psychoanalysis* (Basingstoke: Palgrave Macmillan, 1980).

41. See Elizabeth A. Wilson, *Psychosomatic: Feminism and the Neurological Body* (Durham NC: Duke University Press, 2004), 4.
42. TCD MS 10971/7/1, in Feldman, "Sourcing," 309.
43. TCD MS 10971/7/2, in Feldman, "Sourcing," 310.
44. Karin Stephen, *Psychoanalysis and Medicine: A Study of the Wish to Fall Ill* (Cambridge: Cambridge University Press, 1933), 114, 149, 149, 150.
45. Jean Laplanche and Jean-Bertrand Pontalis, *The Language of Psychoanalysis* (London: Karnac, 1988), 77.
46. TCD MS 10971/8/23, in Feldman, "Sourcing," 342.
47. Ernest Jones, *Treatment of the Neuroses* (London: Ballière, Tindall and Cox, 1920), 195.
48. Beckett, *Letters: Vol I*, 300.
49. For an account of Broca's presentation, see Juergen Tesak and Chris Code, *Milestones in the History of Aphasia: Theories and Protagonists* (Hove: Psychology Press, 2008), 46–54.
50. The qualification 'articulated language' was important, as damage to other areas of the brain were identified later in the century as apparently responsible for other forms of aphasia, including significant language comprehension impairments—*sensory* aphasia.
51. Broca himself preferred the term *aphemia* as describing better the significant problems with the organization and production of articulated speech, despite a lack of paralysis affecting the speech organs, he identified.
52. See L.S. Jacyna, *Lost Words: Narratives of Language and the Brain, 1825–1926* (Princeton: Princeton University Pres, 2000), 3.
53. See Elizabeth A. Franz and Grant Gillett, "John Hughlings Jackson's Evolutionary Neurology: A Unifying Framework for Cognitive Neuroscience," *Brain* 134 (2011), 3114–3120.
54. John Hughlings Jackson, "Evolution and Dissolution of the Nervous System," *Lancet* 1 (1884), 556.
55. John Hughlings Jackson, "Loss of Speech: Its Association with Valvular Disease of the Heart and with Hemiplegia on the Right Side–Defects of Smell–Defects of Speech in Chorea. Arterial Lesions in Epilepsy [1864]," in "Reprint of Some of Dr Hughlings Jackson's Papers on the Affections of Speech," *Brain* 38, nos. 1–2 (1915), 28–42, 40.
56. John Hughlings Jackson, *Selected Writings of John Hughlings Jackson: Vol. II*, ed. J. Taylor (London: Staples Press, 1932), 135.
57. John Hughlings Jackson, "On Affections of Speech from Disease of the Brain [1880]," in "Reprint," 130–146, 139.
58. Hughlings Jackson, "On Affections of Speech from Disease of the Brain [1879]," in "Reprint," 107–129, 111.
59. Beckett, *The Unnamable*, 50
60. Maude, "A Stirring Beyond Coming and Going," 160; Jean-Luc Nespoulous, Chris Code, Jacques Virbel, and André Roch Lecours, "Hypotheses on the Dissociation between 'Referential' and 'Modalizing' Verbal Behaviour in Aphasia," *Applied Psycholinguistics* 19 (1998), 329.
61. Elizabeth Barry, *Beckett and Authority: The Uses of Cliché* (Basginstoke: Palgrave Macmillan, 2006), 65.
62. Barry, *Beckett and Authority*, 89.
63. Beckett, *Complete Dramatic Works*, 138.
64. Beckett, *Complete Dramatic Works*, 140, 143.
65. We are grateful to Mary Bryden for sharing this illuminating detail, which she received in conversation with Billie Whitelaw.
66. See Chris Code, "Neurolinguistic Analysis of Recurrent Utterances in Aphasia," *Cortex* 18 (1982), 149.

67. See Code, "Neurolinguistic Analysis of Recurrent Utterances in Aphasia," 141–152. See also Chris Code, Jeremy J Tree, and Karen Dawe, "Opportunities to say 'Yes': Rare Speech Automatisms in a Case of Progressive Nonfluent Aphasia and Apraxia," *Neurocase* 15, no. 6 (2009), 445–458, 446.
68. Beckett, *Complete Dramatic Works*, 243.
69. Beckett, *Texts for Nothing*, 13.
70. See M. Laine and N. Martin, *Anomia: Theoretical and Clinical Aspects* (Hove: Psychology Press, 2006).
71. Code, "Neurolinguistic Analysis"; Beckett, *The Unnamable*, 103.
72. Beckett, *The Unnamable*, 134.
73. Code, Tree, Dawe, "Opportunities to say 'Yes'," 454–455.
74. Nespoulous, Code, Virbel, and Lecours, "Hypotheses on Dissociation," 323–324.
75. Lawrence Harvey, *Samuel Beckett: Poet and Critic* (Princeton: Princeton University Press, 1970), 249.
76. Lawrence Shainberg, "Exorcising Beckett," *Paris Review* 104 (1987), 103.
77. *The Letters of Samuel Beckett, Vol. II: 1941–1956*, ed. George Craig, Martha Dow Fehsenfeld, Dan Gunn, and Lois More Overbeck (Cambridge: Cambridge University Press, 2011), 140, 149.
78. Shainberg, "Exorcising Beckett," 105.
79. Gabriel D'Aubarède, "Interview with Samuel Beckett," in *Samuel Beckett: The Critical Heritage*, ed. Lawrence Graver and Raymond Federman (London: Routledge & Kegan Paul, 1979), 217.
80. Théophile Alajouanine, "Aphasia and Artistic Realization," *Brain* 79, no. 3 (1948) 229–241, 231.
81. Alajouanine, "Aphasia and Artistic Realization," 239.

WORKS CITED

Alajouanine, Théophile. "Aphasia and Artistic Realization." *Brain* 79, no. 3 (1948): 229–241.

Albright, Daniel. *Beckett and Aesthetics*. Cambridge: Cambridge University Press, 2003.

Aristotle. *The Complete Works of Aristotle: Volumes 1 & 2: Revised Oxford Translation*, ed. Jonathan Barnes. Princeton: Princeton University Press, 1984.

Barry, Elizabeth. *Beckett and Authority: The Uses of Cliché*. Basginstoke: Palgrave Macmillan, 2006.

Beausang, Michel. "*Watt*; Logique, démence, aphasie." In *Beckett avant Beckett: essays sur le jeune Beckett, 1930–1945*, ed. Jean-Michel Rabaté. Paris: Presses de l'Ecole Normale Supérieure, 1984), 153–172.

Beckett, Samuel. *Malone Dies*. London: Faber, 2010.

Beckett, Samuel. *Mercier and Camier*. London: Calder and Boyars, 1974.

Beckett, Samuel. *Molloy*. London: Faber, 2009.

Beckett, Samuel. *Poems: 1930–1989*. London: John Calder, 2002.

Beckett, Samuel. *Texts for Nothing*. London: John Calder, 1999.

Beckett, Samuel. *The Complete Dramatic Works*. London: Faber, 1990.

Beckett, Samuel. *The Letters of Samuel Beckett Vol. I: 1929–40*, ed. Martha Dow Fehsenfeld and Lois More Overbeck. Cambridge: Cambridge University Press, 2009.

Beckett, Samuel. *The Letters of Samuel Beckett, Vol. II: 1941–1956*, ed. George Craig, Martha Dow Fehsenfeld, Dan Gunn, and Lois More Overbeck. Cambridge: Cambridge University Press, 2011.

Beckett, Samuel. *The Unnamable*. London: Faber, 2010.

Boller, Francois. "Valery Larbaud." In *Neurological Disorders in Famous Artists: Part 2*, eds. Julien Bogousslavsky and Francois Boller. Basel: Karger, 2005.

Code, Chris. "Neurolinguistic Analysis of Recurrent Utterances in Aphasia." *Cortex* 18 (1982): 141–152.

Code, Chris, Jeremy J. Tree and Karen Dawe. "Opportunities to Say 'Yes': Rare Speech Automatisms in a Case of Progressive Non-fluent Aphasia and Apraxia." *Neurocase* 15, no. 6 (2009): 445–458.

Critchley, Macdonald. *John Hughlings Jackson: The Father of English Neurology*. Oxford: Oxford University Press, 1998.

D'Aubarède, Gabriel. "Interview with Samuel Beckett." In *Samuel Beckett: The Critical Heritage*, ed. Lawrence Graver and Raymond Federman. London: Routledge & Kegan Paul, 1979.

Descartes, René. *Discourse on the Method*, in *Descartes: Selected Philosophical Writings*. Translated by John Cottingham, Robert Stoothoff and Dugald Murdoch. Cambridge: Cambridge University Press, 1988.

Feldman, Matthew. *Beckett's Books: A Cultural History of Samuel Beckett's "Interwar Notes."* London: Continuum, 2006.

Feldman, Matthew. "Sourcing 'Aporetics': An Empirical Study on Philosophical Influences on the Development of Samuel Beckett's Writing." Ph.D. thesis, Oxford Brookes University, 2004.

Forrester, John. *Language and the Origins of Psychoanalysis*. Basingstoke: Palgrave Macmillan, 1980.

Franz, Elizabeth A. and Grant Gillett. "John Hughlings Jackson's Evolutionary Neurology: A Unifying Framework for Cognitive Neuroscience." *Brain* 134 (2011): 3114–3120.

Garcia Hubard, Gabriela. "En traversant l'aphasie." *Samuel Beckett Today/Aujourd'hui* 20 (2008): 335–345.

Harmon, Maurice, ed. *No Author Better Served: The Correspondence of Samuel Beckett and Alan Schneider*. Cambridge, MA: Harvard University Press, 1998.

Harvey, Lawrence. *Samuel Beckett: Poet and Critic*. Princeton: Princeton University Press, 1970.

Hughlings Jackson, John. "Evolution and Dissolution of the Nervous System." *Lancet* 1 (1884).

Hughlings Jackson, John. "Loss of Speech: Its Association with Valvular Disease of the Heart and with Hemiplegia on the Right Side–Defects of Smell–Defects of Speech in Chorea. Arterial Lesions in Epilepsy [1864]." In "Reprint of Some of Dr Hughlings Jackson's Papers on the Affections of Speech." *Brain* (1915): 28–42, 147–174.

Hughlings Jackson, John. *Selected Writings of John Hughlings Jackson: Vol. II*, ed. J. Taylor. London: Staples Press, 1932.

Jacyna, L. S. *Lost Words: Narratives of Language and the Brain, 1825–1926*. Princeton: Princeton University Pres, 2000.

Jones, Ernest. *Treatment of the Neuroses*. London: Ballière, Tindall and Cox, 1920.

Knowlson, James. *Damned to Fame: The Life of Samuel Beckett*. London: Jonathan Cape, 1996.

Laine, M. and N. Martin. *Anomia: Theoretical and Clinical Aspects*. Hove: Psychology Press, 2006.

Laplanche, Jean and Jean-Bertrand Pontalis. *The Language of Psychoanalysis*. London: Karnac, 1988.

Laranjinha, Natália. "L'Écriture aphasique de Samuel Beckett." *Samuel Beckett Today/Aujourd'hui* 22 (2010): 449–462.

Le Juez, Brigitte. *Beckett Before Beckett: Beckett's Lectures on French Literature*. London: Souvenir Press, 2008.

Maude, Ulrika. "'A Stirring Beyond Coming and Going': Beckett and Tourette's." *Journal of Beckett Studies* 17, nos. 1–2 (2008): 153–168.

Nespoulous, Jean-Luc, Chris Code, Jacques Virbel and André Roch Lecours. "Hypotheses on the Dissociation between 'Referential' and 'Modalizing' Verbal Behaviour in Aphasia." *Applied Psycholinguistics* 19 (1998): 311–331.

Nordau, Max. *Degeneration.* London: William Heinemann, 1895.

Pilling, John, ed. *Beckett's Dream Notebook.* Reading: Beckett International Foundation, 1999.

Salisbury, Laura. "'What Is the Word': Beckett's Aphasic Modernism." *Journal of Beckett Studies* 17, nos. 1–2 (2008): 78–126.

Stephen, Karin. *Psychoanalysis and Medicine: A Study of the Wish to Fall Ill.* Cambridge: Cambridge University Press, 1933.

Tesak, Juergen and Chris Code. *Milestones in the History of Aphasia: Theories and Protagonists.* Hove: Psychology Press, 2008.

Wilson, Elizabeth A. *Psychosomatic: Feminism and the Neurological Body.* Durham NC: Duke University Press, 2004, 1–14.

Windelband, Wilhelm. *A History of Philosophy.* Translated by James Hayden Tufts. London: Macmillan, 1910.

7 Staging Aphasia
Jean-Claude Van Itallie's *The Traveller* and Arthur Kopit's *Wings*

Gene A. Plunka

Ludwig Wittgenstein's *Tractatus Logico-Philosophicus* is largely devoted to the problem of how language, the tool by which humans orient themselves to their physical and social environments, organizes knowledge. In short, language differentiates humans from animals and is the predominant factor in distinguishing what constitutes culture. Wittgenstein investigated cultural acquisition, i.e., how we become linguistically competent or how language is possible. Wittgenstein's theoretical assumptions gain further significance when examined in conjunction with Benjamin Whorf's research into how language shapes culture. One viable method of studying cultural acquisition through the development of language skills is to examine how adult aphasics reacquire their cognitive skills after brain damage has caused severe language deficit. This relationship between language and cultural acquisition is well illustrated in American playwright Jean-Claude van Itallie's 1987 drama, *The Traveller*, a partly fictitious account of director Joseph Chaikin's aphasic condition.

In his *Tractatus Logico-Philosophicus*, Wittgenstein explored the notion of how a sequence of words can have meaning that will be understood. Wittgenstein and the logical positivists believed thoughts are made perceptible to the senses through a proposition of language. Wittgenstein viewed sentences as logical pictures of reality. He wrote that humanity "possesses the ability to construct languages capable of expressing every sense, without having any idea how each word has meaning or what its meaning is—just as people speak without knowing how the individual sounds are produced."[1] But how are sentences learned? Wittgenstein found that there is a relationship between empirical objects and the signs for them. A child learns language through example and practice of using signs in an ordinary way. Signs, however, have meaning only in the context of a proposition, a model of reality as we imagine it. In short, propositions form the basis of language—thought expressed in perceptible signs.

Benjamin Whorf applied Wittgenstein's tenets to linguistic anthropology, the study of language in various societies. The Sapir–Whorf hypothesis (Whorf studied with Edward Sapir when the latter came from the University of Chicago to take a position as Professor of Anthropology at Yale University in fall 1931) states that all higher levels of thinking are dependent on language. Humans perceive the world principally through language. The Sapir–Whorf hypothesis implies that the structure of one's language conditions the manner in which the speaker of that language thinks. In other words, the structures of various languages force the speakers of those tongues to view reality differently. If, as Wittgenstein noted, a sentence is a logical picture of reality, and if, as the Sapir–Whorf hypothesis states, signs change from culture to culture, then individuals do not have the same mental pictures of objects. Speakers of different languages view the universe differently since thinking is relative to the language learned. Linguists argue that the investigation of the internal structure of individual languages helps us to understand the complexity of our own thinking habits. We see, hear, and think the way we do largely because the linguistic habits of our culture predispose certain choices of interpretation. Every language is a vast system in which we channel our thoughts and build our day-to-day consciousness. As Whorf acknowledges, "A change in language can transform our appreciation of the Cosmos."[2] Essentially, the study of linguistics becomes the quest for meaning, a heuristic approach to problems of psychology.

Aphasia, from the Greek *aphatos* (speechless) or "out of phase," is a loss or impairment of language due to some type of brain injury such as a direct blow, trauma, infection, or stroke. The form that aphasia assumes depends upon what area of the brain is damaged. Broca's aphasia, in which there is a lesion in the frontal lobe, results in damage to the area that supplies instructions for muscle movements associated with speech. These aphasics cannot pronounce words, although language comprehension is intact. Wernicke's aphasia, which occurs because of a lesion in the temporal lobe, adversely affects the recollection and interpretation of spoken and written language. Wernicke's aphasics cannot associate learned words with inner thoughts or stored memories and thus speak in gibberish. Generally, the aphasic has lost the capacity for using language to communicate meaning or for what Wittgenstein might refer to as "propositioning." Aphasics have difficulty using signs to express or comprehend ideas and must relearn the relationship between signifieds and signifiers.[3]

Many adult aphasics have not lost judgment or the ability to reason but are instead unable to express thoughts through language. The retraining process is similar to how a child learns language through auditory recognition of words and then by understanding the meaning and concomitant use of words in sentences. The reacquisition of phonemic distinctions by the adult aphasic parallels the same order as observed in the child. However, the adult aphasic's language, previously learned, has been distorted by a lesion in the brain whereas the child is encountering language for the first time. Retraining aphasics to understand language and use it appropriately is a process that enables us to study how language organizes human knowledge, or as Whorf might state, how cognitive differences are related to lexical differences, and therefore how culture is transmitted.[4]

In April 1984, breathing difficulties and angina pain forced Chaikin to quit rehearsals for *Waiting for Godot*, which he was to direct at the Stratford Festival in Canada. An X-ray taken at New York's Presbyterian Hospital confirmed the prognosis: without open-heart surgery, Chaikin would die. On May 7, 1984, Chaikin, for the third time in his life, underwent heart surgery. Before he was anesthetized, Chaikin, in response to his friend Stephanie Lafarge's query about how he felt, recited a speech from *King Lear*, a play that he had been working on in preparation for its staging at the Public Theater in the fall. During the operation, a blood clot momentarily cut off oxygen to his brain, creating a lesion on the left side of the brain, a type of stroke. Van Itallie, who was the first to see Chaikin after the operation, recalled, "His speech was all blather."[5] The stroke resulted in what was diagnosed as severe aphasia, most likely a combination of Broca's aphasia and Wernicke's aphasia. Chaikin could not understand the speech of others and was not able to put words together in an articulate sentence. He did not realize that his inarticulate babble was virtually incomprehensible to those who spoke with him. He could read words but not music, was barely able to write, and had no ability to work with math or sign language. A couple of months after the operation, van Itallie was driving Chaikin to the hospital. Chaikin, who at this time could read much better than he could speak, was reading aloud, as speech therapy, the captions of the Gustave Dore book of illustrations for Dante's *Inferno*. Van Itallie immediately saw that similarities between Chaikin's life and Dante's *Inferno* were perhaps the subject for a new play. In July 1984, van Itallie began work on the play with Chaikin. Van Itallie stated, "It became clear quickly that the Dante story was too abstract by itself—that there was a very personal story as well. So I decided to tell it in parallel."[6]

Much of the play is based upon Daniel Moses's (The Traveller) perceptions of everyday reality, but during periods of aphasia, his distorted vision is depicted on stage stylistically.[7] Van Itallie has stated that experimental stage techniques work better to express the Traveller's aphasic perceptions: "It [*The Traveller*] is within a more Chekhovian framework, if you will, but within this there are other forms that are more appropriate to different realities, such as dreams and hallucinations."[8] Van Itallie said he began with a conventional structure: "It's a passion play which follows the patterns of the old Mysteries—a descent into Hell, a confrontation with the self, ego death and a rebirth into reality. That's a very traditional journey."[9] The play's naturalistic framework, which van Itallie associates with Chekhovian realism, coincides with the real, intense struggle of an aphasic who goes into a type of hell, an Inferno, and when reborn, attempts to find his identity again almost as if he is learning from birth. Van Itallie discussed how he juxtaposed conventional and experimental forms in *The Traveller*:

> The play starts out in "real" reality—whatever you want to call that, Chekhovian reality or high-pressured New York reality. And then the

Traveller begins to get drugs and anesthetic, and his mind begins to fuzz a little. The conceit of the play is that at this point he goes down into the Inferno world, and he's in a dream reality, a very profound dream reality . . . The play has a kind of parabolic shape. It goes down at that point, and then you start coming back up, and as you surface, you come back into the more Chekhovian reality. But there are still some leftovers: when the Traveller sees the horse neighing or when he has hallucinations. And so then there are juxtapositions of realities. But more and more as he deals with people and has to find a new language to do that, is reborn into the world really, there is more of the Chekhovian reality.[10]

Van Itallie's use of the quest as a metaphor for the aphasic's road to recovery is particularly apropos because neurolinguists have often referred to the relearning process as similar to a journey to the "otherworld." The long-term treatment of aphasia may last for years, depending on the severity of the damage to the brain, as well as the patient's age, intelligence, language abilities, and physical condition.[11] Although much of the research on aphasia has focused on its pathology (e.g., the work of Broca and Wernicke), other investigators, such as Hughlings Jackson, have emphasized the psychological disorders associated with the disease and the implications for long-term recovery in which the patient must explore unknown terrain.[12] Aphasia causes severe disruption to an individual's hope for recovery because language, the usual tool for coping (as in swearing or acting out frustrations), has gone awry. Thus, the aphasic feels as if he or she is on a quest in a foreign land or "otherworld" in which language must be reacquired in order to cope psychologically.

In one sense, *The Traveller* conveys the same types of changing realities presented in van Itallie's earlier play, *The Tibetan Book of the Dead*. After the Traveller has a stroke and experiences the effects of aphasia, he is often in a nebulous condition that is similar to the *Bardo*, a Tibetan term that characterizes the state between death and rebirth. In *The Traveller*, Daniel Moses experiences a type of death after his surgery—a descent into hell. His rebirth is the prolonged growth process in which he must learn to recognize language and how it is logically formed. Most of the play, however, represents the agony of the *Bardo* for the Traveller, the state between death and rediscovering his identity through his close association with friends and relatives. Van Itallie acknowledged that the *Bardo* state requires stage techniques that would reflect the protagonist's constantly changing realities and his journey through inner space.[13] When the Traveller transcends this state of mind and begins to interact in the real world of friends, lovers, and family, the form becomes more conventional.

The Traveller begins in the New York City apartment of composer Daniel Moses. Daniel is on the telephone, infuriated that his work, aptly titled *Manhattan Inferno*, was negatively reviewed in *New York Magazine*.[14]

Daniel, himself an inferno, is, as the stage directions indicate, "intense."[15] He is the personification of busy activity, always seeming to be in a hurry: "His hands are continually busy jotting a note, searching for something, playing with the cassette tapes and the volume of the music, or putting something into his mouth" (6). He takes two telephone calls at once, putting one of his friends on hold. His frantic schedule leaves very little time for himself; his appointment calendar confirms that he is booked up days in advance. An unexpected visit by his friend Aaron makes him feel "pressured" (8), and he laments, "I'm going nuts here" (8). Aaron asks Danie if he would like to walk by the pier to watch the sunset. Daniel must attend to his work first, so he refuses the offer. He asks Aaron, "But how about Tuesday at five fifteen? We can go for a walk then" (10). Daniel is obviously allowing work to interfere with life, and his spiritual state is suffering the consequences. Daniel insists that he is free to meet with his friend until 6:30 p.m. but not longer; the conversation with Aaron becomes frustrating to him, and he begins to internalize his pent-up hostilities. We learn that Daniel has been seeing a cardiologist because of his breathing difficulties. Sipping coffee and wine while smoking cigarettes only exacerbates his health problems. He begins to seethe when Linda places him on hold during their telephone conversation. Another telephone call, this time from the Traveller's brother, frustrates him to the extent of nearly banging his fist on the table. Suddenly, the Traveller experiences symptoms of heart failure: fluid in the lungs and shortness of breath. He totters from dizziness as the stage lights black out as well.

The Traveller must undergo open-heart surgery, which he has been through before. Like Chaikin, who was quite independent, admitted to van Itallie, the Traveller says to Aaron, "I'm afraid of living . . . diminished" (20). Chaikin's last words before the surgery were Lear's on the heath; Daniel, commissioned to write an opera version of *King Lear*, recites Lear's speech before receiving the anesthesia. The stage directions reveal, "This moment marks a crossing from one state of the Traveller's mind to another. He is entering an altered state of consciousness" (21). Van Itallie views the play as a Dante-esque journey from the hyperactivity of Manhattan life down into a type of Inferno, the near-death state of open-heart surgery and the aphasia that follows the stroke incurred during the operation.[16] Daniel is a traveller who journeys to undiscovered territory during the surgery. When he awakens, Daniel is in the *Bardo* state; as in *The Tibetan Book of the Dead*, the person in the *Bardo* must choose between death and spiritual rebirth. When the Traveller chooses to live, the remainder of the play then deals with his rebirth, a continual learning process in which Daniel must discover the reality of friends, relatives, physicians, and therapists; as is true of any newborn, he must also acquire language skills. As the Traveller, Daniel journeys into the interior of his soul; he must struggle from within in order to be reborn. The play is a descent into hell followed by a phoenix-like rise from the ashes to mature through struggle and achievement. In this sense, the Traveller is similar to the Journeyor in van Itallie's *A Fable*, who learns to recognize that the Beast lies within the soul.[17]

Choosing rebirth, the Traveller is now in a state of innocence, allowing us to study the relationship between language development and cultural acquisition. He assesses his newborn status: "Like baby. Like angel./Feeling like that/Like traveling to stars, to friends./Beginning./Beginning like baby" (30). The stage directions indicate, "The Traveller is dazed and weak, like a baby. He expresses wonderment at what he is feeling" (33). The Traveller appears to understand that his retraining process will be similar to a child's ability to learn language through auditory recognition of sounds. Daniel muses, "Myself feeling to child/But cannot spitch to child" (97). Unable to use language effectively to communicate meaning, Daniel feels divorced from his environment: "Wow./Foreign to exile. Feeling like that/Exile to earth. It's true./Like baby . . . to earth . . ." (46). He admits to himself, "Difficult . . . to born" (32).

The Traveller's first words to the nurse, "Shalef nosh shaman. Ponly shingle" (39), reveal that he must learn language as if for the first time. Van Itallie has always been interested in how language can be manipulated to control one's thoughts and actions. In this sense, *The Traveller* is similar to Peter Handke's play, *Kaspar*, which is derived from an actual incident in which Kaspar Hauser, at age sixteen, essentially a feral child, turned up in Nuremberg in 1828 virtually unable to speak. Kept imprisoned in a dungeon for sixteen years by demented parents, Kaspar knew only one sentence, which he spoke in an Austrian dialect: "I would like to become a horseman such as my father once was." Kaspar could recite the words but did not know their meaning; this is similar to the Traveller responding "yeah" to whatever question is posed. Handke, working with linguistic principles formulated by Wittgenstein, demonstrates that as Kaspar, the newborn, learns phonetics, then words, and finally sentences, language creates order in his life. Kaspar learns the relationship between signs and objects and then eventually clarifies objects with sentences. To name an object means to control it. The play demonstrates the importance of the Sapir–Whorf hypothesis: Kaspar learns that language influences thought. Kaspar's initial lack of language resulted in disorientation. As his language develops, so does his intelligence and concomitantly his ability to become a productive member of the culture. Handke intimates that language socializes human beings, thus distinguishing them from animals.[18] Like Kaspar, the Traveller gradually accepts the fact that language organizes knowledge and is an integral part of the socialization process.

Even more apropos is a comparison between *The Traveller* and Arthur Kopit's play, *Wings*. Kopit and van Itallie first met as students in Robert Chapman's playwriting course at Harvard University in 1957. Over the years, they shared several acquaintances active in the New York theater scene and would occasionally meet each other at social events. Kopit was also on the *S.S. France* in April 1968 when van Itallie, Chaikin, and other

Open Theatre performers were en route to Europe to stage *The Serpent*. Furthermore, Van Itallie, Kopit, and John Guare all taught together one semester at Yale University. Kopit introduced Chaikin and van Itallie to Jacqueline Doolittle, the model for Amy, the speech therapist who worked with Emily Stilson after her stroke in *Wings*. Like van Itallie, who based *The Traveller* on Chaikin's real bout with aphasia, Kopit modeled *Wings* upon the actual life of a wingwalker who lost the ability to speak coherently after suffering a stroke, and on his father's own aphasic condition due to a stroke that he had in 1976. In an interview that I conducted with him on June 26, 1993, van Itallie explained that while *The Traveller* was conceived with Chaikin's aphasia in mind, Kopit's play was never considered during any of the drafts he wrote.[19] Van Itallie, however, has seen *Wings* performed. Although acknowledging certain similarities between the two plays, he believes that there are substantial differences.

Kopit divides Emily Stilson's stroke into four distinct phases. In "Prelude," the stroke is represented by an alarm clock coinciding with Emily's inner state. The second segment, "Catastrophe," reflects the hospital setting seen through Emily's distorted perceptions. In "Awakening," Emily is essentially reborn, like the Traveller, as she begins to connect words with ideas. Finally, the last segment, "Explorations," indicates Emily's rejuvenated sense of confidence as she conquers her fears and renews the spirit of wingwalking again. Emily Stilson regains her wings by mastering language, viewing sentences as logical pictures of reality and relearning the meanings of signifiers. Both plays reflect the idea that one's identity is established by language, which frames how the universe is depicted for us. However, one substantial difference between *Wings* and *The Traveller* is that, as Doris Auerbach has noted, the former play is a metaphor for the despair of the human condition, whereas the latter drama does not focus *per se* on the difficulty of communication in the modern world.[20] Margot Anne Kelly sees *Wings* as belonging to a series of "disability plays" that offer models for attaining personal freedom within the confining structures of social institutions. She writes, "While Emily is not committing suicide, we do sense that her contentment is in part relief—a liberation from having to try to conform to a social order that had become untenable."[21] In *The Traveller*, van Itallie, however, seems to keep the focus on psycholinguistics rather than on sociology.

This emphasis on psycholinguistics is similar to Susan Yankowitz's treatment of the subject in her play, *Night Sky*, which premiered at the Judith Anderson Theatre in New York City on May 14, 1991. Written at the request of Joseph Chaikin, who directed the play, Yankowitz's stage depiction of Chaikin's recovery from aphasia parallels van Itallie's exploration of cultural acquisition and creates meaning through the use of language. In her "Introduction and Dedication" to the play, Yankowitz wrote, "*Night Sky* is about listening and language, about inner and outer space, about a medical condition, a family's ordeal, an individual triumph—but most of all, it is about communication."[22] The play traces the arduous recovery of Anna, a forty-year-old astronomer, whose aphasia has resulted in acutely impaired syntax, damaged comprehension of verbal formation, and memory loss. Anna, formerly a strong-willed, confident woman, is now frustrated that her inability to use language has left her virtually without a culture and thus without an identity.

Night Sky takes us through the various stages of aphasia as Anna first struggles with nonsense language or gibberish, begins to understand words but cannot verbalize the relationship between objects and their signs, gradually struggles for words and then mouths morphemes, and then finally learns how to string words together without the proper use of prepositions or verbs yet still developing propositions that have meaning and can be understood. Meanwhile, during Anna's long recovery, Yankowitz explores the notion that cultural acquisition is more subtle than merely relearning one's native tongue. Anna must be able to communicate with Jennifer, her fourteen-year-old daughter, who is learning French in school. Daniel, Anna's boyfriend, a baritone who sings operas in French and English, presents a different problem for her as she tries to sing along with him. The Doctor tells Daniel, "Just keep in mind that there are many ways of communicating" (28) and that because the left part of her brain was damaged and the musical area of the brain is located in the right hemisphere, understanding music is not the same process as knowledge of a foreign language. Moreover, since Anna is a scientist and views her full recovery based on her ability to deliver a scientific paper that she has been writing for delivery at an important upcoming international conference, Yankowitz is also investigating how science language acquisition compounds the difficulty in achieving full acculturation. Finally, *Night Sky* explores the notion that relearning the relationships between signifieds and signifiers is insufficient since language must be applied in various cultural milieux; Anna becomes overwhelmed with a world filled with impatient, fast talkers, answering machines, and fashionable party talk, underscored, as the stage directions indicate, by a variety of voices and sounds, "*such as a news report, rap or rock music, a paid political announcement, a football sportscast, a commercial, etc*" (39). Thus, *Night Sky* in its exploration of how various new languages (foreign, musical, and scientific) are acquired and also how language must be framed in its cultural context is similar to van Itallie's investigation into the relationship between language and cultural acquisition in *The Traveller*.

After the operation, the Traveller begins to receive visitors in the hospital. Jodie, the Traveller's sister, visits with Aaron, who realizes that Daniel has had a stroke during surgery. Daniel's brain has trouble processing words; thus, he cannot understand what is being said to him. English has become a foreign language to Daniel. For example, when Laurie, the nurse, speaks to the aphasic, her language appears to be gibberish because Daniel cannot make any correspondence between words and signs: "Share. Shash mush me nore momargible" (38). In response to questions, he can only utter "yeah" even when the expected response should be "no." Asked to put matches in an ashtray, Daniel lights a candle with a match. Van Itallie also notes, "His words and speech rhythms are relearned, so his speech sounds clipped, as if he had a slight British accent" (24). When encouraged to identify a brush, Daniel refers to it as "klipklop," much in the same manner that Emily Stilson struggled with "tooovebram" and "tooove-britch" but could not articulate "toothbrush." In short, Daniel cannot make the relationship between empirical objects and the signs for them. He is forced to relearn the relationship between the signified and the signifiers. This linguistically fragmented world of the aphasic is represented stylistically on stage. As the nurse hops like a kangaroo or as Doctor Steiff whinnies and then paws the ground like a horse, the audience perceives the protagonist's altered state. As the Sapir–Whorf hypothesis suggests, a change in language does indeed alter our perception of the cosmos. As Daniel learns the structure of language, he will gradually be socialized to think like others in the culture.

The Traveller begins to learn how to express thoughts through language. His quandary is the same as the dilemma that plagued Emily Stilson, who frankly asked her therapist how names of objects are derived. What we see on stage in *The Traveller* is essentially the transmission of knowledge through language acquisition, similar to the learning process observed in children. Through language, the Traveller will unite self and universe. Aaron must use charades in order to communicate with his friend. The charades allow Aaron to use signs in an ordinary way, as Wittgenstein suggested, to transmit language. Meanwhile, Doctor Sullivan is instructing Daniel through auditory recognition of words. She explains the technique to the Traveller's nephew: "Don't ask him to repeat your pronunciation. He must retrieve words from his mind. A subtle process. There's no prescribed methodology. We hope speech exercises help a little, but mainly we must help him surprise himself into going around the blocked area in the brain" (101–102). By watching television, Daniel is inculcated with the notion of inflection and tone: "Words myself nothing, of course—/It's 'tone.'/It's word: 'tone.'/Tone': it's 'secret language'" (64). Television provides Daniel with a logical picture of reality in which the relationship among signs, tone of voice, and morphemes becomes more meaningful. Daniel is gradually being acculturated through linguistics. While watching television, Daniel states, "It's 'secret language.'/'Communication.' Wow. It's word./Humans' face communication to me" (64). He then switches channels quickly, trying to mimic the faces on television.

After ten days, the Traveller begins to connect words with ideas and to learn the meanings of individual signifiers. When Daniel sees a lightning storm outside his window, he begins to speak in cadences: "Crash, fash, crash pash pash mash!/Pash! Crash! Plash flashpash crash!/Mashafalash, prash" (76). Aaron determines that the Traveller is trying to recite Lear's words on the heath in the storm. For the first time during his rebirth, the

Traveller has associated words with meanings and is beginning to interpret language denotatively. This is the initial step toward how Wittgenstein
believed thoughts are made perceptible through logical pictures of reality
that cement the relationship between signifieds and signifiers.

The latter part of the play takes place in Daniel's New York apartment
where he is receiving therapy as an outpatient. The Traveller's once incomprehensible language is now interspersed with recognizable words. As the
weeks go by, Doctor Sullivan's therapy, which includes slow repetition of
words while instructing Daniel, becomes more effective. Soon, the Traveller begins to read words and attempts to articulate their meanings. Aaron
has placed markers throughout the Traveller's apartment. When he sees the
sign marked "aphasia," the Traveller says, "A-phasia—it's word/It's Greek:
a-phasia./It's 'rats.'/It's to cancer—/Peoples running away" (112–3). Daniel
then mimics people running in fear of his condition. As an aphasic, Daniel
has had his culture taken from him. Daniel is no longer a composer; he is
incapable of composing even a sentence. He is considered to be a foreigner,
and when a stranger asks him about his native country, Daniel amusingly
replies "Poland." Yet he has actually made considerable progress on his
journey toward full rebirth because he is soon able to carry on a partial
conversation with someone and can even recognize the names of close relatives. He is trying to make sense of his condition through a proposition of
language in which signs are related to ideas:

THE TRAVELLER: Wow.
        It's improv-e-ment.
        Slow improv-e-ment . . . but stroke—it's
        quick—
        It's
        (He mimes lightning.)
AARON: Lightning. It's lightning.
THE TRAVELLER: Yeah . . . to brain.
        Stroke, it's, of course—
AARON: Say it slowly.
THE TRAVELLER: Stroke, it's curse.
        Everything puzzle. (115)

The puzzle is slowly being unraveled as the Traveller learns to apply words
to various contexts.

By the end of the drama, the Traveller is able to put nouns, verbs, articles,
and prepositions together to form a picture of reality. His goal is to speak in
sentences, a proposition of language. Daniel realizes, "Sentence: it's organization—/It's human organization" (126), the first vestige of cultural acquisition. He reads, "Take off your gloves, please," puts the newspaper down,
and proudly announces, "It's a sentence" (126). As an aphasic devoid of
intelligible language, the Traveller was culturally deprived. Language

acquisition now allows the Traveller to view the universe differently. He makes the connection between language acquisition and acculturation: "Sentence, it's—/(He reads from his notebook.)/'Civilization'" (128). Daniel understands that language is the key to his rebirth and will influence one's cultural distinctions: "It's a sentence: coming to earth" (128). The last lines of the play indicate his achievement in which Daniel is using thoughts as a proposition of language to create a sense of order in which there is meaning in his life: "I am a composer./My name is Daniel" (129).

Staging the drama of aphasia allows us to understand the importance of language in determining cultural acquisition. Daniel Moses's progression from an aphasic who has lost his artistic heritage to an intelligent composer who is trying to regain an appreciation for an operatic version of *King Lear* is accomplished by language acquisition. Van Itallie's play demonstrates how language creates order in our lives and influences our various cultures. In his prelinguistic state, Daniel was close to an unthinking animal; loss of speech means an inability to create propositions. Language has socialized him, providing meaning in his life, albeit through a system of external conditioning controlled by "prompters." The world may not be as we perceive it, but language offers the means for us to construct logical pictures that provide an orientation to the universe.

NOTES

1. Ludwig Wittgenstein, *Prototractatus*, trans. D.F. Pears and B.F. McGuinness (Ithaca: Cornell University Press, 1971), 83.
2. Benjamin Lee Whorf, "Language, Mind, and Reality," *Language, Thought, and Reality: Selected Writings of Benjamin Lee Whorf*, ed. John B. Carroll (New York: John Wiley, 1956), 263.
3. For more information, see Harold Goodglass and Sheila Blumstein, *Psycholinguistics and Aphasia* (Baltimore: Johns Hopkins University Press, 1973), passim.
4. In this sense, aphasia is particularly pertinent to psycholinguistics, which studies the decoding process by which messages to the brain are received and interpreted, as well as encoding processes in which the message is conceived and articulated.
5. Bernard Ohanian, "The Lost Words of Joseph Chaikin," *Hippocrates* (January/February 1989), 76.
6. Philip Reed, "Author Jean-Claude van Itallie," *Drama-Logue* 5–11 (March 1987), 5.
7. The genesis of the play began with a workshop; during October, van Itallie brought actress Rosemary Quinn and director Robert Woodruff in to work on the project. They discussed the structure of the play and how Chaikin might have a role in it. These ideas reached fruition on the boards when, during the winter of 1985, Ellen Stewart provided space for Joan Mcintosh and a few other performers to experiment with the piece. Van Itallie spent two months during summer 1985 writing *The Traveller*. A staged reading of the play was given at the River Arts Theater in Woodstock. Van Itallie was also keeping a journal of Chaikin's progress during his recovery; some of this information would eventually be incorporated into *The Traveller*. The

role of the Traveller was originally conceived of as a female because, as van Itallie explained to me in an interview that I conducted with him on June 26, 1993, "The Traveller was a woman for a little while because we were thinking of using Joan Mcintosh, an actress that Joe and I both admire a great deal." However, when the play was later staged in Los Angeles, Joan was not able to leave her son in New York to play the role, so the Traveller became a man. The play premiered at the Mark Taper Forum in Los Angeles on March 4, 1987 and ran until April 5. Van Itallie revised *The Traveller* before it was performed at the Leicester Haymarket Theatre in Leicester, England, from September 30, 1987 to October 24; afterwards, it transferred to London's Almeida Theatre from December 8, 1987 to January 9, 1988. Van Itallie continued to revise and tighten the play. The next major draft of *The Traveller* was completed in March 1990. Two years and five months later, at the end of August 1992, van Itallie finished the final draft of the play. In this version, Aaron is a male in his mid-forties and Jed Moses, originally the Traveller's brother, is now Jodie Moses, the Traveller's sister, modeled in part upon Shami Chaikin and upon Joe's brother Ben. Van Itallie is more comfortable with this edition of the play in which he can identify with Aaron as the Traveller's friend and confidant. Obviously, this version required some rewriting during the segments between the Traveller and Aaron, but, for the most part, the August 1992 edition remains essentially the same as the March 1990 draft.

8. Steven Simmons, "Opposites Attract," *A.C.T. Preview* (Spring 1987), 6.
9. Kevin Jackson, "One From the Inferno," *Face* 90 (October 1987), 37.
10. Alexis Greene, "An Interview with Jean-Claude van Itallie," *Studies in American Drama, 1945-Present* 3 (1988), 143.
11. See Aleen Agranowitz and Milfred Riddle McKeown, *Aphasia Handbook for Adults and Children* (Springfield: Charles C. Thomas, 1964), 8.
12. See Theodore Weisenburg and Katherine E. McBride, *Aphasia: A Clinical and Psychological Study* (New York: Hafher, 1964), 19.
13. Kathryn Bernheimer, "Their Lives in Art," *Sunday Camera* (25 January 1987): 2D.
14. The reference to *New York Magazine* may not be evident to someone unfamiliar with van Itallie's theater. Van Itallie, an artist, like Daniel Moses, is taking a swipe at John Simon's vicious attacks on his plays, all of those reviews published in *New York*.
15. Jean-Claude van Itallie, *The Traveller*, unpublished manuscript, August 29, 1992, 5. Subsequent references will appear parenthetically in the text.
16. Reed, "Author Jean-Claude van Itallie," 5.
17. The origins of this archetypal quest derive from van Itallie's interests in fairy tales, in myths discussed by Joseph Campbell in his books, and in Tibetan lore.
18. Handke's play goes one step further than *The Traveller* by suggesting that language can also brainwash people, destroying their individuality. The prompters manipulate Kaspar into sounding like everyone else. Kaspar becomes an automaton, a cipher reciting the inanities espoused by the Other. In this sense, *Kaspar* is similar to Ionesco's *La Cantatrice chauve* in which the Smiths and Martins recite nonsense language without any meaning, almost as if they were mouthing cliches that they frequently have heard others speak.
19. Gene A. Plunka, interview with Jean-Claude van Itallie, June 26, 1993, Rowe, Massachusetts.
20. Doris Auerbach, *Sam Shepard, Arthur Kopit, and the Off Broadway Theater* (Boston: Twayne, 1982), 105–106.

21. Margot Anne Kelley, "Order Within Fragmentation: Postmodernism and the Stroke Victim's World," *Modern Drama* 34, no. 3 (1991), 390.
22. Susan Yankowitz, "Introduction and Dedication," *Night Sky* (London: Samuel French, 1997), [unpaginated]. All subsequent citations are from this edition and are included within parentheses in the text.

WORKS CITED

Agranowitz, Aleen and Milfred Riddle McKeown. *Aphasia Handbook for Adults and Children.* Springfield: Charles C. Thomas, 1964.

Auerbach, Doris. *Sam Shepard, Arthur Kopit, and the Off Broadway Theater.* Boston: Twayne, 1982.

Bernheimer, Kathryn. "Their Lives in Art." *Sunday Camera* (25 January 1987).

Goodglass, Harold and Sheila Blumstein. *Psycholinguistics and Aphasia.* Baltimore and London: Johns Hopkins University Press, 1973.

Greene, Alexis. "An Interview with Jean-Claude van Itallie." *Studies in American Drama, 1945-Present* 3 (1988).

Jackson, Kevin. "One From the Inferno." *Face* 90 (October 1987).

Kelley, Margot Anne. "Order Within Fragmentation: Postmodernism and the Stroke Victim's World." *Modern Drama* 34, no. 3 (1991).

Ohanian, Bernard. "The Lost Words of Joseph Chaikin." *Hippocrates.* January/February 1989.

Plunka, Gene A. Interview with Jean-Claude van Itallie. Rowe, Massachusetts (26 June 1993).

Reed, Philip. "Author Jean-Claude van Itallie." *Drama-Logue* 5, no. 11 (March 1987).

Simmons, Steven. "Opposites Attract." *A.C.T. Preview* (Spring 1987).

Van Itallie, Jean-Claude. *The Traveller.* Unpublished Manuscript (29 August 1992).

Weisenburg, Theodore and Katherine E. McBride. *Aphasia: A Clinical and Psychological Study.* New York: Hafner, 1964.

Whorf, Benjamin Lee. "Language, Mind, and Reality." *Language, Thought, and Reality: Selected Writings of Benjamin Lee Whorf,* edited by John B. Carroll. New York: John Wiley, 1956.

Wittgenstein, Ludwig. *Prototractatus.* Translated by D.F. Pears and B.F. McGuinness. Ithaca: Cornell University Press, 1971.

Yankowitz, Susan. "Introduction and Dedication." *Night Sky.* London: Samuel French, 1997.

8 The Poetics of Tourette's Syndrome
Language, Neurobiology, and Poetry

Ronald Schleifer

The "I" of the lyricist . . . sounds from the depth of his being: its "subjectivity" in the sense of modern aestheticians is a fiction.

—Friedrich Nietzsche, *The Birth of Tragedy*

The neural bases of human language are intertwined with other aspects of cognition, motor control, and emotion.

—Philip Lieberman, *Human Language and our Reptilian Brain*

In this chapter, I want to examine the relationship of poetry to the neurobiological condition known as Tourette's Syndrome. Tourette's syndrome is clearly an organic condition that involves, among other symptoms, the seeming emotion-charged use of language, the spouting forth of obscene language that, as researchers note, "may represent," among other symptoms, "a common clinical expression of underlying central nervous system dysfunction."[1] The uncanny verbalizations of Tourette's, as David Morris has argued, are apparently connected "to subcortical structures [of the brain] that permit them to tumble out unbidden, like a shout or cry."[2] Poetry also, in the description of the semiotician A. J. Greimas, attempts to create the "meaning-effect" of a "primal cry," an "illusory signification of a 'deep meaning,' hidden and inherent in the plane of expression," in the very sounds of language.[3] Language, as neuroanatomy has demonstrated, involves various regions of the brain, especially Broca's area in the frontal region of the neocortex and Wernicke's area in the posterior area of the cortex. Both the cortex and neocortex have been consistently associated with more abstract modes of reasoning.[4] But subcortical regions of the brain, especially the thalamus, the hypothalamus, the amygdala, and the basal ganglia—regions that have been called our "reptilian brain" since humans and other primates inherit them from earlier and less complex life forms—have also been associated with language.[5] Studies in experimental neurobiology have closely correlated these areas of the "reptilian" or "old brain" with motor activity, basic instincts, and emotions.

Poetry, I am contending, in its more or less intentional and willful activity, calls upon all of these neurological resources of language—so that in poetry, as in the neurobiology of language more generally, the strict distinction between language and motor activities is less and less apposite. This contention, I believe, is illuminated by an examination of Tourette's syndrome in its more or less unintentional and impulsive activity. Just as the facial tattoos of Maori warriors create the "effect" of the facial signaling of aggression, which is part of the behaviors of many primate species and has clearly been associated with cortical and subcortical regions of the brain (especially the amygdala, the seat of emotions in primates containing what researchers describe as "face-responsive [neuronal] cells"), so poetry creates the effect of the vocal signalings of primates, which, it seems clear, manifest themselves involuntarily in Tourette's syndrome.[6] In this chapter, I argue that the conventions and resources of poetry and of what Roman Jakobson calls the "poetic function" of literary language more generally— fascinations with the sounds and rhythms of language, with rhymes and repetitions, with its chants and interpersonal powers—haunt the terrible and involuntary utterances of Tourette's syndrome in its powerful connections between motor activity and phonic activity.[7]

But before I begin in earnest, let me make clear what I am *not* doing. I do not want to suggest that Tourette's syndrome is not a terrible ailment, occasioning powerful distress and appalling disruptions in people's lives. Oliver Sacks makes this clear in his book *Awakenings*, in which he describes the "immense variety of involuntary and compulsive movements [that] were seen" in post-encephalitic patients after they were treated with L-DOPA, including virtually all of the involuntary and compulsive symptoms of Tourette's syndrome I will describe in a moment.[8] Describing these symptoms shared by his patients and people suffering from Tourette's syndrome, Sacks quotes a line from Thom Gunn's poem "The Sense of Movement": "One is always nearer by not being still." "This poem," Sacks writes, "deals with the basic *urge* to *move*, a movement which is always, mysteriously *towards*" (my italics). This is not so, he says, for the patients he encounters: they are "*no* nearer for not being still. [They are] no nearer to anything by virtue of [their] motion; and in this sense, [their] motion is not genuine movement."[9] In the same way, the motor/phonic symptoms of Tourette's I describe do *not* constitute poetry: the language uttered by people who have Tourette's may no more resemble poetry than their involuntary movements resemble pantomime. But the powerful connections between linguistic and motor activity—between the meanings and materialities of discourse exhibited in the meaningless rhymes, rhythms, and invectives of Tourette's—manifest, I believe, the fact that the sources and resources of poetry are seated deeply within our primate brains.

PART ONE

Let me begin, then, by quoting Sacks's elegant description of Tourette's syndrome he wrote several decades after the first edition of *Awakenings*:

In 1885, Gilles de la Tourette, a pupil of Charcot, described the astonishing syndrome which now bears his name. 'Tourette's syndrome', as it was immediately dubbed, is characterised by an excess of nervous energy, and a great production and extravagance of strange motions and notions: tics, jerks, mannerisms, grimaces, noises, curses, involuntary imitations and compulsions of all sorts, with an odd elfin humour and a tendency to antic and outlandish kinds of play. In its 'highest' forms, Tourette's syndrome involves every aspect of the affective, the instinctual and the imaginative life; in its 'lower', and perhaps commoner, forms, there may be little more than abnormal movements and impulsivity, though even here there is an element of strangeness. . . . It was clear to Tourette, and his peers, that this syndrome was a sort of possession by primitive impulses and urges: but also that it was a possession with an organic basis—a very definite (if undiscovered) neurological disorder.[10]

Tourette's syndrome, Sacks noted a few years later in *An Anthropologist on Mars*, is "characterized, above all, by convulsive tics, by involuntary mimicry or repetition of others' words or actions (echolalia and ecopraxia), and by the involuntary or compulsive utterances of curses and obscenities (coprolalia)" leading some to "strange, often witty" associations, others to "a constant testing of physical and social boundaries," and still others to "a constant, restless reacting to the environment, a lunging at and sniffing of everything or a sudden flinging of objects."[11] As this suggests, Tourette's syndrome inhabits the juncture between biological formations and cultural formations, between the motor tics of Tourette's syndrome—squinting, tapping, arm waving, sticking out the tongue, even licking objects—and its phonic tics—clearing the throat, sniffing, barking, repeating verbal sounds, rhymes, puns, shouting obscenities. There is a strange energy to Tourette's syndrome that Sacks describes throughout his work and that, as I will display later in this chapter, Jonathan Lethem embodies in his recent novel, *Motherless Brooklyn*.

What fascinates me about this syndrome—as it does Sacks, Lethem, and even David Morris in his powerful study of late twentieth-century illness, *Illness and Culture in the Postmodern Age*—is the continuity it presents between motor and verbal activity. The latest experimental work on the neurology of language, as outlined in Philip Lieberman's remarkable book, *Human Language and Our Reptilian Brain*, argues forcefully and persuasively for tight connections between motor activity and language skills by focusing on the seat of vertebrate motor activity in the subcortical basal ganglia.[12] Lieberman cites studies that suggest that "the cerebellum and basal ganglia should no longer be considered as purely motor structures" but instead involved "in cognitive processes"; he even suggests that the evolution of hominid upright walking is closely connected to the evolution of language.[13] This connection between body and language—between seemingly immaterial cognitive activity and our bodily life—is under-lined in Tourette's syndrome (even though Lieberman doesn't mention it) which, by definition, essentially combines, in the words of a handbook on Tourette's, "the presence of multiple motor tics (twitches) and one or more vocal tics (or noises)."[14]

At least since the Enlightenment, the connection between body and spirit has often been denied. In a defining instance, René Descartes argued that language is the very sign of the immaterial soul in humankind and that automatic, mechanical phonic responses to experience, were they possible, would have nothing to do with meaningful language or meaningful ges-ture. "We can certainly conceive of a machine so constructed," Descartes wrote in the *Discourse on Method*, "that it utters words . . . if you touch it in one spot [and] if you touch it in another it cries out that you are hurting it," but "it is not conceivable that such a machine should produce different arrangements of words so as to give an appropriately meaningful answer to whatever is said in its presence, as the dullest of men can do."[15] Like Des-cartes's machine, tics of Tourette's syndrome, whether they are phonic or motor, respond to the world in a machine-like way without presenting any of the "appropriately meaningful" responses that Descartes describes.

Yet the tics of Tourette's syndrome convey meaning and provoke responses that raise questions about the ways in which the "appropriate-ness" of response is measured and the ways in which the materialities and meanings of discourse are bound together. "Tics," Sacks argues,

> can have an ambiguous status, partway between meaningless jerks or noises and meaningful acts. Though the tendency to tic is innate in Tourette's, the particular *form* of tics often has a personal or historical origin. Thus a name, a sound, a visual image, a gesture, perhaps seen years before and forgotten, may first be unconsciously echoed or imi-tated and then preserved in the stereotypic form of a tic.[16]

In a more scientific discourse, James Leckman and Donald Cohen describe "severe tic disorder as a model neuropsychiatric disorder that exists at the interface of mind and body."[17] Sacks's narrative descriptions in "Witty, Ticcy Ray" and "A Surgeon's Life," Leckman and Cohen's scientific accounts, and Jonathan Lethem's first-person novelistic treatment offer a wide array of discussions of Tourette's syndrome and allow for its being taken up, like the sounds of language themselves, to a host of differing ends. Tourette's syndrome, then, situated "partway between meaningless jerks or noises and meaningful acts" at the "interface of mind and body," seems to take up the very materiality of language and underlines its materiality even as it also preserves it *as* language. Thus Dr. Carl Bennett, the subject of Sacks's most recent essay on Tourette's, "A Surgeon's Life," notes that "it is just the sound [of particular words] that attracts me. Any odd sound, any odd name, may start repeating itself, get me going." "Echolalia," Sacks goes on, "freezes sounds, arrests time, preserves stimuli as 'foreign bodies' or echoes in the mind, maintaining an alien existence, like implants. It is only the sound of the words, their 'melody,' as Bennett says, that implants them in his mind; their origins and meanings and associations are irrelevant."[18]

Such frozen and arrested sound is a resource for poetry, its rhymes, alliteration, its "melody," even (or especially) the odd sense of the impersonalness of its most intimate references. Nietzsche's *The Birth of Tragedy*, as I suggest in my first epigraph, offers a fine meditation on the impersonalness of lyric poetry.[19] Nietzsche repeatedly associates lyric poetry with "primordial" existence and even the "primal cry" that Greimas mentions. In Dionysian art, he writes, "we are pierced by the maddening sting" of the pains of "primordial being itself,"

> just when we have become, as it were, one with the infinite primordial joy in existence, and when we anticipate, in Dionysian ecstasy, the indestructibility and eternity of this joy. In spite of fear and pity, we are the happy living beings, not as individuals, but as the *one* living being, with whose creative joy we are united.[20]

Nietzsche came to disavow the exuberance of this writing, but what I want to suggest is that the impersonal energies he sees called upon and transformed in lyric and tragedy may well be connected to primordial, "reptilian" brain structures. Gilles Deleuze describes a version of this impersonalness in Nietzsche when he argues that, for Nietzsche, "a phenomenon is not an appearance or even an apparition but a sign, a symptom which finds its meaning in an existing force. The whole of philosophy is a symptomatology, and a semeiology."[21] It is the genius of art to apprehend impersonal phenomena—perhaps even unintentional phenomena—as meaningful. Similarly, Sacks argues in the 1982 Epilogue to *Awakenings* that "Nietzsche, almost alone of philosophers, sees philosophy as grounded in our understanding (or misunderstanding) of the body, and so looks to the ideal of the Philosophic Physician."[22] Thus Nietzsche describes "the catharsis of Aristotle" as a "pathological discharge" which philologists are not sure "should be included [either] among medical or moral phenomena."[23] While I do not argue that poetry is in any way an "impersonal" medical condition, the physiological condition of Tourette's syndrome sheds light upon its working and its power.

A striking example, that makes the seeming unintentional impersonalness of meaning and poetry its very theme, is D.H. Lawrence's poem, "Tortoise Shout." This poem articulates the sexual cry of a male tortoise, its "tortoise eternity, / Age-long, reptilian persistence."[24] Before offering a Lawrentian baroque sexual allegory, the poem reduces itself, so to speak, to sounds that are almost unintelligible, "This last / Strange, faint coition yell / Of the male tortoise at extremity, / Tiny from under the very edge of the farthest far-off horizon of life."[25]

A far, was-it-audible scream,
Or did it sound on the plasm direct?

Worse than the cry of the new-born,
A Scream,
A yell,
A shout,
A paean,
A death-agony,
A birth-cry,
A submission,
All tiny, tiny, far away, reptile under the first dawn.[26]

"The Tortoise Shout" is attempting to articulate—or, at least to describe—
"deep," primordial meaning, a primal reptilian cry.

PART TWO

Here, then, is precisely my thesis: that resources of language most starkly
apprehensible in the extremity and dysfunctionality of Tourette's syndrome
are a source of much of poetry's power. More specifically, human language,
as Lieberman contends, "is overlaid on sensorimotor systems that originally
evolved to do other things and continue to do them now," and that poetry
calls upon all the resources of what he calls the "functional language system," based upon the subcortical or the "reptilian" brain as well as the
neocortex, to achieve its power and its meanings.[27] To make this argument,
I want to reiterate Greimas's semiotic description of poetry. Greimas has
noted that "at the moment of perception" a listener eliminates "about 40%
of the redundancies of the distinctive phonological features unnecessary for
the apprehension of meaning."[28] "Inversely," he argues, "the reception of
the poetic message can be interpreted as the valorization of redundancies
which become significative with the changing of the level of perception,
valorization which would give rise to the apprehension of regularities . . . of
sound, of connotation as it were, and not only of denotation."[29] By "valorization" Greimas means that superfluous redundancies of sound—but also
redundancies of grammar or even semantics—come to constitute a level of
meaning or a "meaning-effect" rather than simply a vehicle for meaning
that can be eliminated once meaning is communicated. Such "meaning-effects" are the *phenomena* of meaning: the felt sense of comprehension, the
signifying whole beyond the individual elements of a sentence, for instance,
or the logic of an argument, the genre of an extended discourse, the moral
of a tale.[30] But the phenomena of meaning-effects include other "felt senses"
discourse provokes, such as sadness, anxiety, fear, joy.[31] And poetry, Greimas is arguing, creates or provokes all of these effects by taking up and

using—in Sacks's language, by freezing and arresting—the "disposable" material redundancies of language in ways that make them essential.

This description of poetry, emphasizing as it does the phenomenal *materiality* of language, is at odds with the traditional opposition between matter and spirit. Again, Descartes makes this clear when he notes that, "it may happen that we hear an utterance whose meaning we understand perfectly well, but afterwards we cannot say in what language it was spoken."[32] In *The World* he uses this example to argue for a mechanical description of light:

> if words, which signify nothing except by human convention, suffice to make us think of things to which they bear no resemblance, then why should nature not also have established some sign which would make us have the sensation of light, even if the sign contained nothing in itself which is similar to this sensation? Is it not thus that nature has established laughter and tears, to make us read joy and sadness on the faces of men?[33]

Descartes's subject reads rather than participates in emotion: language is always a vehicle for meaning, never a provocation, a meaning-effect.

Moreover, his reference to the "joy and sadness on the faces of men" is particularly apt because it is probable that the neurobiology of emotions—which include joy, sadness, and a seemingly innate ability of primates to respond to faces—is closely connected to the strength and strange fascination of Tourette's syndrome,[34] its *situation* at the juncture of motor and verbal resources, between the intentional verbal meanings of discourse and its seeming unintended force. That is, in its combinations of motor and phonic tics Tourette's syndrome uncovers redundancies that are often ignored. Lionel Essrog, the Tourettic narrator of Jonathan Lethem's novel *Motherless Brooklyn*, says as much: "Tourette's teaches you what people will ignore and forget, teaches you to see the reality-knitting mechanism people employ to tuck away the intolerable, the incongruous, the disruptive—it teaches you this because you're the one lobbing the intolerable, incongruous, and disruptive their way."[35]

Early in the novel, Essrog introduces himself in ways that demonstrate how Tourette's syndrome seems to depend upon and emphasize (if not valorize) the materiality of language:

> Lionel, my name. Frank and the Minna Men pronounced it to rhyme with *vinyl*. Lionel Essrog. *Line-all.*
> Liable Guesscog.
> Final Escrow.
> Ironic Pissclam.
> And so on.
> My own name was the original verbal taffy, by now stretched to filament-thin threads that lay all over the floor of my echo-chamber skull. Slack, the flavor all chewed out of it.[36]

"Filament thin threads." There is a strange hauntingness of the phonological and metaphorical language here: even the extended metaphor of "taffy" possesses a filament-thin materiality, and its combination of slackness and flavorlessness in the context of the almost metaphysical wittiness of the conceit presents almost intolerable incongruity.

These aspects of Tourette's syndrome—its hovering between meaning and meaninglessness in the sounds and meanings of language, its revelations of the "reality-knitting" aspects of discourse, its playfulness and wit, its pathos and bathos—all these things, as Greimas says, are what poetry does as well, are sources and resources for poetry. "What is common to all [poetic] phenomena," he argues in a precise semiotic description,

> is the shortening of the distance between the signifier and the signified: one could say that poetic language, while remaining part of language, seeks to reachieve the 'primal cry,' and thus is situated midway between simple articulation and a linguistic double articulation. It results in a 'meaning-effect' . . . which is that of 'rediscovered truth' which is original and originary. . . . It is [an] illusory signification of a 'deep meaning', hidden and inherent in the [phonological] plane of expression . . . [37]

The double articulation of language *is* the opposition between material signifier and immaterial signified, between the "distinctive phonological features" Greimas describes and the semantic wholes apprehended as meaning that do not seem, phenomenally, reducible to any part or even any precise combinations of parts.[38] Poetry, in this definition, attempts to create the illusion, the "meaning-effect," that the signifier of the symbolic and communicative system of language becomes what cognitive neuroscience calls the "vocal signals" of primates.[39] The "vocal signals" neuroscience describes, even when they make possible or manifest primate social organization, are themselves not structures of communication. They are "primal cries" in which the distance between signifier and signified, between sound and import, does not exist. Unlike the language Descartes describes in *The World*, the import of a vocal signal cannot "eliminate" its material manifestation, the mechanical signals of primates.

In important ways the phonic tics of Tourette's syndrome seem to be *simply* mechanical, self-stimulating vocal signals. The fact that in clinical trials three decades ago both motor and phonic tics were suppressed by dopamine-blocking drugs—haloperidol, in early instances—suggests its mechanical nature.[40] Indeed, as Leckman, Riddle, and Cohen note,

> the basal ganglia and the substantia nigra are widely considered to be the neuroanatomical regions associated with a variety of movement disorders including Parkinson's disease, encephalitis lethargica, Huntington's disease, and tardive dykinesia. Although the neuropathological

correlates of TS remain to be fully established, the presence of abnormal movements in TS, suggestive neuropathological data, and a substantial body of pharmacological and metabolic data implicating neurochemical systems localized in these regions have led to the hypothesis that the pathophysiology of TS and related disorders may involve some dysfunction of these areas.[41]

Here, as in the neurobiology of emotion—which is, like Tourette's syndrome, associated with subcortical regions of the brain—Tourette's syndrome seems to realize itself in relation to what has been called our "reptilian brain." Tourette's syndrome, Sacks writes, like,

> Parkinsonism and chorea, reflects what Pavlov called 'the blind force of the subcortex,' a disturbance of those primitive parts of the brain. . . . In Tourette's, where there is excitement of the emotions and the passions, a disorder of the primal, instinctual bases of behaviour, the disturbance seems to lie in the very highest parts of the 'old brain': the thalamus, hypothalamus, limbic system and amygdala, where the basic affective and instinctual determinants of personality are lodged.[42]

Echoing, repetition, puns, punctuated language—erasing in its barks and noises the distance between the signifier and signified even as it excites the emotions and passions: this description of Tourette's might help us to see some of the resources of language poetry attempts to "reachieve."

The most well-known aspect of Tourette's, its coprolalic barking of obscenities, is tied up with the materiality of language—both its material soundings but also its material neuroanatomic pathways. In fact, David Morris has argued that, in important ways "midbrain and limbic structures [function] in the control of obscene words."[43] In this argument, Morris assumes that cognitive/expressive language *simply* originates in the neocortex and, for that reason, is distinctly "human." "Human speech," he writes, "however it developed during the long history of evolution, did *not* develop from the cries and vocalizations of nonhuman primates. Human speech differs fundamentally from animal cries in the sense that it proceeds from an entirely different region of the brain."[44] Certainly neurological studies have shown, as both Lieberman and Deacon note, that "neocortical areas do not appear to regulate voluntary vocalizations in nonhuman primates; neither cortical lesions nor stimulations affects their vocalizations."[45] And more strikingly, Jane Goodall observes that "chimpanzee vocalizations are closely bound to emotion. The production of a sound in the *absence* of the appropriate emotional state seems to be an almost impossible task for a chimpanzee."[46]

But, as might already be clear, I am suggesting that Morris is not altogether correct in his contention that all speech differs simply and fundamentally from the primal cries of primates.[47] In fact, even Morris suggests some aspects of primal discourse inhabit language when he cites studies that demonstrate that "aphasias that cripple or destroy normal speech, leaving patients unable to talk or write, sometimes preserve untouched the ability to swear like a sailor," and he goes on to argue that "an obscenity, after all, is more like a cry than a word. Or rather, it belongs to a special class of words that serve as the direct expression of emotion."[48] A friend and brilliant scholar who suffers from Tourette's has warned me not to romanticize Tourette's syndrome in the ways that R. D. Laing romanticized schizophrenia a generation ago. Morris, in this passage, comes close to such romanticization insofar as he is suggesting that the tics of Tourette's are interpersonally expressive. There is, as Morris says, a class of words that serve in powerful ways to express emotion, but their use—or really "mention"—in Tourette's syndrome is not expressive even if they can create the "effect" of expression. Still, the phonic "mention" in Tourette's of sounds which function in verbal "use" most forcefully juxtaposes the biological and cultural formations inhabiting language which I mentioned earlier.[49] In his study, Morris argues that "the obscene achieves its apparently ineradicable place by weaving together powerful elements of our biology, psychology, and social life."[50] These "weavings" involve "old brain" subcortex as well as the neocortex, including the basal ganglia that Lieberman argues constitutes an essential part of the functional language system, and together—as elements of biology, psychology, and social life—they serve poetry.

Finally, the tics of Tourette's syndrome, both motor and phonic, are closely associated with obsessive-compulsive behavior.[51] Such behavior blurs or suspends the opposition between intentional and involuntary actions insofar as it shapes itself in relation to context.[52] A host of scientific studies have demonstrated that 10 to 40 percent of patients subject to tic disorders "report *obsessional thoughts* and exhibit *compulsive behaviors*," and Sacks's case histories also make this abundantly clear, as does Lethem's powerful fictional portrayal of Tourette's.[53] As I already suggested, the verbal manifestations of Tourette's are often context sensitive, taking the form of repetition of sounds including echolalia, but also palilalia, "the repetition of the patient's own last word, phrase, or syllable," and, as both Sacks and Lethem portray, they often take the forms of verbal rhymes and puns.[54] Neurobiologists suggest that obsessive-compulsive behavior may be closely connected to grooming behavior in other mammals, and Lieberman argues that such behavior—regulated in the subcortical basal ganglia—is parallel to the syntax of language.[55] Thus, the very neurobiology of language—including "phylogenetically 'primitive' neuroanatomical structures found in the brains of 'lower' animals, such as the cerebellum and basal ganglia"—suggests the opposition between the intentional activities of mind and the automatic activities of body is more complicated than we thought.[56] Terrence Deacon notes that "even for humans, the essentially automatic and unconscious nature of many stereotypic calls ["primal cries"] causes them to erupt without warning, often before there is time to interfere with their expression. . . . This curious conflict between simultaneously produced intentional and unintentional behaviors offers a unique insight into the nature of language. The superimposition of intentional cortical motor behaviors over autonomous subcortical vocal behaviors is, in a way, an externalized model of a neural relationship that is internalized in the production of human speech."[57] This conflict is present, in notably different ways, in Tourette's syndrome and in poetry.

PART THREE

That is, even if Tourette's syndrome arises from biological grounds, it involves, as Morris suggests, elements of psychology and social life as well. Sacks notes that, in the momentary freedom from Tourette's syndrome when Dr. Bennett's performs surgery, "one is seeing something at a much higher level than the merely rhythmic, quasi-automatic resonance of the motor patterns; one is seeing (however it is to be defined in psychic or neural terms) a fundamental act of incarnation or personation, whereby the skills, the feelings, the entire neural engrams of another self, are taking over in the brain, redefining the person, his whole nervous system, as long as the performance lasts."[58] Sacks is talking about the ways in which Tourette's seems to be "suspended," momentarily, by rhythmic activity in general and, in this specific case, by the art of surgery. In "Witty, Ticcy Ray" he presents Tourette's in the opposite fashion, when he quotes Ray claiming that he can't imagine his life without his tic: "I consist of tics," he says, "—there is nothing else."[59] "He said," Sacks concludes, "he could not imagine life without Tourette's, nor was he sure he would care for it."[60] In both these cases Sacks is depicting what the neurologists Cohen, Bruun, and Leckman describe in the "Preface" to *Tourette's Syndrome and Tic Disorders: Clinical Understanding and Treatment*. Tourette's syndrome, they say, "affects individuals at the core of their experience of themselves as being in control of their own movements, statements, and thoughts."[61] At the heart of this "core" is language. Tourette's syndrome affects this core as it manifests a kind of "material language" in relation to what Sacks describes as "selfness" and its connection to the seeming intentionality of language. It is "often difficult for Touretters," Sacks writes, "to see their Tourette's as something external to themselves, because many of its tics and urges may be felt as intentional, as an integral part of the self, the personality, the will."[62] Early in *Motherless Brooklyn* Lethem describes the progression from early motor tics in patients suffering from Tourette's syndrome to phonic tics.[63] For a time, Lionel's ticcing took the form of kissing the other boys in the Brooklyn orphanage. "The kissing cycle was mercifully brief," he writes.

> I found other outlets, other obsessions. . . . [Instead, I was] prone to floor-tapping, whistling, tongue-clicking, winking, rapid head turns, and

wall-stroking, anything but the direct utterances for which my particular Tourette's brain most yearned. Language bubbled inside me now, the frozen sea melting, but it felt too dangerous to let out. Speech was intention, and I couldn't let anyone else or myself know how intentional my craziness felt. Pratfalls, antics—those were accidental lunacy, and more or less forgivable. Practically speaking, it was one thing to stroke Leshawn Montrose's arm or even kiss him, another entirely to walk up and call him Shefawn Mongoose, or Lefthand Moonprose, of Fuckyou Roseprawn.[64]

Lionel's description of unwilled intention, so to speak, is the problem of Tourette's and, in a way, the problem of poetry. Words call themselves forth by sound and rhythm, by their performability, that—however "crazy" they seem—*feels* intentional.

In "Tradition and the Individual Talent" T.S. Eliot describes "the bad poet" as one who "is usually unconscious where he ought to be conscious, and conscious where he ought to be unconscious. Both errors tend to make him 'personal.'"[65] Another way to say this is to describe poetry as the articulation of the kind of language I have been describing throughout this: the *material* articulations of language that gather up the power and emotions of seeming subcortical primal cries within its discourses. "T.S. Eliot." Neuroscientists repeatedly abbreviate Tourette's syndrome as "TS." Could there be a link here? If there is, such a link is "Tourettic": it traffics in the materiality of language, making material *sound* intentional and meaningful, making impulse seem conscious. That is, the mechanical echoings, repetitions, rhythms, and emotionally-charged phonic tics of TS present themselves as meaningful sounds and, as perhaps obscenities themselves do, trigger or are simply associated with more or less automatic emotional responses. Behind this "link" between the sounds and energies of poetry and discourse is the assumption that lyric poetry does not only—or does not simply—"express" the poet, but that it also articulates what I described earlier in relation to Nietzsche as "impersonal energies," articulations which are *apprehended* in particular conscious and unconscious manners.[66]

This is, I believe, at least a part of what Eliot—and in their different ways Nietzsche and Lawrence—mean by "impersonal" poetry, and what Lethem repeatedly figures in *Motherless Brooklyn* as the "boiling" of language. "Beneath that frozen shell of sea," Lionel says,

a sea of language was reaching full boil. It became harder and harder not to notice that when a television pitchman said *to last the rest of a lifetime* my brain went *to rest the lust of a loaftomb*, that when I heard "Alfred Hitchcock," I silently replied "Altered Houseclock" or "Ilford Hotchkiss . . ."[67]

Language boils in poetry. Listen, for instance, to T.S. Eliot's "Ash Wednesday":

If the lost word is lost, if the spent word is spent
If the unheard, unspoken
Word is unspoken, unheard;
Still is the unspoken word, the Word unheard,
The Word without a word, the Word within
The world and for the world;
And the light shone in darkness and
Against the Word the unstilled world still whirled
About the centre of the silent Word.
   O my people, what have I done unto thee.[68]

All the material resources of poetry are here: rhymes, alliteration, repetition, the puns of *rime riche*, unmarked quotation, incantation that almost barks. Signifier and signified approach one another to the point of signal, to the point of primal cry: "the Word without a word, the Word within / The world and for the world." In this poetry an insistent material discourse pushes, almost Tourettically, towards a word without a word within the world whirling and still.

In the passage from "Ash Wednesday," for instance, Eliot gathers together the energies of language to make the unheard word whirl the world provokingly, startlingly, affectingly. "Tics," Sacks says, "are like hieroglyphic, petrified residues of the past and may, indeed, with the passage of time become so hieroglyphic, so abbreviated, as to become unintelligible (as 'God be with you' was condensed, collapsed, after centuries, to the phonetically similar but meaningless 'goodbye')."[69] Hugh Kenner describes the mechanism by which the signifiers of what he calls "post-Symbolist" poetry float, tic-like, above meaning. Citing a couplet from Shakespeare's *Cymbeline*, "Golden lads and girls all must / As chimney-sweepers, come to dust," he describes the "magic" that "irradiates the stanza" so that "we, the heirs of Mallarmé and Valéry and Eliot, do not simply pass over 'golden' but find it richly Shakespearean." Moreover, he goes on to describe what Sacks would call the hieroglypic abbreviations of this poetry: he notes that in Shakespeare's Warwickshire "golden boys" are the name for dandelions, and they are called "chimney-sweepers" when they go to seed. "We may want to say," he argues, "that Shakespeare wrote about happenings in the world, the world that contains mortal men and sunlight and dandelions, and that a post-Symbolist reading converts his work into something that happens in the language, where 'golden' will interact with 'dust' and 'wages' and 'lads' and 'girls' and 'chimney-sweepers,' and where 'dust' rhymes with 'must,' mortality with necessity."[70]

Greimas describes the phenomena of modern poetry very much in these terms: modern poetry aims, he argues, at "'abolishing syntax,' that is to say, diminishing as much as possible the number of functional messages" in order to iterate "a certain number of semic categories" which constitute poetic communication.[71] For Greimas, the "semic categories" are the "distinctive features" of meaning or semantics parallel in organization to the distinctive phonological features I cited him mentioning earlier. Semic categories, he argues, "probably contain the universals of language," by which he means categories organizing experience shared by all people.[72] Many of these categories—of spatial relationships, of emotional response to experience, of motor balance in the world—neurology suggests, depend in important degree to subcortical regions of the brain. And many of them are mimicked, disrupted, incongruously enacted in the motor and phonic symptoms of Tourette's syndrome.[73] In Greimas's analysis, then, modern poetry aims at creating a semantics that is seemingly without syntax, which is to say a semantics in which the opposition between word and thing— between the two articulations of language or between the opposition of linguistic and motor activity—pushes towards the "rediscovered truth" of a simple rather than a double articulation.

The verbal tics of Tourette's syndrome are, like the modern poetry both Kenner and Greimas describe (in their remarkably different idioms), something that happens in the language that disrupts and dislodges by means of the intolerable, incongruous, and disruptive materiality of language. Such materiality is no simple metaphor: it is literally materially inscribed within our brain structure and brain chemistry, powers we share with primates and other mammals that bubble forth to disturb and affect us in the impulsive utterances in Tourette's syndrome and that are gathered up to one degree or other in poetic discourses. Poetry enacts what I'd like to call the "intentional materiality" of discourse we can hear in Tourette's syndrome and in T.S. Eliot. Listen to the end of section V of "Ash Wednesday" (earlier, I cited the beginning of this section):

> Will the veiled sister between the slender
> Yew trees pray for those who offend her
> And are terrified and cannot surrender
> And affirm before the world and deny between the rocks
> In the last desert between the last blue rocks
> The desert in the garden the garden in the desert
> Of drouth, spitting from the mouth the withered apple-seed.
>   O my people.[74]

Eliot's feminine rhymes, "slender," "offend her," "surrender," slide "her," the unnamed Mary, into an unaccented schwa, an unheard word, a vocal signal. Like Lionel's "Altered Houseclock," Eliot's echoed sounds, repeated words, even the spondee of "the last blue rocks" slowing down the line, or his archaic "drouth," mispronouncing our English to rhyme with mouth, all play with sounds and meanings to create an illusion of articulated but not quite apprehensible meaning hidden and inherent in the seeming "signals" of poetry.

Such play is, of course, more than play. As Dr. Bennett told Sacks, Tourette's syndrome is not gentle. . . . You can see it as whimsical, funny—be tempted to romanticize it—but Tourette's comes from deep down in the nervous system and the unconscious. It taps into the oldest, strongest feelings we have. Tourette's is like an epilepsy of the subcortex; when it takes over, there's just a thin line of control, a thin line of cortex, between you and it, between you and that raging storm, the blind force of the subcortex. One can see the charming things, the funny things, the creative side of Tourette's, but there's also that dark side.[75]

Poetry, too, sometimes taps the oldest strongest feelings we have, even as it puts up a thin line of control. Moreover, it does so in uses of language that, again at times, picks up the *materials* of language that Tourette's articulates, cursing, rhyming, patterning discourse—above all *embodying* discourse—to provoke and arouse elements of our oldest emotional lives.

NOTES

1. Stanley Fahn and Gerald Erenberg, "Differential Diagnosis of Tic Phenomena: A Neurologic Perspective," in *Tourette's Syndrome and Tic Disorders: Clinical Understanding and Treatment*, ed. Donald Cohen, Ruth Bruun and James Leckman (New York: John Wiley & Sons, 1988), 51. For a remarkably detailed history describing the controversy of whether Tourette's syndrome is an organic or a psychogenic illness, see Kushner 1999. Kushner thoroughly examines the major scientific studies of and cultural conflicts surrounding Tourette's in the last century and concludes that "Tourette syndrome is an organic disturbance brought about by malfunctions connected with signaling in the basal ganglia." (Howard I. Kushner, *A Cursing Brain? The Histories of Tourette Syndrome* [Cambridge: Harvard University Press, 1999], 192–193).
2. David Morris, *Illness and Culture in the Postmodern Age* (Berkeley and Los Angeles: University of California Press, 1998), 170.
3. A. J. Greimas, "La linguistique structurale et la poétique," in *Du Sens* (Paris: Seuil, 1970); Cited and trans. in Ronald Schleifer, *A. J. Greimas and the Nature of Meaning* (London: Croom Helm, 1987), 152–153.
4. Chomskian linguists limit language to these areas. Thus, Steven Pinker argues that "we can narrow down our search" for the brain centers of language "by throwing away half of the brain." Steven Pinker, *The Language Instinct* (New York: Harper Perennial, 1994), 299. Others suggest that language, like many other brain functions, is a distributed network that utilizes wide areas of the brain (see Lieberman *Human Language and our Reptilian Brain: The Sybcortical Bases of Speech, Syntax, and Thought* [Cambridge: Harvard University Press, 2000], and Terrence Deacon *The Symbolic Species: The Co-Evolution of Language and the Brain* [New York: Norton, 1998]). But all agree that the cortex and neocortex are important, especially in more abstract forms of thinking: "functional magnetic resonance imaging (fMRI) data confirm the cognitive role of the dorsolateral-prefrontal-striatal circuit [the "frontal lobe"] in intact human subjects." (Lieberman, *Human Language and our Reptilian Brain*, 113; see also Deacon, *The Symbolic Species*, esp. Chapter 10; and Philip Leiberman, *Eve Spoke: Human Language and Human Evolution* [London: Picador, 1998], 70).

5. See Lieberman, *Human Language and our Reptilian Brain*.
6. Daniel McNeill, *The Face* (Boston: Little Brown, 1998), 302; John Aggleton and Andrew Young, "The Enigma of the Amygdala: On Its Contribution to Human Emotion," in *Cognitive Neuroscience of Emotion*, ed. Richard Lane and Lynn Nadel (Oxford: Oxford University Press, 2000), 113. (See also Nathan Emery and David Amaral, "The Role of the Amygdala in Primate Social Cognition," in *Cognitive Neuroscience of Emotion*, ed. Richard Lane and Lynn Nadel [Oxford: Oxford University Press, 2000] 179).
7. By "poetic function" Jakobson is describing that aspect of language which exists outside its referential, emotive, conative, communicative, and semiotic functions. He most fully describes this in "Linguistics and Poetics," where he argues that "any attempt to reduce the sphere of the poetic function to poetry or to confine poetry to the poetic function would be a delusive over-simplification." Roman Jakobson, "Linguistics and Poetics," in *Language and Literature* (Cambridge: Harvard University Press, 1987), 69. "Poetics in the wider sense of the word," he writes, "deals with the poetic function not only in poetry, where this function is superimposed upon the other functions of language, but also outside poetry, where some other function is superimposed upon the poetic function." (Jakobson, "Linguistics and Poetics," 73). Derek Attridge situates Jakobson's poetics within the opposition between conceiving poetry as functioning "to heighten attention to the meanings of words and sentences" and conceiving poetry as "a linguistic practice that specifically emphasizes the material properties of language . . . [that] provide pleasure and significance independently of cognitive content." (Derek Attridge, *Peculiar Language* [Ithaca: Cornell University Press, 1988], 130). The second of these conceptions, that of the "poetics" of the material properties of language, can be discerned in the neurobiological dysfunctions of Tourette's syndrome. In fact, many of the technical descriptions Jakobson offers as manifestations of the poetic function—including paronomasia, echo rhyme, alliteration, and, more globally, focus on syllabic phonemes, which is to say the material sounds of language–describe phonic symptoms of Tourette's syndrome. (Jakobson, "Linguistics and Poetics," 70, 73). The second of these conceptions emphasizes the reception or apprehension of poetic discourse rather than its intentional production.
8. Oliver Sacks, *Awakenings* [1990] (New York: Vintage Books, 1999). Howard Kushner identifies post-encephalic tics and those of Tourette's (Kushner, *A Cursing Brain*, 66–71). L-DOPA stimulates the production of the biochemical neurotransmitter dopamine, and drugs that suppress the symptoms of Tourette's, such as haloperidol, block dopamine.
9. Sacks, *Awakenings*, 16–17. It is notable that Gunn is describing in this poem the felt *coincidence* between semantic "sense"–the mysterious future-oriented "purport" of language that Louis Hjelmslev describes as the best definition of meaning–and physical movement, a coincidence that Tourette's, in its combinations of phonic and motor tics, clarifies by disrupting. (Louis Hjelmslev, *Prolegomena to a Theory of Language*, trans. Francis Whitfield [Madicson: University of Wisconsin Press, 1961]). Here, I need to acknowledge, and I hope to participate in, Sacks's remarkable and powerful sympathy and respect for people suffering from the "variety of involuntary and compulsive" motor and phonic tics, including people suffering from Tourette's syndrome. In *Awakenings*, but also in later essays more directly focused on Tourette's syndrome I quote throughout this chapter, Sacks, like W.H. Auden's father, Dr. G.A. Auden, does not always regard Tourette's syndrome "as purely deleterious or destructive in nature. Less zealous to 'pathologize' than many of his colleagues," Sacks observes, "Dr Auden noted that some of

those affected, especially children, might be "awakened" into a genuine (if morbid) brilliance, into unexpected and unprecedented heights and depths." (Sacks, *Awakenings*, 17). This is certainly the phenomena he describes in the two case histories of Tourette's I cite, "Witty, Ticcy Ray" (1987) and "A Surgeon's Life" (1995).

10. Oliver Sacks, *The Man who Mistook his Wife for a Hat* (New York: Harper and Row, 1987), 92.

11. Oliver Sacks, *An Anthropologist on Mars* (New York: Vintage Books, 1995), 78.

12. Lieberman argues "what is offered here is a starting point, a theory that relates phenomena that are seemingly unrelated, such as why the pattern of deficits associated with the syndrome of Broca's aphasia involves certain aspects of speech production, lexical access, and the comprehension of distinctions in meaning conveyed by syntax, why similar effects occur in Parkinson's disease, why children are able to learn language after massive cortical damage, why recovery from certain types of brain damage is problematic, and why aged people who speak slowly also have difficulty comprehending distinctions in meaning conveyed by complex syntax or long sentences." (Lieberman, *Human Language and our Reptilian Brain*, 16–17). Lieberman does not examine Tourette's syndrome, yet it seems clear that his attempt to relate "phenomena that are seemingly unrelated" helps to establish the connection between the motor and phonic tics of Tourette's syndrome. Neuroanatomical studies as well as Oliver Sacks's narrative histories argue for the connection between the complex symptoms of Tourette's and the "movement disorders" (the motor dysfunction) of Parkinson's disease. (See James Leckman, Mark Riddle, and Donald Cohen, "Pathobiology of Tourette's Syndrome," in *Tourette's Syndrome and Tic Disorders: Clinical Understanding and Treatment*, ed. Donald Cohen, Ruth Bruun, and James Leckman [New York: John Wiley & Sons, 1988], 104–105), as well as Sacks's repeated references to Tourette's in the latest revision of *Awakenings* (1999). What is striking about Tourette's is that its motor dysfunction is combined with phonic (and sometimes verbal) tics.

13. Leiberman, *Human Language and our Reptilian Brain*, 89; citing F. A. Middleton and P. L. Strick, "Anatomical Evidence for Cerebellar and Basal Ganglia Involvement in Higher Cognition," *Science* 31 (1994), 460; Lieberman, *Human Language and our Reptilian Brain*, 143, 151. (See also Damasio for an extended argument about the role "emotion, feeling, and biological regulation in human reason." Antonio Damasio, *Descartes' Error: Emotion, Reason, and the Human Brain* [New York: Avon, 1994], xiii).

14. Mary Robertson and Simon Baron-Cohen, *Tourette Syndrome: The Facts* (Oxford: Oxford University Press, 1998), 45.

15. René Descartes, *Discourse on Method* René Descartes, in *The Philosophical Writings*, trans. John Cottingham, Robert Stoothoff, and Dugald Murdoch, 3 vols. (Cambridge: Cambridge University Press, 1984–85), I.140.

16. Sacks, *Anthropologist on Mars*, 81.

17. James Leckman and Donald Cohen, "Descriptive and Diagnostic Classification of Tic Disorders," in *Tourette's Syndrome and Tic Disorders: Clinical Understanding and Treatment*, ed. Donald Cohen, Ruth Bruun, and James Leckman (New York: John Wiley & Sons, 1988), 9.

18. Sacks, *Anthropologist on Mars*, 88–89.

19. Friedrich Nietzsche, *The Birth of Tragedy and The Case of Wagner*, trans. Walter Kaufmann (New York: Vintage Books, 1967), 49.

20. Nietzsche, *The Birth of Tragedy*, 104–05.

21. Gilles Deleuze, *Nietzsche and Philosophy*, trans. Hugh Tomlinson (New York: Columbia University Press, 1983), 3.

22. Sacks, *Awakenings*, 279.

23. Nietzsche, *The Birth of Tragedy*, 132.

24. D.H. Lawrence, "Tortoise Shout," in *The Complete Poems* ed. Vivian de Sola Pinto and Warren Roberts (New York: Viking Press, 1964), 365.

25. Lawrence, "Tortoise Shout," 366.

26. Lawrence, "Tortoise Shout," 364.

27. Lieberman, *Human Language and our Reptilian Brain*, 1. (See also Lieberman, *Human Language and our Reptilian Brain*, 123, 156; and Deacon, *The Symbolic Species*, 298).

28. Lieberman describes such redundancies in discussing the difficulties of following "even 'well-formed' speech recorded under ideal conditions." "We are generally unaware of these problems," he writes, "because we 'fill in' missing information, overriding acoustic phenomena that conflict with our internally generated hypotheses concerning what was *probably* said, and the probability involves a weighting of semantic and pragmatic information derived from parallel, highly redundant processing. Many of these phenomena can be explained if we take into account the distributed, parallel processing that appears to typify biological brains." (Lieberman, *Human Language and our Reptilian Brain*, 24–25). This description takes its place within Lieberman's larger argument of the redundant and overdetermined nature of Darwinian evolution. "Indeed," he writes, "speech perception is not a strictly 'bottom-up' process in which only primary acoustic or articulatory information is available to a listener. Many studies have demonstrated that what a listener 'hears' also depends on lexical and pragmatic information." (Lieberman, *Human Language and our Reptilian Brain*, 58). Such pragmatics, he argues, is not "logical" but "proximate": "evolution is a tinkerer, adapting existing structures that enhance reproductive success in the ever-changing conditions of life." (Lieberman, *Human Language and our Reptilian Brain*, 166; see also Lieberman, *Eve Spoke*, 18–20, and Damasio, *Descartes' Error*, 190). A chief example of this aspect of his argument is what he calls "motor equivalence," "the ability of animals and humans to accomplish the same goal using different muscles or different body parts." (Lieberman, *Human Language and our Reptilian Brain*, 39). Terrence Deacon, in his richly detailed neurological study, *The Symbolic Species: The Co-Evolution of Language and the Brain*, also describes evolution as different from a simple logical hierarchy, organized around "different ways of achieving the same goal" so that "neural distribution of language functions need not parallel a linguistic analysis of those same functions." (Deacon, *The Symbolic Species*, 286).

29. A.J. Greimas, "Introduction," *Essais de Sémiotique Poétique*, ed. A.J. Greimas. Paris: Librairie Larousse, 1972; cited and trans. in Schleifer, *Greimas and the Nature of Meaning*, 152.

30. Oliver Sacks describes a similar phenomenal "signifying whole" in terms of the permanence of a biological "engram." "Many neuropsychologists," he writes, ". . . have spent their lives "in search of the Engram" [that more or less permanence-effect produced by stimulation by means of which] . . . individual skills and memories may survive massive and varied extirpations of the brain. Such experimental observations . . . indicate that one's *persona* is in no way 'localizable' in the classical sense, that it cannot be equated with any given 'center,' 'system,' 'nexus,' etc. but only with the intricate totality of the whole organism, in its ever-changing, continuously modulated, afferent-efferent relation with the world." (Sacks, *Awakenings*, 239).

31. See Schleifer, *Greimas and the Nature of Meaning*, xix.
32. Descartes, *The Philosophical Writings*, I.81.
33. Descartes, *The Philosophical Writings*, I.81
34. One of the oddest of the symptoms of Tourette's syndrome—one I return to later when I discuss the impulse to kiss other orphans that the narrator of Lethem's novel, *Motherless Brooklyn*, feels–is the urge to bite and lick things. A similar symptom (found in rhesus monkeys investigating "objects with their mouth instead of their hand") often accompanies Klüver-Bucy syndrome surgically induced in primates. This syndrome also includes "profound emotional disturbances." (Emery and Amaral, *Cognitive Neuroscience of Emotion*, 162; see also Aggleton and Young, "The Enigma of the Amygdala," 108). In fact, the Klüver-Bucy syndrome is a significant part of the evidence of the role of the subcortical amygdala in emotion (including "verbal signals" in primate mating. (Emergy and Amaral, *Cognitive Neuroscience of Emotion*, 174).
35. Lethem, *Motherless Brooklyn*, 43.
36. Lethem, *Motherless Brooklyn*, 7.
37. Greimas, "La linguistique structurale et la poétique"; cited and trans. in Schleifer, *Greimas and the Nature of Meaning*, 152–153.
38. For a short discussion of double articulation, see Ronald Schleifer, *Analogical Thinking: Post-Enlightenment Understanding in Language, Collaboration, and Interpretation* (Ann Arbor: University of Michigan Press, 2000), 55–57, 64.
39. Emergy and Amaral, *Cognitive Neuroscience of Emotion*, 174. In his translation of Saussure's *Course in General Linguistics*, Roy Harris renders *signifier* as "signal" rather than signifier. (Ferdinand de Saussure, *Course in General Linguistics*, trans. Roy Harris [La Salle, IL: Open Court Press, 1983]). This is a problem–in a translation, I should add, that vastly improves the existing one–on two levels. First is the level of culture: for decades "signifier" has been the common term, and one can hardly ignore a term's history and currency in making a translation. And second on the level of sense: Saussure's *signifier* is precisely *not* a signal insofar as it exists in a structure of double articulation.
40. See Kushner, *A Cursing Brain*, 133–143; he cites Janice R. Stevens and Paul H. Blachly, "Successful Treatment of the Maladie des Tics, Gilles de la Tourette's Syndrome," *American Journal of Diseases in Children* 112 (1966).
41. Leckman, Riddle, and Cohen, *Tourette's Syndrome and Tic Disorders*, 105.
42. Sacks *The Man who Mistook his Wife for a Hat*, 95–96.
43. Morris, *Illness and Culture in the Postmodern Age*, 174.
44. Morris, *Illness and Culture in the Postmodern Age*, 174.
45. Lieberman, *Human Language and our Reptilian Brain*, 99; he is citing P. D. MacLean and J. D Newman, "Role of Midline Frontolimbi Cortex in the Production of the Isolation Call of Squirrel Monkeys," *Brain Research*, 450 (1988), and D. Sutton and U. Jurgens, "Neural Control of Vocalization," in *Comparative Primate Biology*, ed. H. D. Stiklis and J. Erwin, Vol. 4 (New York: Arthur D. Liss, 1988). (See also Deacon, *The Symbolic Species*, 235–236).
46. Jane Goodall, *The Chimpanzees of Gombe: Patterns of Behavior* (Cambridge: Harvard University Press, 1986), 125.
47. Terrence Deacon notes that "language evolved in a parallel, alongside calls and gestures, and dependent on them—indeed, language and many human nonlinguistic forms of communication probably co-evolved. . . . This is demonstrated by the fact that innate call and gesture systems, comparable to

what are available to other primates, still exist side by side with language in us. Their complementarity with and distinction from language are exemplified by the fact that they are invariably produced by very different brain regions than are involved in speech production and language comprehension." (Deacon, *The Symbolic Species*, 54).

48. Morris, *Illness and Culture in the Postmodern Age*, 174; see also Pinker, *The Language Instinct*, 301. Morris, *Illness and Culture in the Postmodern Age*, 174.

49. For a fine discussion of the philosophical opposition between the "use" of a term in discourse and its "mention" when it is being discussed, metalinguistically, without functioning within discourse, see Jonathan Culler, "Convention and Meaning: Derrida and Austin," *New Literary History*, 13 (1983): note 11. While Culler is arguing for the deconstruction of this opposition, I employ it here to distinguish between more or less intentional "use" and unintentional "mention." Later, however, I note the manner in which behaviors that Sacks describes as "pseudo-actions" complicates the force of the Tourettic mention of obscenities (see note 74 below).

50. Morris, *Illness and Culture in the Postmodern Age*, 166.

51. See J. A. Gray, *The Neuropsychology of Anxiety: An Enquiry into the Functions of the Septo-Hippocampal System* (Oxford: Oxford University Press, 1982), 50; he cites D.L. Pauls, J.F. Leckman, K.E. Towbin, G.E.P Zahner, and D.J. Cohen, "A Possible Genetic Relationship Exists between Tourette's Syndrome and Obsessive-Compulsive Disorder," *Pschopharacology Bulletin*, 22 (1986); Kushner, *A Cursing Brain*, 205, 216.

52. Kushner, *A Cursing Brain*, 197–199. The *Diagnostical and Statistical Manual of Mental Disorders-IIIR* categorizes obsessive-compulsive behavior as "intentional": compulsions, it states, requires "representative, purposeful and intentional behavior that is performed according to certain rules or in a stereotyped fashion." (Cited in Kushner, *A Cursing Brain*, 197). This definition has generated strong disagreements concerning whether obsessive-compulsive behavior is part of Tourette's *syndrome* between those who contend that TS is *simply* organic and completely unintentional in its manifestations and those who contend it is psychogenic. Leiberman notes that "many neurological disturbances in humans (such as Parkinson's and Huntington's diseases, obsessive-compulsive behavior, depression) can be traced to disrupted basal ganglia circuits." (Lieberman, *Eve Spoke*, 106). The ability to "suspend" or postpone motor and phonic tics in response to contexts also creates the effect of blurring the opposition between intentional and unintentional behavior. (Kushner, *A Cursing Brain*, 7; see also Sacks, *The Man who Mistook his Wife for a Hat*, and Sacks, *An Anthropologist on Mars*).

53. Leckman and Cohen, *Tourette's Syndrome and Tic Disorders*, 10. (See also Kenneth Towbin, "Obsessive-Compulsive Symptoms in Tourette's Syndrome," in *Tourette's Syndrome and Tic Disorders: Clinical Understanding and Treatment*, ed. Donald Cohen, Ruth Bruun, and James Leckman [New York: John Wiley & Sons, 1988]).

54. See Kushner, *A Cursing Brain*, 2–3; Robertson and Baron-Cohen, *Tourette Syndrome*, 21; Sacks, *The Man who Mistook his Wife for a Hat*.

55. Gray, *The Neuropsychology of Anxiety*, 443; Lieberman, *Human Language and our Reptilian Brain*, 87.

56. Lieberman, *Human Language and our Reptilian Brain*, 20.

57. Deacon, *The Symbolic Species*, 244.

58. Sacks, *An Anthropologist on Mars*, 98.

59. Sacks, *The Man who Mistook his Wife for a Hat*, 98.

60. Sacks, *The Man who Mistook his Wife for a Hat*, 98.

61. Donald J. Cohen, Ruth Bruun, and James Leckman, "Preface," to *Tourette's Syndrome and Tic Disorders: Clinical Understanding and Treatment*, ed. Donald Cohen, Ruth Bruun, and James Leckman (New York: John Wiley & Sons, 1988), xiii.

62. Sacks, *An Anthropologist on Mars*, 102; see also Sacks, *Awakenings*, 109–111.

63. Clinicians note that motor tics usually start occurring at about age 7 while phonic tics usually occur between 4 and 7 years later. Ruth Bruun, "The Natural History of Tourette's Syndrome," in *Tourette's Syndrome and Tic Disorders: Clinical Understanding and Treatment*, ed. Donald Cohen, Ruth Bruun, and James Leckman (New York: John Wiley & Sons, 1988), esp. 23–25.

64. Lethem, *Motherless Brooklyn*, 47.

65. T.S. Eliot, "Tradition and the Individual Talent," in *Selected Prose*, ed. Frank Kermode (New York: Harcourt Brace Jovanovich, 1974), 43. We can provocatively compare Eliot's description of poetry to Antonio Damasio's description of cognition in an experiment designed to elicit reasoned predictions from subjects, some of whom suffer from brain damage. "I suspect that before and beneath the conscious hunch there is a nonconscious process gradually formulating a prediction for the outcome of each move, and gradually telling the mindful player, at first softly but then ever louder, that punishment or reward is about to strike *if* a certain move is indeed carried out. In short, I doubt that it is a matter of only fully conscious process, or only fully nonconscious process. It seems to take both types of processing for the well-tempered decision-making brain to operate. (Damasio, *Descartes' Error*, 214).

66. Again, this comports with the structural linguistics in the context of which Greimas and Jakobson offer their analyses of poetry. Early in his career, Greimas describes the transformation of historical to formal or structural linguistics in the twentieth century as the creation of "a linguistics of perception and not of expression." (A.J. Greimas, "La Linguistique statistique et la linguistique structural," *Le Français moderne*, 31 [1963]; cited and trans. in Schleifer, *Greimas and the Nature of Meaning*, xix). By this he means that linguistics turned to phenomenology and pursued the manner in which signification is apprehended rather than (or along with) the ways it is generated. Certainly, the language of Tourette's syndrome can be understood to be subject to a phenomenological poetics. In fact, I would suggest that a neurological examination of some of the "impersonal energies" inhabiting Tourette's syndrome particularly and language more generally lends itself nicely to a phenomenological materialism.

67. Lethem, *Motherless Brooklyn*, 46.

68. T.S. Eliot, "Ash Wednesday," in *Selected Poems* (New York: Harvest/HBJ Book, 1964), 90.

69. Sacks, *An Anthropologist on Mars*, 81.

70. (Hugh Kenner—ref details? 1971: 122, 123)

71. A.J. Greimas, *Structural Semantics*, trans. Daniele McDowell, Ronald Schleifer, and Alan Velie (Lincoln: University of Nebraska Press, 1983), 153–154.

72. A.J. Greimas and J. Courtés, *Semiotics and Language: An Analytical Dictionary*, trans. Larry Crist, Daniel Patte, and others (Bloomington: Indiana University Press, 1982), 278. For Greimas, such semantic categories, following the structures of Saussurean linguistics, are purely *relational*: in *Structural Semantics*, for instance, he "sketches" what he calls "the *semic system of spatiality*" in terms of binary oppositions. Greimas, *Structural*

Semantics, 36. (That is, he analyzes "spatiality" as consisting of "dimentionality" vs. "nondimentionality"; and "dimentionality" consisting, in turn, of "horizontality" vs. "verticality"; and "horizontality" consisting, in turn, of "perspectivity" vs. "laterality"; etc.) In a similar fashion, in an appendix to *Awakenings*, "Parkisonian Space and Time," Sacks aligns Parkinsonian experiences of time and space with Leibniz's relative conceptions of time and space as opposed to Newton's absolute conceptions, calling them "convenient (or conventional) constructions or 'models.'" (Sacks, *Awakenings*, 339). Similarly, Darwinian accounts of natural selection describe adaptive strategies as "proximate," and, like the Saussurean notion of the "arbitrary nature of the sign" or Sacks's notion of the conventionality of space-experience, as more or less "convenient." Thus, for instance, sounding a lot like Claude Lévi-Strauss, Lieberman argues that "evolution is a tinkerer, adapting existing structures that enhance reproductive success in the ever-changing conditions of life." (Lieberman, *Human Language and our Reptilian Brain*, 166). In arguing for the continuity of reason with our bodily life, Damasio also describes evolution as "thrifty and tinkering." (Damasio, *Descartes' Error*, 190).

Still, biological adaptations are not quite *purely* relational—or as *purely* non-referential–as language is sometimes described in Saussure or even Greimas. Deacon offers a finely textured account of referentiality in relation to brain function and learning. (Deacon, *The Symbolic Species*, 59–92.) Thus the "convenient" and thereby "arbitrary" nature of a primate's "normal" spatial sense, as opposed as it could be to the very different experiences of space of frogs or even dogs, is always *contingently arbitrary*: it is contingent, that is, on the "ever-changing conditions of life." (Katherine Hayles, "Constrained Constructivism: Locating Scientific Inquiry in the Theater of Representation," *New Orleans Review*, 18 [1991], 76–78). Thus, when Sacks describes the "violently deforming forces" his post-encephalitic patients are subject to that "drive" them to "misperformance and miscognition" in experiences in which "normal" spatial and temporal relationship do not function, those "universals" of spatial and temporal apprehension–the "universals" of meaning, experience, and language–are governed by contingent adaptive needs particular to primates. (Sacks, *Awakenings*, 344–345; see also Sacks's discussion of spatial experience for people with Tourette's in *An Anthropologist from Mars*, 83). "Eating fruit," Emery and Amaral argue,

> is a relatively simple task for most primates. Good color vision is required to locate specific types of fruit and to assess the level of ripeness or toxins that may be present. Olfaction and taste are also important indicators of the palatability of food. Highly distributed resources such as ripe fruit require a highly developed spatial memory system to remember where a previously encountered desirable or plentiful food source is located within a forest environment. A fine level of dexterity may be required to reach fruits in the high branches of trees, and fine manipulative ability may be required for removing the skin and seeds of some fruits. (Emery and Amaral, "The Role of the Amygdala," 170)

Fruit eaters, they also argue, "are usually highly social" since "the majority of fruit-eating primates eat green or bitter fruits, which are plentiful and clumped in large resources, thereby enabling many animals to feed in one tree," which thus "provides increased opportunities for social interaction." (Emery and Amaral, "The Role of the Amygdala," 170). Here, then, they argue for the adaptiveness of dexterity, fine vision, spatial sense, and communicative systems based upon the arbitrary contingencies of adaption to an ever-changing world. They also argue that all of these adaptations use and modify subcortical resources of the brain, especially the amygdala.

The"universal" primate and human sense of space—our performance and cognition of it, and even the misperformances in some of the symptoms of Tourette's–offers a way of bringing together the "cultural formations" of structural semantics and the biological formations of Darwinian materialism. It offers the possibility of emphasizing an (arbitrary) materialism that can, in fact, be accommodated by structuralist and semiotic accounts of meaning and experience.

73. Sacks calls such mimicking "pseudo-actions" and "simulacra of action and meaning": "Mrs. Y.'s tics," he writes in *Awakenings*, "*look* like actions or deeds–and not mere jerks or spasms or movements. One sees, for example, gasps, pants, sniffs, finger-snappings, throat-clearing, pinching movements, scratching movements, touching movements, etc., etc., which could all be part of a normal gestural repertoire . . . These pseudo-actions, sometimes comic, sometimes grotesque, convey a deeply paradoxical feeling, in that they *seem* at first to have a definite (if mysterious) organization and purpose and then one realizes that in fact they do not." (Sacks, *Awakenings*, 109). Here Sacks is describing the kind of "pseudo-intentionality" that Lionel Essog describes in opposing the "accidental lunacy" of kissing to the seeming intention of his verbal tics. And this phenomena gets even more complicated in that the subjects of Tourette's syndrome often "camouflage," as my friend told me, unintentional action with seeming intentional gestures. Lethem narrates such "camouflage" throughout *Motherless Brooklyn*, and Sacks describes it explicitly: "When I questioned Miss H. about this symptom [a lightening-quick movement of the right hand to the face] . . . she replied that it was 'a nonsense-movement'. . . . Within three days of its appearance, however, this tic had become associated with an intention and a use: it had become a mannerism, and was now used by Miss H. to adjust the position of her spectacles." (Sacks, *Awakenings*, 136).
74. Eliot, *Selected Poems*, 91.
75. Sacks, *An Anthropologist on Mars*, 100.

WORKS CITED

Aggleton, John and Andrew Young. "The Enigma of the Amygdala: On Its Contribution to Human Emotion." In *Cognitive Neuroscience of Emotion*, ed. Richard Lane and Lynn Nadel. Oxford: Oxford University Press, 2000, 106–128.

Attridge, Derek. *Peculiar Language*. Ithaca: Cornell University Press, 1988.

Bruun, Ruth. "The Natural History of Tourette's Syndrome." In *Tourette's Syndrome and Tic Disorders: Clinical Understanding and Treatment*, ed. Donald Cohen, Ruth Bruun, and James Leckman. New York: John Wiley & Sons, 1988, 21–39.

Cohen, Donald J., Ruth Bruun and James Leckman. "Preface." In *Tourette's Syndrome and Tic Disorders: Clinical Understanding and Treatment*, ed. Donald Cohen, Ruth Bruun, and James Leckman. New York: John Wiley & Sons, 1988, xi–xv.

Culler, Jonathan. "Convention and Meaning: Derrida and Austin." *New Literary History*, 13 (1983): 15–30.

Damasio, Antonio. *Descartes' Error: Emotion, Reason, and the Human Brain*. New York: Avon, 1994.

Deacon, Terrence. *The Symbolic Species: The Co-Evolution of Language and the Brain*. New York: Norton, 1998.

Deleuze, Gilles. *Nietzsche and Philosophy*, trans. Hugh Tomlinson. New York: Columbia University Press, 1983.

Descartes, René. *The Philosophical Writings*, trans. John Cottingham, Robert Stoothoff, and Dugald Murdoch. 3 vols. Cambridge: Cambridge University Press, 1984 (Vol 2), 1985 (Vol 1).

Eliot, T.S. *Selected Poems*. New York: Harvest/HBJ Book, 1964.

Eliot, T.S. "Tradition and the Individual Talent." In *Selected Prose*, ed. Frank Kermode. New York: Harcourt Brace Jovanovich, 1974, 37–44.

Emery, Nathan and David Amaral. "The Role of the Amygdala in Primate Social Cognition." In *Cognitive Neuroscience of Emotion*, ed. Richard Lane and Lynn Nadel. Oxford: Oxford University Press, 2000, 156–191.

Fahn, Stanley and Gerald Erenberg. "Differential Diagnosis of Tic Phenomena: A Neurologic Perspective." In *Tourette's Syndrome and Tic Disorders: Clinical Understanding and Treatment*, ed. Donald Cohen, Ruth Bruun, and James Leckman. New York: John Wiley & Sons, 1988, 41–54.

Goodall, Jane. *The Chimpanzees of Gombe: Patterns of Behavior*. Cambridge: Harvard University Press, 1986.

Gray, J. A. *The Neuropsychology of Anxiety: An Enquiry into the Functions of the Septo-Hippocampal System*. Oxford: Oxford University Press, 1982.

Gray, J. A. "Framework for a Taxonomy of Psychiatric Disorder." In *Emotions: Essays on Emotion Theory*, ed. Stephanie Van Gooze, Nanne Van de Poll, Joseph Sergeant. Hillsdale, NJ: Lawrence Erlbaum Associates, 1994, 29–59.

Greimas, A.J. "La Linguistique statistique et la linguistique structural." *Le Français moderne*, 31 (1963): 55–68.

Greimas, A.J. "La linguistique structurale et la poétique." In *Du Sens*. Paris: Seuil, 1970, 271–283.

Greimas, A.J. "Introduction." *Essais de Sémiotique Poétique*, ed. A.J. Greimas. Paris: Librairie Larousse, 1972, 6–24.

Greimas, A. J. *Structural Semantics*, trans. Daniele McDowell, Ronald Schleifer and Alan Velie. Lincoln: University of Nebraska Press, 1983.

Greimas, A.J., and J. Courtés. *Semiotics and Language: An Analytical Dictionary*, trans. Larry Crist, Daniel Patte and others. Bloomington: Indiana University Press, 1982.

Hayles, Katherine. "Constrained Constructivism: Locating Scientific Inquiry in the Theater of Representation." *New Orleans Review*, 18 (1991): 76–85.

Hjelmslev, Louis. *Prolegomena to a Theory of Language*, trans. Francis Whitfield. Madicson: University of Wisconsin Press, 1961.

Jakobson, Roman. "Linguistics and Poetics." In *Language and Literature*. Cambridge: Harvard University Press, 1987, 62–94.

Kushner, Howard I. *A Cursing Brain? The Histories of Tourette Syndrome*. Cambridge: Harvard University Press, 1999.

Lawrence, D.H. *The Complete Poems*, ed. Vivian de Sola Pinto and Warren Roberts. New York: Viking Press, 1964.

Leckman, James and Donald Cohen. "Descriptive and Diagnostic Classification of Tic Disorders." In *Tourette's Syndrome and Tic Disorders: Clinical Understanding and Treatment*, ed. Donald Cohen, Ruth Bruun, and James Leckman. New York: John Wiley & Sons, 1988, 3–19.

Leckman, James, Mark Riddle and Donald Cohen. "Pathobiology of Tourette's Syndrome." In *Tourette's Syndrome and Tic Disorders: Clinical Understanding and Treatment*, ed. Donald Cohen, Ruth Bruun and James Leckman. New York: John Wiley & Sons, 1988, 103–116.

Lethem, Jonathan. *Motherless Brooklyn*. New York: Doubleday, 1999.

Lieberman, Philip. *Eve Spoke: Human Language and Human Evolution*. London: Picador, 1998.

Lieberman, Philip. *Human Language and our Reptilian Brain: The Sybcortical Bases of Speech, Syntax, and Thought*. Cambridge: Harvard University Press, 2000.

MacLean, P.D., and J.D Newman. "Role of Midline Frontolimbi Cortex in the Production of the Isolation Call of Squirrel Monkeys." *Brain Research* 450 (1988): 111–123.

McNeill, Daniel. *The Face*. Boston: Little Brown, 1998.

Middleton, F.A., and P.L. Strick. "Anatomical Evidence for Cerebellar and Basal Ganglia Involvement in Higher Cognition." *Science* 31 (1994): 458461.

Morris, David. *Illness and Culture in the Postmodern Age*. Berkeley: University of California Press, 1998.

Nietzsche, Friedrich. *The Birth of Tragedy and The Case of Wagner*, trans. Walter Kaufmann. New York: Vintage Books, 1967.

Pauls, D.L., J.F. Leckman, K.E. Towbin, G.E.P Zahner and D.J. Cohen. "A Possible Genetic Relationship Exists between Tourette's Syndrome and Obsessive-Compulsive Disorder." *Pschopharacology Bulletin* 22 (1986): 730–733.

Pinker, Steven. *The Language Instinct*. New York: Harper Perennial, 1994.

Robertson, Mary and Simon Baron-Cohen. *Tourette Syndrome: The Facts*. Oxford: Oxford University Press, 1998.

Sacks, Oliver. *The Man who Mistook his Wife for a Hat*. New York: Harper and Row, 1987.

Sacks, Oliver. *Awakenings* [1990]. New York: Vintage Books, 1999.

Sacks, Oliver. *An Anthropologist on Mars*. New York: Vintage Books, 1995.

Saussure, Ferdinand de. *Course in General Linguistics*, trans. Roy Harris. La Salle, IL: Open Court Press, 1983.

Schleifer, Ronald. *A.J. Greimas and the Nature of Meaning*. London: Croom Helm, 1987.

Schleifer, Ronald. *Modernism and Time: The Logic of Abundance in Literature, Science, and Culture, 1880–1930*. Cambridge: Cambridge University Press, 2000.

Schleifer, Ronald. *Analogical Thinking: Post-Enlightenment Understanding in Language, Collaboration, and Interpretation*. Ann Arbor: University of Michigan Press, 2000a.

Stevens, Janice R., and Paul H. Blachly. "Successful Treatment of the Maladie des Tics, Gilles de la Tourette's Syndrome." *American Journal of Diseases in Children* 112 (1966): 541–545.

Sutton, D., and U. Jurgens. "Neural Control of Vocalization." In *Comparative Primate Biology*, ed. H.D. Stiklis and J. Erwin. Vol. 4. New York: Arthur D. Liss, 1988, 635–647.

Towbin, Kenneth. "Obsessive-Compulsive Symptoms in Tourette's Syndrome." In *Tourette's Syndrome and Tic Disorders: Clinical Understanding and Treatment*, ed. Donald Cohen, Ruth Bruun, and James Leckman. New York: John Wiley & Sons, 1988, 137–149.

9 The Visualization of the Twisted Tongue

Portrayals of Stuttering in Film, Television, and Comic Books

Jeffrey Johnson

There is a well-established tradition within the entertainment and publishing industries of depicting mentally and physically challenged characters. While many of the early renderings were sideshowesque amusements or one-dimensional melodramas, numerous contemporary works have utilized characters with disabilities in well-rounded and non-stereotypical ways. Although it would appear that many in society have begun to demand more realistic portrayals of characters with physical and mental challenges, one impediment that is still often typified by coarse caricatures is that of stuttering. The speech impediment labeled stuttering is often used as a crude formulaic storytelling device that adheres to basic misconceptions about the condition. Stuttering is frequently employed as visual shorthand to communicate humor, nervousness, weakness or unheroic/villainous characters. Because almost all of the monographs written about the portrayals of disabilities in film and television fail to mention stuttering, the purpose of this paper is to examine the basic categorical formulas used in depicting stuttering in the mainstream popular culture areas of film, television and comic books.[1] Though the subject may seem minor or unimportant, it does in fact provide an outlet to observe the relationship between a physical condition and the popular conception of the mental and personality traits that accompany it.

One widely accepted definition of stuttering is, "the interruption of the flow of speech by hesitations, prolongation of sounds and blockages sufficient to cause anxiety and impair verbal communication."[2] This cumbersome and unwieldy definition does not prevent a substantial majority of the population from believing they understand the concept of stuttering.[3] Most people know someone who stutters; it is estimated that there are around fifty million stutterers worldwide.[4] It is a condition that is rarely viewed as either mysterious or extraordinary but rather often seen as a mundane and trivial ailment. Possibly because stuttering is relatively common and because it involves a 'simple' aspect of everyday life (speaking), theories abound among the laity about the probable causes and cures of the malady. Stuttering is often attributed to nervousness or weakness and cures such as "breathe differently," "speak slower," or "snap your fingers when you talk" are routinely prescribed by helpful listeners. This familiarity and perceived understanding of the speech impediment has been transferred to popular culture outlets where stuttering characters have long been included. Unfortunately, the portrayals of these characters have often pandered to the public's base ideas of stuttering and thus have been stereotypical, unrealistic and even at times derogatory.[5]

The oldest and most basic portrayal of stuttering in film and television is that of the simple comedic device or gag. This characterization follows a long theatrical tradition in which a physical, mental, emotional, ethnic or social condition is lampooned in order to provide low level comedy. The basis for this type of character is the need to provide lighter moments that are aesthetically or viscerally humorous. Often these roles are created to showcase a malady or humorous oddity much in the tradition of Barnumesque sideshows. Examples of this are cowboy sidekicks with 'funny' voices or mannerisms like Gabby Hayes, the racial/ethnic 'other' in the vein of Jack Benny's Rochester or the Green Hornet's Kato or the physically challenged such as the visual impaired Mister Magoo. The most notable fictional comic stutterer is undoubtedly the Warner Brothers cartoon character Porky Pig. Created in 1935, Porky Pig is a severe stutterer who often is lampooned because of his speech impediment. In Porky's 1935 debut *I Haven't Got a Hat* he fails to recite "The Ride of Paul Revere" to the amusement of the audience while in 1938's *Porky's Poppa* he becomes so enraged after hearing himself speak that he smashes the phonograph on which his voice is being played. Additionally, Porky's words often become so entangled that he is forced to replace words or phrases or even give up though the viewer knows what he wishes to say. These and many other examples, along with Porky's signature "Th-Th-That's all folks," seem to indicate that a sizable number of people find Porky's stuttering amusing. Porky is mainly a reactionary character in his films and often his scenes are chances for the audience to hear the cartoon pig 'talk funny.' In 1987, researcher Gerald Johnson conducted a clinical analysis of Porky's stuttering and determined that the animated swine was disfluent on a rather high 23 percent of his words and displayed atypical and exaggerated characteristics of stuttering.[6] In other words, not surprisingly one of Porky's main purposes is to be funny when he speaks and to be an easy auditory gag for those who find stuttering humorous.

Porky Pig is far from the only example of stuttering being used for humorous affect in popular culture. Mel Tillis (a real life stutterer) uses his speech to create low brow comedy in films like *Cannonball Run, The Villain* and *Smokey and the Bandit II*. While, *The Maltese Falcon* (1941), staring Humphrey Bogart, contains this dialogue about stuttering:

Gangster: "You've got a smart answer for everything don't you?"
Sam Spade: "What do you want me to do, learn to stutter?"[7]

Again, this comic tradition seems to be used with characters that stutter because on a foundational level stuttering is funny to many. To some, it is amusing to think of the smooth-talking Bogart fighting for words and arriving at a less than 'smart' answer. Equally funny is the idea that the loquacious Sam Spade would voluntarily teach himself to stutter. Another example of pithy comedic dialogue about stuttering is the 1956 film *The Court Jester*, in which comedian Danny Kaye becomes involved in an elaborate ruse and pretends to interpret the sign language of his supposedly deaf granddaughter. During one exchange, the woman gives a lengthy sign answer that is interpreted by Kaye as merely, "no." When asked why it took so many hand signs for such a short answer Kaye responds, "she stutters."[8] It seems that the implication that a person can stutter while 'speaking' with her hands is amusing. Additionally, a recent episode of *Curb Your Enthusiasm* features a man who stutters and wishes to park in handicap parking because of his disability.[9] Here the debate over stuttering's significance provides an opportunity for base level humor. No matter if one finds such low-brow comedy to be entertaining of not, it cannot be denied that this device is an important element in many films and television shows.[10] It is significant that when used as a comic element the stutterer is not a true representation of a person but rather is the physical embodiment of his speech impediment. His only purpose is to stutter and thus amuse. In this context, a stutterer's narrative role is to provide light-hearted moments and then exit so that the more important characters can fill the screen.

The stutterer as comic relief is an important narrative device in popular media but certainly not the only one. Likely, the most common way in which stuttering is used in visual media is to easily display that a character is weak or nervous. This storytelling shorthand has developed out of the popular misconception that stuttering is a sign of weakness. Experts, like author Barry Guitar, assert that, "research has shown that most people, even classroom teachers and speech-language pathologists, stereotype people who stutter as tense, insecure, and fearful."[11] Since many in the general public already believe stutterers to be anxious, unconfident and timid, writers need not spend precious time explaining that a character possesses these traits. They instead assume the audience will make the mental leap from the speech impediment to the weak behaviors in which it is associated. Examples of this characterization of weakness abound probably because it is such an easy and popular association with stuttering. One interesting example of this depiction of stuttering is the character of Lieutenant Reginald Barclay in the popular science fiction television series *Star Trek: The Next Generation*. In the futuristic world of *Star Trek*, Barclay is a nervous and socially inept starship engineer. Barclay is shown to be a shy hypochondriac, who fears the ship's transporters (a common method of transportation on the show) and is so uncomfortable with people that he would rather interact with computer simulated characters. In early episodes featuring Barclay, a young character, Wesley Crusher, nicknames him "Lieutenant

Broccoli" in order to emphasize his limitations.[12] In addition to Barclay's other shortcomings, he also stutters. On a starship filled with courageous and often heroic personnel, the one character who is shown to have multiple anxieties and weaknesses is also the one who stutters. Contrast this depiction to that of the chief engineer, Geordi La Forge, who happens to be blind. La Forge's blindness is partially overcome, by a device called a VISOR, that allows him to see in a different way than his crewmates. Throughout the series, La Forge is shown to be capable and heroic and his blindness is often depicted as a beneficial quality as in episode #113 "The Masterpiece Society" in which La Forge's VISOR helps to save a doomed colony.[13] Other physical disabilities are also portrayed positively, an example being a character in the episode entitled "Loud as a Whisper" in which a deaf mediator is revered for his strong character and excellent communication skills.[14] Barclay's stuttering is never portrayed as noble or even mentioned aloud; instead it serves to reinforce his weak nature. Barclay is not a person who stutters but rather is a shy, backward phobic person and stuttering is a symptom of these things. In an episode of *Star Trek Voyager*, a possible future version of Barclay is shown as confident, assertive and non-stuttering. The apparent message being that when he overcomes his fears and shyness, Barclay also stops stuttering.[15]

Probably the most famous motion picture to invoke images of a nervous and weak stutterer is the 1988 comedy *A Fish Called Wanda*. In this film Michael Palin plays Ken Pile, a hitman who stutters. Throughout the movie, Ken is tormented by a thief named Otto West, played by Kevin Kline, who constantly makes fun of his stuttering. Otto repeatedly mocks Ken's speaking and often imitates his stuttering. Although Ken is a professional hitman, he is a soft-hearted animal lover who routinely cannot find the courage to defend himself against Otto's taunts. As the film draws to a close, Otto and Ken have a final showdown and Otto still ridicules Ken by exclaiming, "It's K-K-K-Ken, coming to k-k-kill me."[16] Eventually, Ken attempts to kill Otto by running over him with a large motor vehicle and finds that this act of violence and revenge has cured his stuttering. In essence, Ken finds that although this action is morally questionable, it was indeed an act of strength and this means that he is no longer a weak person. As his weak characteristics disappear so does his stuttering, which served as a sign of the person he no longer is. As a hitman, Ken has always been a murderer but because now he can murder people for personal reasons he has gained potency which makes his stuttering unnecessary.

Examples of the characterization of stuttering as weakness and its contrast with the strength of action abound in films and television. 1998's *The Waterboy* is the tale of a shy, socially backward, young man from Louisiana who becomes the hero of a small university's football team. In order to play football, the hero, Bobby Boucher, acted by Adam Sandler, must channel all of his aggression from years of being teased about many things including his stuttering. On the playing field, Bobby is the quintessential tough, aggressive, strong male that no longer stutters because he no longer is weak. In the same vein is a wrestling character that has appeared in both *Extreme Championship Wrestling* and *World Wrestling Entertainment* name Buh Buh/Bubba Ray Dudley. Although not physically weak, Bubba Ray suffers the taunts of his opponents who make fun of his backwoods background and his stuttering. Bubba Ray stutters so badly that he is unable to pronounce his name until an opponent hits him in the chest with a crutch. This action "toughens up" Bubba Ray and allows him to lose his stutter. Because Bubba Ray has become a "real man," he no longer suffers from stuttering.[17] In the comic book *The Sandman*, a weak stuttering version of the biblical character Abel inhabits the Dream Lord's realm. Abel is portrayed as a nervous cowardly character that is constantly being murdered by his compulsive, aggressive and overbearing brother Cain. Abel does little to stop this cycle of violence and instead allows Cain to do what he wishes. In the film *Primal Fear* (1996), Edward Norton plays a murderer that pretends to have multiple personalities in order to receive a courtroom acquittal. The 'weaker' personality Aaron stutters badly and is contrasted to Roy, a dominant and violent personality that speaks fluently. When Norton becomes Roy, his power is not only demonstrated in the words he uses but also in his fluency. Similarly, in the film (and book) *Harry Potter and the Sorcerer's Stone*, the villain Professor Quirrell feigns stuttering in order to appear weaker and thus not be suspected of his crimes. Quirrell appears to be nervous, timid and rather harmless and his stuttering showcases these traits. When he stops pretending to be meek, Quirrell also stops stuttering and is shown to be a powerful villain. In the novel on which the film is based, when asked about his criminal ways, Quirrell states ". . . who would suspect p-p-poor, st-stuttering P-Professor Quirrell?"[18]

One additional example of stuttering signifying weakness can be found in the John Wayne movie *The Cowboys* (1972). In the film, John Wayne hires a group of young men to work on a cattle drive. One of the boys (about age 10) clearly stutters and as the film progresses an accident takes place that forces the boy to come to the John Wayne character for help. The boy is so shaken that he is unable to speak fluently, and when it becomes clear what has happened, John Wayne verbally abuses him and tells him that he can talk normally if he wishes to. The exchange is as follows:

Wayne: "You almost let your friend drown out there in that river."
Kid: "I'da rather d-d-died then do that."
Wayne: "And you're a liar!"
Kid: "It ain't my fault I stutter."
Wayne: "Listen to me you whining little welt. You're gonna stop that stuttering or get the hell out of here. You're gonna stop it or go home, Do ya hear me?"
Kid: "Son of a Bitch!"
Wayne: "What did you say?"

Kid: "You God damned son of a bitch!"
Wayne: "Say that again."
Kid: "You God damned mean son of a bitch."
Wayne: "Say it faster."
Kid: "You god damned mean dirty son of a bitch."
Wayne: "Wouldn't make it a habit calling me that, Son."[19]

Miraculously, this violent verbal outburst cures the boy and he does not stutter again in the film. Many speech therapists would argue that John Wayne's stuttering therapy was in fact the opposite of how the situation should be handled. Most clinicians report that bouts of disfluency should be dealt with in a patient and understanding manner. In fact, in an essay written in rebuttal to the film, Hans-Georg Basshardt notes that John Wayne's therapy would likely make a stutterer less fluent by making him more anxious and struggle more.[20] Wayne's message to the young stutterer was the same as in all the above-mentioned films: that stutterers stutter because of weakness and fear. The morale of the films is that if the stutterer becomes stronger and more in charge of his life then he can stop his stuttering. Like Oedipus blinding himself so that he could truly see, the disappearance of stuttering reflects a symbolic change within a character. No longer should he be seen as weak or passive, but rather he has now overcome those difficulties and can be viewed with respect and approval.

Because stuttering is often used as visual shorthand for weakness, characters who stutter are rarely cast in the role of the hero. The archetypal hero must be strong and confident and those qualities are often lacking among stutterers in visual media. Revisiting the relationship between the stutterer and John Wayne in the film *The Cowboys*, it is unimaginable that the roles could be reversed. Although many speech disfluency experts like Hans-Georg Basshardt argue that John Wayne handled the situation incorrectly, one cannot envision a scenario in which the stuttering boy argues this point and wins. John Wayne in this motion picture, and most of the others he starred in, is the quintessential American hero. He is strong, rugged and assertive; the classic man of action. Notice that Wayne equates stuttering with a moral deficiency. In his mind, the kid will not stop stuttering because he does not have the will to do so. The young man is too lazy, weak-willed or selfish to make a change and is lying to himself and those around him by claiming his stuttering is not his fault. Wayne accepts the kid's stuttering, and the moral failings that come with it, so long as it does not harm the group, but once an innocent is endangered Wayne acts. In doing so, Wayne behaves as the hero by not allowing the selfishness and denial of an individual to potentially harm the whole. The educated viewer knows that the kid is right, his stuttering is not a mental light switch that can be flipped off and on, but that matters little because he does not possess the important elements that would allow him to defeat John Wayne in a battle of wits. Wayne is the motion picture's hero and there is little chance that a stuttering child will be allowed to better him in a contest of any kind. The writers only allow the kid to verbally retaliate against Wayne because it proves that Wayne was correct in his assessment of the proper cure for the kid's speech impediment. Even when the kid acts boldly in a manner that Wayne wishes by cursing at him, Wayne is certain to keep the upper hand by warning the kid about his language. In this film, like many others, stuttering is a deficiency that prevents a character from ever being seen as a true hero.

In the world of comic books, the distinction between hero, villain and supporting cast is often well defined. In general, like motion pictures, comic books have tightly structured rules as to what constitutes a hero. Much like a John Wayne cowboy, comic book heroes are usually strong, confident, aggressive and morally superior. They are men and women of action who overcome outside evils and internal flaws. Often their secret identities have a physical defect or weakness but traditionally none of these imperfections manifest themselves while the superhero identity is present. Clark Kent may be near-sighted, clumsy and bumbling, but Superman is not. Freddy Freeman is a physically handicapped newsboy, but Captain Marvel Jr. is a supremely powerful being. Likewise, Marvel Comics' version of the Norse god Thor shows no sign of the paralyzed leg that his alter ego possesses. These impediments, much like stuttering, are unheroic and only serve as guidelines to what a hero is not. Like the above-mentioned handicaps, stuttering is used as an example of an unheroic trait in the Marvel Comics' hero known as Cloak. Tyrone Johnson is a teenage runaway who lives in New York City. Tyrone leaves home because he feels responsible for his best friend Billy's death. At ages seventeen, Tyrone and Billy witness a robbery and murder. When the police arrive, Tyrone stutters so violently that he is unable to tell the police that Billy did not commit the crime. When Billy is fatally shot by one of the officers, Tyrone blames himself for being unable to speak to the authorities and defend his friend. At this point, Tyrone is the antithesis of the hero. His mental weakness and physical frailty prevent him from saving his best friend's life. Tyrone cannot live with the guilt and drops out of society. Eventually, through a series of convoluted events, he and a wealthy female runaway are given superpowers and turn to fighting crime.[21] When Tyrone receives his powers, and becomes the hero Cloak, he no longer stutters but instead speaks fluently and his words are often in dark bold print to make them seem more aggressive and authoritative.[22] In this text, the very symbol of Tyrone's weakness is his stuttering. It is what prevents him from being a hero and what he blames for ruining his life. Tyrone is incapable of being a hero while he stutters; the two things are in such conflict that heroic actions are inconceivable. When Tyrone gains superpowers, he transforms into another person that is heroic, aggressive, and does not stutter. As Tyrone's weakness departs, so does his stuttering and he is capable of being a true hero.

Both examples of the stutterers' inability to be heroic in visual media have focused on the way that stuttering prevented a character from performing a heroic act. In each case, the person who stuttered was unable to 'do the right thing' in a life or death situation. Sometimes, the heroism in a visual narrative comes not from a single act but rather from a job done well. Such is the case in *My Cousin Vinny*, a 1992 film about a New York lawyer (Joe Pesci) defending two youths accused of murder in the southern United States. Although Pesci's character seems incompetent throughout the motion picture, in the end he proves himself to be a good lawyer by finding evidence that acquits the defendants. Pesci is poorly trained, ill mannered and unprofessional but becomes the hero of the film by using trickery, self-confidence and verbal blustering. In contrast, Austin Pendleton plays a public defender who is briefly assigned to the case and at first seems lawyerly in every way. He is well dressed and groomed, understands the intricacies of the law, and seems to be an altogether better lawyer than Pesci. When the two lawyers enter the courtroom though, Pesci proves to be a skilled cross-examiner, while Pendleton stutters severely and has difficulty asking any questions. In this moment, Pesci proves himself to be the film's hero and Pendleton becomes an also-ran that is never seen again. Pendleton is better trained, more knowledgeable, and undoubtedly has more legal experience than Pesci. Pendleton has been hired as a public defender while Pesci has never tried a case before and has just passed the New York state bar exam on the sixth try. This matters little though because the sight of Pendleton stuttering reveals his weakness, incompetence, and his inability to be heroic. No matter how well trained he may be, a stuttering lawyer is too weak, vulnerable and amusing to be the hero and win the big case.

Stuttering is often depicted for base amusement, to portray weakness or to contrast and define heroic qualities. Additionally, it sometimes serves as a brand that marks a villain. Narrative tradition is rife with examples of disfigured or deformed evildoers ranging from Peter Pan's Captain Hook to latter-day Bond villains. Like the deformities used with these characters, stuttering is sometimes employed to portray a physical defect that hints at a greater moral or spiritual deformity. A villain's stuttering helps relay to the audience there is something sinister about him. Such is the case in several television crime dramas including *CSI: Crime Scenes Investigation* and *Criminal Minds*. Mandy Patinkin plays Jason Gideon, a genius FBI profiler, who has the knack for being able to solve difficult cases in CBS's *Criminal Minds*. In an ongoing storyline, Patinkin is tracking a serial murder known as the Footpath Killer. After hearing that the killer likes to surprise his victims in isolated places and physically overpower them, Patinkin concludes that the killer must be a stutterer. In his professional opinion, stuttering would cause the murderer to act in such a way because it would make him incapable of verbally beguiling would-be victims. Although there would seem to be a multitude of alternative explanations, Patinkin is nonetheless right and eventually catches the killer because he recognizes the telltale stutter. Throughout the storyline, it is clear that the agents are not merely looking for a criminal that stutters but that his stuttering is a part of his criminal makeup. Like the Victorian concept of a criminal class, the Footpath Killer's stuttering marks him physically as a delinquent. Within this context, stuttering is an unnatural perversion that signals a moral/ spiritual deficiency. The Footpath Killer's stuttering proves that something evil exists within him. The criminal is not someone who has committed a crime, but he is a person whose nature it is to commit crimes. His stuttering is the mark that his animalistic criminal impulses make him unfit for society and is a danger to all those around him. While other visual genre characters stutter to be funny, to display weakness or to be unheroic, characters like the Footpath Killer stutter to prove they are unnatural.

A similar character to *Criminal Minds*'s Footpath Killer is *CSI*'s Paul Milander, a murdering sociopath who has appeared in multiple episodes including the pilot. Milander is a brilliant criminal who plays a game of cat and mouse with the CSIs as his tally of murder victims steadily increases. Eventually, Gil Grissom, the lead CSI investigator, is able to deduce that Milander is a murderer because of a line of evidence that revolves around his stuttering. Once again, as with the Footpath Killer, Milander's stuttering marks him as unnatural and evil. He is the opposite of the clean, efficient, law observing CSIs who process his case. His stuttering is an outward manifestation of an inward evil. Unlike the Footpath Killer, Milander displays other more aberrant behaviors like manipulating his victims' lives and toying with the authorities but our passage into his inner deviancy is the discovery of his stuttering. Notice that both of these television crime dramas profess to be concerned with the mastery of science over superstition and ignorance, yet their handling of stuttering and criminals does not work within this overall focus. Both programs have chosen to portray stuttering not as a physical characteristic or impediment but rather as a sign of a greater evil.

Television is not the only visual media that has portrayed stuttering as a sinister brand. As mentioned before, films often present physical deformities or maladies as representations of evil. One such motion picture is 1991's *Dead Again*, a neo-film noir about a reincarnated murderer and victim. Throughout the film, the audience is led to speculate at the relationship between the two main characters, played by Kenneth Branagh and Emma Thompson, and encouraged to guess which was victim and murderer in a past life. Branagh is the prime suspect throughout the film, but in the end it is revealed that a minor character in fact committed the crime. While Branagh's and Thompson's characters have been reincarnated, their current hypnotist was a young boy named Frankie that in their past lives had a severe stutter and committed the brutal murder. The older present day Frankie does not stutter throughout the film until he is unmasked as the murderer. When his criminal ways become evident so does his stuttering. Unlike the villains in *CSI* and *Criminal Minds*, Frankie is able to disguise his true nature and thus 'cure' his stuttering. When his criminal behavior is revealed though, he can no longer lie about his unnatural makeup and the return of his stuttering showcases his downfall.

While crime stories in television and films sometimes portray stutterers as inhumane criminals, comic books extend this idea and often invent evil stuttering villains that have non-human/animalist characteristics. In comic books, unlike films or television, it is a widely accepted practice that villains are evil by nature so they must be dehumanized further by being given physical/mental impediments and often being linked to animalistic traits. As Marc Shell discusses in his monograph *Stutter*, there is a long history of animals that stutter in literature and films but generally these animals are not categorized as evil. Comic books uniquely fuse animalistic personas/behaviors with impediments like stuttering to create a subhuman predator. Unlike the television and film criminal, the comic book villain does not stutter to mark himself as inhuman. His animal-like abilities showcase, rather, that he stutters to display that his wildness makes him less than human. Like villains many comic book superheroes possess superpowers based on animal traits (Aquaman, Animal Man, Beast Boy, etc.), but heroes use their abilities to control and civilize nature. Instead of becoming animalistic and cruel, heroes use their powers to elevate themselves and society and thus become 'kings of the jungle' in a Tarzan-like manner. Conversely, villains with animal-like superpowers or accelerated abilities do not rise above nature but rather sink into its depths and become subhuman. Stuttering marks and notes this lack of humanity and displays that the villain's powers control him instead of him controlling them. The comic book narratives seem to state that a person who cannot manage a simple act like speaking cannot be expected to manage abilities beyond the dreams of most humans. Accordingly, a character who stutters lacks the self-control to elevate himself above his base wants and desires. Multiple examples of this exist: Animal-Master, a criminal circus trainer who attempts to defeat Aquaman while stuttering out threats[23]; Peepers, an evil stuttering mutant with exceptional visual abilities that does not take an animal identity but possesses superpowers that suggest animal-like dexterity. Additionally, multiple villains possessing snake-like powers have spoken with an elongated 's-s-s' stutter in an attempt to mimic a serpent's hiss. These villains, and others like them, were crafted as stutterers to emphasize animalistic weakness rather than their human strengths.

While many visual media portrayals of characters that stutter have resorted to comic or negative stereotypes, others have attempted to present stutterers positively. The most common seemingly positive way that stuttering is showcased is when a storyline is crafted that aims to teach the audience how to behave. These narrative versions of public service announcements often attempt to educate and promote understanding. Although these storylines can be about any number of subjects, stuttering has been singled out multiple times. Among the most notable is an episode of the popular television show *M*A*S*H* entitled "Run for the Money" (1982) in which Charles Emerson Winchester (David Ogden Stiers) befriends a patient that stutters.[24] Winchester attempts to convince the young soldier that stuttering does not make him unintelligent or inferior, and eventually the young man that stutters gains a higher degree of self respect. It is revealed at the end of the episode that Winchester's sister also stutters. Likewise, in two different episodes of *Little House on the Prairie,* children that stutter are taunted but later lessons about proper behavior towards others are learned.[25] Furthermore, in *Justice League of America* #36 (1965), each of the team's superheroes become handicapped: Superman goes blind, Green Arrow loses his arms, the Flash has only one leg, Hawkman develops asthma and Green Lantern begins to stutter. Evidentially, the heroes learn to adapt to their newly found disabilities and learn the lesson that everyone is important no matter what challenges they face. Each of these teaching narratives attempts to help stutterers by making the world more understanding towards them. The characteristics of the people who stutter are little different from the other visual media portrayals though. The main detail that changes is how people react to them. The stutterers are still presented as weak, nervous and unheroic.[26] Even though these visual narratives have seemingly good intentions, they fail to create characters that are complex enough to be real and instead fall back upon the old stereotypes.[27]

Stereotypical depictions are not unusual in film, television or comic books. These visual media make use of clichés to create easy connections with the viewer or reader. Stuttering is just one of the many ideas, conditions or maladies that has been used as visual shorthand for other internal characteristics. These stereotypical associations differ for each condition, but undoubtedly they exist. In recent years, other physical or mental challenges such as blindness and deafness have begun to be portrayed more realistically in the visual media. Alternatively, stuttering has rarely been shown in a positive or even-handed manner, but rather, the speech impediment is often used as a narrative code to help facilitate commonly held stereotypes. People that stutter are frequently portrayed as humorous, nervous, weak, unheroic or villainous. These generalizations rarely allow a given character an opportunity to become well-rounded, and instead he commonly becomes a personification of his stuttering or a trait that is associated with it. This in turn serves to perpetuate a greater misunderstanding about people that stutter. In doing so, both stutterers and those they come in contact with are harmed and that is the most unfortunate visualization of all.

NOTES

1. For works about disabilities in film and television, see Guy Cumberbatch and Ralph Negrine, *Images of Disability on Television* (New York: Routledge, 1992); Lauri E. Klobas, *Disability Drama in Television and Film* (Jefferson, NC: McFarland & Company, Inc., 1988); Martin F. Norden, *The Cinema of Isolation: A History of Physical Disability in the Movies* (New Brunswick, NJ: Rutgers University Press, 1994).
2. Jock A. Carlisle, *Tangled Tongue: Living with a Stutter* (Toronto: University of Toronto Press, 1985), 4.
3. For the purpose of this chapter the American word "stuttering" is being used as opposed to the British "stammering."

4. Marc Shell, *Stutter* (Cambridge, MA: Harvard University Press, 2005), 1.
5. Numerous studies have been conducted about the attitudes of various members of the general public towards stutterers. These include: I. Doody, J.A. Kalinowski and A. Stuart, "Stereotypes of Stutterers and Nonstutterers in Three Rural Communities in Newfoundland," *Journal of Fluency Disorders* 18, no. 4 (1993): 363–374; M. Dorsey and R.K. Guenther, "Attitudes of Professors and Students toward College Students Who Stutter," *Journal of Fluency Disorders* 25 (2000): 77–83; Rodney M. Gabel, "The Attitudes of University Students towards Career Choices for People who Stutter," (Diss. The Pennsylvania State University, 1999); Thomas R. Klassen, "Perceptions of People who Stutter: Re-assessing the Negative Stereotype," *Perceptual and Motor Skills* 92, no. 2 (2001): 551.
6. Gerald Johnson, *Journal of Fluency Disorders*, 12 (1987), 235–238.
7. John Huston (dir.), *Maltese Falcon* (Warner Brothers, 1941).
8. Judith Maginnis Kuster, *Movies that Portray People Who Stutter* (1 May, 2006), http://www.mnsu.edu/comdis/kuster/media/movietext.html.
9. *HBO: Curb Your Enthusiasm*, (HBO, 25 April, 2006), http://www.hbo.com/larrydavid/episode/season5/keywords42.html.
10. It should be noted that the use of stuttering characters for comic purposes appears to be non-existent within the comic book medium. Most likely this is because the audio element of stuttering, which is lacking in comic books, is often a key component of the impediment's humorous affect on many.
11. Barry Guitar, *Stuttering: An Integrated Approach to Its Nature and Treatment* (Philadelphia: Lippincott Williams & Wilkins, 2006), 17.
12. *Reginald Barclay* (Wikipedia, 17 April 2006), http://en.wikipedia.org/wiki/Reginald_Barclay.
13. *Star Trek the Next Generation Episode Guide* (Episode Guide: Season Five, 11 April, 2006), http://www.durfee.net/startrek/tng_5.html.
14. *Star Trek.com* (11 April, 2006), http://www.durfee.net/startrek/tng_5.html.
15. *Reginald Barclay* (Wikipedia, 17 April 2006).
16. Charles Crichton (dir.), *A Fish Called Wanda* (MGM, 1988).
17. *Talk Wrestling Online* (Talk Wrestling, 13 April, 2006), http://www.talk-wrestlingonline.com/forum.
18. J.K. Rowling, *Harry Potter and the Sorcerer's Stone* (New York: Scholastic, 1998), 209.
19. Mark Rydell (dir.), *The Cowboys* (Warner Brothers, 1972).
20. Hans-Georg Basshardt, "What is Wrong with John Wayne's Stuttering Therapy?" *International Stuttering Internet Conference* (11 April, 2006), http://www.mnsu.edu/comdis/isad/papers/bosshardt.html.
21. *Marvel Comics Character Profile* (Marvel Comics Character Profile: Cloak, 17 April, 2006), http://www.chezcomics.com/comics-resources-information-pages/marvel-comics-information-resources/marvel-comics-superhero-character-profiles/cloak-marvel-comics-profile.htm.
22. An example of this can be found in *Runways* #9–10 (second series).
23. "Aquaman Duels the Animal-Master," *Adventure Comics* 261 (June 1959).
24. Nell Cox, "Run For the Money," *M*A*S*H* (CBS, 1982).
25. Michael Landon (dir.), "The Music Box" (1977) and "No Beast so Fierce" (1982), *Little House on the Prairie* (Goldhil Home Media).
26. Even though the Justice League claims that all handicapped people can be heroes, they look and act nothing like heroes when they developed physical impediments. Green Lantern even states, "S-Sure am g-glad my m-m-muscles d-don't s-s-stutter." *Justice League* 36 (June 1965), 12.

27. Occasionally, biopic films like *The Right Stuff* (1983) portray a motion picture version of a real life person that stutters (in this case John Glenn's wife Annie) and entertainers that stutter in real life ask for a character to stutter realistically, as is the case with stutter James Earl Jones's character in the film *A Family Thing* (1996). (Surprisingly, it is rare for real life stutterers to act in narratives that include non-stereotypical characters that stutter. Often, as is the case with stutterer Bruce Willis in *Color of Night* and *Die Hard with a Vengeance*, a very clichéd character who stutters is showcased. These instances of seemingly positive portrayals of people that stutter are greatly outnumbered by the more stereotypical ones discussed earlier.

WORKS CITED

"Aquaman Duels the Animal-Master." *Adventure Comics* 261 (June 1959): 1–24.

Basshardt, Hans-Georg. "What is Wrong with John Wayne's Stuttering Therapy?" *International Stuttering Internet Conference*. 11 April 2006. http://www.mnsu.edu/comdis/isad/papers/bosshardt.html.

Carlisle, Jock A. *Tangled Tongue: Living with a Stutter*. Toronto: University of Toronto Press, 1985.

Guitar, Barry. *Stuttering: An Integrated Approach to Its Nature and Treatment*. Philadelphia: Lippincott Williams & Wilkins, 2006.

Curb Your Enthusiasm. HBO, 25 April 2006. http://www.hbo.com/larrydavid/episode/season5/keywords42.html.

Johnson, Gerald F. *Journal of Fluency Disorders*, 12 (1987): 235–238.

Kuster, Judith Maginnis. *Movies that Portray People Who Stutter*. 1 May 2006. http://www.mnsu.edu/comdis/kuster/media/movietext.html.

"Marvel Comics Character Profile: Cloak." *Marvel Comics Character Profile*. 17 April, 2006. http://www.chezcomics.com/comics-resources-information-pages/marvel-comics-information-resources/marvel-comics-superhero-character-profiles/cloak-marvel-comics-profile.htm.

Reginald Barclay. Wikipedia: 17 April, 2006. http://en.wikipedia.org/wiki/Reginald_Barclay.

Rowling, J.K. *Harry Potter and the Sorcerer's Stone*. New York: Scholastic, 1998.

Shell, Marc. *Stutter*. Cambridge, Mass: Harvard University Press, 2005.

Star Trek.com. 11 April 2006. Star Trek.com. 11 April 2006. http://www.durfee.net/startrek/tng_5.html.

Star Trek the Next Generation Episode Guide: Season Five. 11 April 2006. http://www.durfee.net/startrek/tng_5.html.

"Talk Wrestling." *Talk Wrestling Online*. 13 April 2006. http://www.talkwrestlingonline.com/forum.

FILMS AND TELEVISION SHOWS

Branagh, Kenneth (dir.). *Dead Again*. Paramount, 1991.

Cannon, Danny (dir.). "Anonymous." *CSI: Crime Scenes Investigation*. CBS, 2000.

Cannon, Danny (dir.). "Pilot." *CSI: Crime Scenes Investigation*. CBS, 2000.

Charles, Larry (dir.). "The Bowtie." *Curb Your Enthusiasm*. HBO, 2005.

Clampett, Robert (dir.). *Porky's Poppa*. Warner Brothers, 1938.

Columbus, Chris (dir.). *Harry Potter and the Sorcerer's Stone.* Warner Brothers, 2001.

Coraci, Frank (dir.). *The Waterboy.* Walt Disney, 1998.

Cox, Nell (dir.). "Run For the Money." *M*A*S*H.* CBS, 1982.

Crichton, Charles (dir.). *A Fish Called Wanda.* MGM, 1988.

Fink, Kenneth (dir.). "Identity Crisis." *CSI: Crime Scenes Investigation.* CBS, 2002.

Frank, Melvin and Norman Panama (dir.). *The Court Jester.* Paramount, 1956.

Haid, Charles (dir.). "Compulsion." *Criminal Minds.* CBS, WLNS, Lansing. 28 September 2005.

Hoblit, Gregory (dir.). *Primal Fear.* Paramount, 1996.

Huston, John (dir.). *Maltese Falcon.* Warner Brothers, 1941.

Kolbe, Winrich (dir.). "The Masterpiece Society." *Star Trek: The Next Generation.* Paramount, 1992.

Landon, Michael (dir.). "No Beast So Fierce." *Little House on the Prairie.* Goldhil Home Media, 1982.

Landon, Michael (dir.). "The Music Box." *Little House on the Prairie.* Goldhil Home Media, 1977.

Lang, Fritz (dir.). *I Haven't Got a Hat.* Warner Brothers, 1935.

Lynn, Jonathan (dir.). *My Cousin Vinny.* 20th Century Fox, 1992.

Needham, Hal (dir.). *Cannonball Run.* Warner Brothers, 1981.

Needham, Hal (dir.). *Smokey and the Bandit II.* Universal, 1980.

Needham, Hal (dir.). *The Villain.* Sony, 1979.

Rydell, Mark (dir.). *The Cowboys.* Warner Brothers, 1972.

Shaw, Larry (dir.). "Loud as a Whisper." *Star Trek: The Next Generation.* Paramount, 1989.

Shepard, Richard (dir.). "Extreme Aggressor." *Criminal Minds.* CBS, WLNS, Lansing. 22 September 2005.

Contributors

Chris Code (University of Exeter) "Jackson's Parrot: Samuel Beckett, Aphasic Speech Automatisms, and Psychosomatic Language" Professor Chris Code, MA, PhD, Fellow of the Royal College of Speech and Language Therapists, Fellow of the British Psychologists, Chartered Psychologist, trained as a speech-language pathologist-therapist with degrees in psychology and linguistics. He is Professorial Research Fellow in Psychology, College of Life and Environmental Sciences, Washington Singer Labs, University of Exeter, England, Foundation Professor of Communication Sciences and Disorders (Hon) at the University of Sydney, past Research Manager for Speakability, Visiting Professor at the Universities of Bremen, Germany and Louisiana at Lafayette, USA. He is *Speakability's* National Adviser on Aphasia in the UK and is Patron of *AphasiaNow*. He is co-founding Editor of *Aphasiology*. His research interests include the neuropsychology of language and speech, psychosocial consequences of aphasia, recovery and treatment of aphasia, the public awareness of aphasia, the history of aphasia, aphasia and the evolution of language and speech, number processing and apraxia.

Laura Davies (Cambridge) "Samuel Johnson and the Frailties of Speech" Laura Davies is a research fellow at the Centre for Christianity and Culture, University of Oxford, where she is currently working on an interdisciplinary study of speech and listening in eighteenth- and nineteenth-century England. She completed her PhD on this subject at the University of Cambridge in 2009. Her publications include articles and book chapters on Samuel Johnson, oral tradition, Methodism and literature, and women's life-writing.

Chris Eagle (Writing and Society Research Centre) "Editor's Introduction: Talking Normal" "'Stuttutistics': On Speech Disorders in *Finnegans Wake*" Chris Eagle is research lecturer in the Writing and Society Research Centre of the University of Western Sydney. Before that, he was a postdoctoral fellow in the Humanities at the California Institute of Technology. In 2009, he received his PhD in English Literature from U.C. Berkeley. He has been a visiting scholar at the Antwerp Joyce Center as well as the Institute of Texts and Modern Manuscripts in Paris. He is also a former Fulbright Scholar. He is the author of *Dysfluencies: On Speech Disorders in Modern Literature* (Bloomsbury, 2013). His articles have appeared in journals including *Modern Language Notes, James Joyce Quarterly, Milton Quarterly, Epoche* and *Comparative Literature Studies,* on figures ranging from Plato to Milton, Proust, Joyce, and Heidegger.

Jeffrey Johnson (Joint POW/MIA Accounting Command Honolulu) "The Visualisation of the Twisted Tongue: Portrayals of Stuttering in Film, Television and Comic Books" Dr. Jeffrey K. Johnson earned a PhD in American Studies from Michigan State University and served as a Peace Corps Volunteer teacher in Turkmenistan. He currently is a World War II historian for the Joint POW/MIA Accounting Command in Honolulu, Hawaii and is the author of several books and articles including *Super-History: Comic Book Superheroes and American Society, 1938 to the Present* and *American Advertising in Poland: A Study of Cultural Interactions Since 1990.*

Herbert Marks (Indiana University) "On Prophetic Stammering" Herbert Marks is Professor of Comparative Literature at Indiana University, where he also directs the Institute for Biblical and Literary Studies and edits the monograph series Indiana Studies in Biblical Literature. His edition of the King James Version of the Old Testament with complete commentary was published last year by W.W. Norton.

Gene A. Plunka (University of Memphis) "'Staging Aphasia': Jean Claude Van-Itallie's *The Traveller* and Arthur Kopit's *Wings*" Gene A. Plunka is professor of English at the University of Memphis, where he teaches courses on modern and contemporary drama. His books include *Peter Shaffer: Roles, Rites, and Rituals in the Theater* (1988); *The Rites of Passage of Jean Genet: The Art and Aesthetics of Risk Taking* (1992); *Antonin Artaud and the Modern Theater* (ed., 1994); *Jean-Claude van Itallie and the Off-Broadway Theater* (1999); *The Black Comedy of John Guare* (2002); *The Plays of Beth Henley: A Critical Study* (2005); *Holocaust Drama: The Theater of Atrocity* (2009); and *Staging Holocaust Resistance* (2012).

Laura Salisbury (Birbeck College) "Jackson's Parrot: Samuel Beckett, Aphasic Speech Automatisms, and Psychosomatic Language" Laura Salisbury is RCUK Fellow in Science, Technology and Culture at Birkbeck College, University of London. She is the author of *Samuel Beckett: Laughing Matters, Comic Timing* (Edinburgh University Press 2012) and co-editor, with Andrew Shail, of *Neurology and Modernity: A Cultural History of Nervous Systems, 1800–1950* (Palgrave, 2010). She has published an article on Beckett's 'aphasic modernism' in *The Journal of Beckett Studies* (2008) and is currently completing a monograph entitled *Aphasic Modernism* on the relationships between literary modernism, critical theory, and neuroscientific conceptions of language.

Ronald Schleifer (University of Oklahoma) "The Poetics of Tourette's Syndrome: Language, Neurobiology, and Poetry" Ronald Schleifer is George Lynn Cross Research Professor of English and Adjunct Professor in the College of Medicine at the University of Oklahoma. From 1976 to 2000 he served as Editor of Genre: Forms of Discourse and Culture; and from 1986 to 1999 he served as co-editor of The Oklahoma Project for Discourse and Theory, a series of books published by the University of Oklahoma Press. Professor Schleifer has written, translated, or edited nineteen books. The most recent include *Intangible Materialism: The Body, Scientific Knowledge, and the Power of Poetry* (Minnesota, 2009); *Medicine and Humanistic Understanding*, a DVD-ROM (Pennsylvania, 2005), co-authored with Jerry Vannatta, MD and Sheila Crow; *Modernism and Time: The Logic of Abundance in Literature, Science, and Culture 1880–1930*, (Cambridge, 2000); and *Analogical Thinking: Post-Enlightenment Understanding of Language, Collaboration, and Interpretation* (Michigan, 2000). He also edited (with David Jobling and Tina Pippin) *A Postmodern Bible Reader* (Blackwell, 2001) and (with Robert Con Davis) *Contemporary Literary Criticism*, now in its fourth edition (Longman, 1998). Professor Schleifer has authored more than seventy scholarly articles on literary modernism, critical theory, semiotics, science/medicine and literature, and the cultural study of music.

Valéria M. Souza (Washington University—St. Louis) "'Irately and ineloquently': Stuttering, Logorrhea, and Disordered Speech among Male Characters in Luís Vaz de Camões' The Lusiads (1572)" Valéria M. Souza holds a PhD in Luso-Afro-Brazilian Studies and Theory from the University of Massachusetts Dartmouth and is a lecturer of Portuguese at Washington University—St. Louis. She is the co-editor, with Victor K. Mendes, of Garrett's Travels Revisited (Tagus Press, 2011) and has had an article, a translation, and a review published in the journals Portuguese Literary & Cultural Studies and Brasil/Brazil. Her dissertation examined representations and the aesthetics of disability in João Guimarães Rosa's Brazilian masterpiece The Devil to Pay in the Backlands (1956).

Joshua St. Pierre (University of Alberta) "The Construction of the Disabled Speaker: Locating Stuttering in Disability Studies" Joshua St. Pierre is a PhD student in philosophy at the University of Alberta. He has published in the Canadian Journal of Disability Studies and has presented numerously on speech, bioethics, disability studies, and ableism in posthumanist discourse. His current research examines the relations between speech, reason, embodiment and disability, looking specifically at the breakdown of speech as a socio-political performance of rational human identity.

Index